A COMPANION TO CRIME, HARM AND VICTIMISATION

Edited by Karen Corteen, Sharon Morley,
Paul Taylor and Jo Turner

D1476723

P

First published in Great Britain in 2016 by

Policy Press   North America office:
University of Bristol   Policy Press
1-9 Old Park Hill   c/o The University of Chicago Press
Bristol BS2 8BB   1427 East 60th Street
UK   Chicago, IL 60637, USA
t: +44 (0)117 954 5940   t: +1 773 702 7700
pp-info@bristol.ac.uk   f: +1 773 702 9756
www.policypress.co.uk   www.press.uchicago.edu
                                             sales@press.uchicago.edu

© Policy Press 2016

British Library Cataloguing in Publication Data
A catalogue record for this book is available from the British Library

Library of Congress Cataloging-in-Publication Data
A catalog record for this book has been requested

ISBN 978-1-4473-2572-7 paperback
ISBN 978-1-4473-2571-0 hardcover
ISBN 978-1-4473-2573-4 ePub
ISBN 978-1-4473-2575-8 Mobi

The right of Karen Corteen, Sharon Morley, Paul Taylor and Jo Turner to be identified as editors of this work has been asserted by them in accordance with the 1988 Copyright, Designs and Patents Act.

Cover design by Andrew Corbett
Front cover image: Kuzma / Bigstock
Printed and bound in Great Britain by CPI Group (UK) Ltd,
Croydon, CR0 4YY
Policy Press uses environmentally responsible print partners

Contents

Contents

Contributors

David Balsamo is professor of social science and dean of faculty at the University of Chester, UK. He has worked as a painter and decorator, operating theatre technician, probation officer, and, latterly, as an academic. His varied career has provided the impetus for a sustained interest and commitment to the sociology and political economy of work. David's doctorate examined the management of teaching and research in the neo-corporate university and was informed by the perspectives and cognitive dissonances of being an academic manager.

Hannah Bows is a doctoral researcher and research assistant in the Centre for Research into Violence and Abuse (CRiVA) at Durham University, UK. Her research interests include gender, violence against women, sex offenders and women's involvement in crime. Her current research examines rape against older people in the UK.

Iain Brennan is a chartered research psychologist and senior lecturer in criminology and psychology in the School of Social Sciences at the University of Hull, UK. His research interests include weapon use, alcohol-related violence and victim responses to crime.

Samantha Bricknell is research manager of the Violence and Exploitation Research Program at the Australian Institute of Criminology (AIC), Australia. She has had extensive experience leading and undertaking research relevant to both violent and transnational organised crime, with a particular interest in male victimisation, human trafficking and slavery, and environmental crime. Samantha's research at the AIC has covered a diverse range of topics, including forced marriage, the attrition of human trafficking matters through the criminal justice system, homicide, missing persons classification, the support needs of male victims of violence, environmental crime in Australia, corruption in Australian sport and the illicit firearms market. She holds a PhD from the Australian National University.

Rob Canton is professor in community and criminal justice at De Montfort University, Leicester, UK. He worked in the Probation Service for many years in a variety of different practice, management and training roles before joining De Montfort. In recent years, Rob has been extensively involved in work to help other countries to develop their practices in supervising offenders, mostly in Eastern Europe. He was appointed by the Council of Europe to contribute to framing the recommendation that was subsequently adopted (in 2010) by the Council of Europe as the European Probation Rules. He has a career-long interest in the challenges involved in working with mentally disordered offenders.

Sheila Coleman is a former senior lecturer and researcher in higher education. She has been involved in researching the aftermath of the Hillsborough Disaster since 1989 and initially monitored the legal proceedings, with a particular emphasis on the inquests. She gave up full-time employment to work voluntarily with the Hillsborough Justice Campaign for many years and continues to work alongside families and survivors. Her main focus of interest is on miscarriages of justice and challenging state power. She currently works as the north-west region community coordinator for the union Unite.

Nancy Contreras is a graduate teaching assistant and master's candidate in criminal justice at the University of Colorado Denver, USA. Her current research explores social media, protests and police–community relations. She has work experience in the juvenile justice system, homeless services and mental health care.

Vickie Cooper is a lecturer in social policy and criminology and co-director of the Harm and Evidence Research Collaborative (HERC), at the Open University, UK. Vickie's research focuses on homelessness in relation to: housing, hostels, the criminal justice system, community punishment and geographical displacement. She is interested in how society contains and manages homeless groups through these various institutions. Currently, she is looking at the relationship between welfare reforms, evictions and homelessness.

Karen Corteen is a senior lecturer in criminal justice at Liverpool John Moores University, UK. Areas that Karen has researched and published in include victimology, critical criminology and sexuality. Her research interests comprise: zemiology; victims and harm; harm and sports entertainment; hate crime; and sexual violence. She is a member of networks concerned with crime, harm and victimisation within and beyond academia.

Pamela Davies is principal lecturer in criminology and teaching fellow in the Faculty of Arts, Design and Social Sciences at Northumbria University, Newcastle upon Tyne, UK. Pam has research interests connected to gender, crime and victimisation. She has published on topics related to experiences of victimisation and support for those affected, invisible crimes and social harms, and criminological research methodologies. She is chair of the British Society of Criminology Victims Network.

Mary Dodge is a professor at the University of Colorado, Denver, USA, in the School of Public Affairs. She earned her PhD in 1997 in criminology, law and society from the School of Social Ecology at the University of California, Irvine. She received her BA and MA in psychology from the University of Colorado at Colorado Springs. Her research and writing interests include gender and crime, white-collar crime, policing, prostitution, and courts.

Marian Duggan is a lecturer in criminology at the University of Kent, UK. Her research focuses on sexuality and gender-based victimisation, in particular, the factors informing and sustaining homophobic and misogynistic violence and the possibilities for preventing such harm. Marian's published work addresses hate crime in Northern Ireland, culturally specific analyses of homophobic victimisation, the efficacy of domestic violence prevention strategies and criminal justice responses to victimisation. Marian is the author of *Queering conflict: Examining lesbian and gay experiences of homophobia in Northern Ireland* (2012, Ashgate) and (with V. Heap) *Administrating victimization: The politics of anti-social behaviour and hate crime policy* (2014, Palgrave Macmillan).

Jennifer L. Dunn is a professor of sociology at Texas Tech University, USA. Her research interests focus on the social construction of individual and collective identities, with substantive scholarship in victimology, deviance, social psychology, social problems and social movements. Her new research is on the criminalisation of victims of police violence.

John P.J. Dussich is professor emeritus of criminology and victimology, Department of Criminology, California State University, Fresno, USA. His primary interest areas of research and theory are in: international victimology; psychosocial coping theory; dynamics of recovery; and, very recently, measuring trauma among refugees. His specialty concerns are in: international femicide; US victim service models; disaster victimisation, crisis response and policy options; and advocacy for elder abuse shelters.

Kathryn Dutton is senior lecturer in law at the University of Bradford Faculty of Management and Law, UK. Her research and teaching expertise lie in the fields of criminal law and criminology, with particular interests in domestic violence and pedagogy.

Sarah Fletcher is a programme and policy officer with the Commissioner for Victims' Rights, South Australia. Before working with the Commissioner, Sarah taught sociology and victimology at the Department of Justice Technical and Further Education College, South Australia. She has spoken at local, national and international events on victims' rights and victim assistance, and writes on these topics. She is a delegate on the Australia National Victims of Crime Working Group. She is a member of the World Society of Victimology, and in 2015, received the Victim Support Service Victim Support Worker of the Year (Professional) Award.

Claire Fox is a senior lecturer in criminology at the University of Manchester, UK. Claire's research interests lie in the area of victimology, in particular, relating to experiences and policies around undocumented migrants and 'difficult' victims, the role of the third sector, and responses and representations of victimisation.

Peter Francis is a professor and criminologist at Northumbria University, UK. His most recent publication (with Dr Pamela Davies and Dr Tanya Wyatt) was the book *Invisible crime and social harms* (2014) for the Critical Criminological Perspectives Series in Palgrave Macmillan. Currently, he is completing the second edition of *Victims, crime and society* for Sage Publications, and the third edition of *Doing criminological research*, also for Sage Publications.

Sam Garkawe is an associate professor at the School of Law and Justice at Southern Cross University, Australia. His main research interests are in criminal justice issues, and he has published particularly in the field of victimology, concentrating on the role of victims in international justice. He has taught victimology since 1996, this being the only subject in an Australian law school that is solely devoted to victim issues, and also presently teaches criminal procedure and international criminal justice. Sam is a life member of the World Society of Victimology and has been on its United Nations Liaison Committee since July 2003, and was an Executive Member from 2009 to 2015.

Jo Goodey is head of the Freedoms and Justice Department at the European Union Agency for Fundamental Rights (FRA), which is based in Vienna. She is responsible for the FRA's research and related work in the fields of access to justice and victims of crime, as well as asylum, migration and borders, and information society, privacy and data protection. In addition, the FRA's statistics and surveys work falls under her department. Her personal research specialisms include: victims of crime; hate crime; trafficking in human beings; discriminatory ethnic profiling; masculinities and crime; violence against women; and survey research methodologies. She was previously a research fellow at the United Nations Office on Drugs and Crime, and has held lectureships in criminology and criminal justice at the Universities of Sheffield and Leeds in the UK.

Simon Green is senior lecturer in community justice and criminology in the Centre for Criminology and Criminal Justice at the University of Hull, UK. He teaches and researches in the areas of criminological theory, victimology, restorative justice and crime reduction. His most recent book is *Crime, community and morality* (2014, Routledge) and he is currently writing and researching about police triage schemes, cultural victimology and restorative justice theory.

Nic Groombridge has played and watched sport most of his life. His PhD involved observing young 'joyriders' at projects that used the prospect of motor sport as a 'hook' to encourage desistance from crime. An early advocate of green criminology, he saw the harm that both joyriders and legal car users caused. He tweets @criminology4u and blogs on public and sports criminology. His book, *Sports criminology*, is to be published by Policy Press. A former head of sociology at St Mary's University, Twickenham, UK, he is now a visiting scholar there.

Matthew Hall is a professor of law and criminal justice in the College of Social Science, University of Lincoln, UK. His particular research interests include victimisation and the place of victims in the criminal justice system, and, more recently, he has worked extensively in the growing field of green criminology. With regard to victims' rights, Matthew has contributed to the European Commission, the South African Department of Justice and Constitutional Development and the South Korean and Irish governments, and he is a pioneer in environmental victimisation.

Katherine Harrison is a senior lecturer in sociology at the University of Chester, UK. Her research and teaching focus on visual culture and gender. She is currently investigating the rise in popularity of knitting for leisure among young women in 21st-century Britain. Katherine is series editor of Issues in the Social Sciences, a themed book series published by the University of Chester Press, which aims to present current academic research in accessible language for scholars at all levels.

Vicky Heap is a senior lecturer in criminology at Sheffield Hallam University, UK, where she has worked since 2012. Her research interests centre around anti-social behaviour, particularly public perceptions, policy developments and victims' provisions. She has newly published on the UK Coalition government's victim-focused anti-social behaviour policy and recently co-authored a book (with Marian Duggan) entitled *Administrating victimization: The politics of anti-social behaviour and hate crime policy* (Palgrave, 2014). She is a steering group member of the British Society of Criminology Victims Network and is co-chair of her department's Criminal Justice Institutions Research Cluster.

Jill Jameson is a senior lecturer in criminology at the University of Lincoln, UK. She coordinates and teaches on a number of degree courses, where her teaching interests include criminological theories, gender and crime, penology, research methodologies, criminal justice professions, and student employability. Her research interests take in work on student employability and engagement, pedagogy in higher education, and student bystander intervention programmes addressing gender-based violence.

Akilah Jardine is a doctoral researcher in the School of Law at Liverpool John Moores University, UK. Her research interest lies in international law on modern-day slavery and the trafficking of human beings. She aims to recommend new approaches to identifying and combating the trafficking of human beings and to highlight the strengths and weaknesses in current international human trafficking legislation in order to contribute to the discovery and development of legal doctrines.

Timothy W. Jones is senior lecturer in history at La Trobe University, Australia. He is a historian of sexuality and religion in modern Britain and Australia, interested in the relationship between religion, medicine and law in shaping sexual politics. Current research projects include researching the influence of the moral welfare movement, the rise of the New Christian Right and treatments of sexual deviancy, particularly clerical child sex offenders.

Andrew Karmen received his PhD in sociology from Columbia University, USA, in 1977. Since 1978, he has been a professor at John Jay College of Criminal Justice, USA, where he was a co-director of the Master's Program in Criminal Justice for nearly 20 years. He is the author of *New York murder mystery: The true story of the crime crash of the 1990s* (NYU Press, 2006), as well as *Crime victims: An introduction to victimology* (9th edn) (Cengage, 2016).

Tammy Landau is associate professor in the Department of Criminology at Ryerson University, Toronto, Canada. She was a senior research and policy advisor to the Arbour Commission regarding events at the Prison For Women, and is a former member of the Board of Directors of Aboriginal Legal Services of Toronto. Tammy was appointed to the Ontario Civilian Commission on Police Services, where she served from 2004 to 2012. Her current research interests include police accountability and critical victimology. She is currently working on a project on the racial profiling of women in the community.

Carly Lightowlers is an academic fellow at the University of Leeds, UK. She has previously worked as a senior lecturer in criminal justice and alcohol researcher at Liverpool John Moores University, UK, as well as having held research positions in local and central government. She completed her PhD on the development of drinking patterns and violent behaviour among young people at the University of Manchester, UK, and conducted research on the 2011 English summer riots. Her methodological expertise is in applying quantitative methods in the study of substance use, crime and justice.

Rob I. Mawby is visiting professor of criminology and criminal justice at the University of South Wales and visiting professor of rural criminology at Harper Adams University, UK. He previously worked at the UK universities of Sheffield, Leeds, Bradford and Plymouth, where he was professor of criminology and criminal justice for 15 years. He was the academic expert on European Forum for Urban Security's 'Security and Tourism' initiative (2013–2015), and works with the European Union in producing the UK reports on victims' rights and victims' services. He is editor of *Crime Prevention and Community Safety: An International Journal*, is on the editorial board of *The Police Journal* and has published numerous articles and books.

Liam McCann is a critical criminologist and principal lecturer in criminology at the University of Lincoln, UK, and has been programme leader there for the BA (Hons) Criminology, and its nine joint honours programmes, and the MAs in Criminology and Globalising Justice. Liam is from West Belfast but was forced to leave due to the threat of sectarian violence posed to his bar manager father, he therefore considers himself a political refugee and economic migrant from Western Europe. His research interests include state crime, racism, policing and the pedagogy of students' use of feedback.

Beth McJury currently works as a visiting lecturer in the Department of Social and Political Science at the University of Chester, UK. Her main interests are zemiology, social movements and protest. She is undertaking a PhD at the university that seeks to explore resistance to unconventional gas and oil extraction.

Linda Moore is senior lecturer in criminology in the School of Criminology, Politics and Social Policy at Ulster University, Northern Ireland. Her research interests are children's rights, youth justice and human rights within the penal context. With Professor Phil Scraton, she published *The incarceration of women: Punishing bodies, breaking spirits* (Palgrave Macmillan, 2014).

Sharon Morley is a senior lecturer in criminology and deputy head of the Department of Social and Political Science at the University of Chester, UK. Her research interests include; young women and their everyday experiences of violence, dating violence, precautionary strategies, and narrative research. Most recently, her research and publications have spanned the areas of violence in society and the victimisation of health and social care professionals, as well as media representations of mentally disordered offenders.

Emma Murray is a senior lecturer in Criminal Justice at the School of Law in Liverpool John Moores University, UK. Central to Emma's PhD is dignity and justice for veterans' in post-conflict settings. Her work aims to critically address the multiple agencies and actors involved in the governance of veterans in the UK, aiming to give veterans a voice within academic and policy debates.

Michael Naughton is a reader in sociology and law, University of Bristol, UK. He has published widely on miscarriages of justice and wrongful convictions for academic and non-academic sources. His books include *The innocent and the criminal justice system* (Palgrave Macmillan, 2013), *Rethinking miscarriages of justice* (Palgrave Macmillan, 2007), *Claims of innocence: An introduction to wrongful convictions and how they might be challenged* (with Gabe Tan) (University of Bristol, 2011) and (as editor) *The Criminal Cases Review Commission: Hope for the innocent?* (Palgrave Macmillan, 2009).

Michael O'Connell is the commissioner for victims' rights, South Australia. Previously, he was the first victims of crime coordinator in that state and served for over 20 years as a police officer (during which time he was appointed the inaugural victim impact statement coordinator). Michael lectures and writes on victimology and criminal justice. He is a life member of the World Society of Victimology and its current secretary-general, as well as a member of The Alliance of NGOs on Crime Prevention and Criminal Justice. For his work in promoting victims' rights and advancing victimology, Michael has received the Australia Police Medal, been a finalist in the Australian of the Year and been honoured with the National Victim Support Australasia award.

Cassandra A. Ogden is senior lecturer and programme leader for sociology at the University of Chester, UK. Her PhD thesis explored the experiences of children with inflammatory bowel disease, which fuelled her interest in exploring the social disgust of particular bodies and the stigma that people face due to perceived differences of the body. Much of Cassandra's current work utilises a critical disability studies perspective but she has also published and co-published on disability hate crime, childhood illness experiences, the social and legal responses to smoking in public and its impact upon the incarcerated, quality of life research, the narrative inquiry technique, and the use of food banks in Cheshire.

Nicola O'Leary is a lecturer in criminology at the University of Hull, UK, where she previously studied, gaining her PhD in 2012. She teaches in the areas of criminological theory, punishment and the media and crime. Her principal research interests are based around the intersections between crime, media and culture, with an emphasis on notions of identity, victimisation, resilience and stigma. Current interests include a particular concern with ethical methods of researching victims of harm.

Nikos Passas is professor of criminology and criminal justice, and co-director of the Institute for Security and Public Policy, at Northeastern University, US. He is also consortium member at the International Anti-Corruption Academy and editor-in-chief of *Crime, Law and Social Change*. He specialises in the study of corruption, terrorism, illicit flows, informal fund transfers, white-collar crime, targeted sanctions and international crimes. He has over 180 publications in 13 languages. He offers public and private sector training, and consults with law firms, banks, international organisations (United Nations, World Bank, International Monetary Fund, European Union, Interamerican Development Bank, International Anti-Corruption Academy) and government agencies in many countries.

Tina Patel is a senior lecturer in criminology at the University of Salford, UK. Tina's research interests are in 'race' and ethnicity, experiences of racism in a post-race state, social exclusion, and policing (mis)behaviour. She has recently carried out research into: the policing of racist violence in Northern Ireland; vehicle crime in deprived neighbourhoods; and the foster care and identity development of refugee-status children. Tina is currently undertaking research into racist hate crimes. Tina has authored several books, and is currently writing *Race and society*, due to be published by Sage in 2016.

Eleanor Peters is a senior lecturer in criminology and criminal justice and the programme leader for the BA (Hons) Criminology and Criminal Justice programme at Edge Hill University, UK. She graduated from the University of Central England with a BA (Hons) in Sociology and has a PhD from Bristol University. She has previously worked in a research capacity for Barnardo's, the University of Central Lancashire and the Children's Society. She has published a range of reports, articles in scholarly journals and chapters in edited books in the areas of youth justice and social care.

Diana Sankey is a lecturer in law at Liverpool John Moores University, UK. Her research interests are in the areas of international criminal law, transitional justice and gender. She has previously published work on gendered harms and on the recognition of socio-economic forms of violence in transitional justice.

David Scott is senior lecturer in criminology at Liverpool John Moores University, UK. He is a former coordinator of the European Group for the Study of Deviance and Social Control and a founding editor of the journal *Justice, Power and Resistance*. He has written widely on prisons, punishment and critical criminology and his main research focus is on the ethics and politics of penal abolitionism.

David W. Selfe is director of the School of Law, Liverpool John Moores University, UK. He teaches criminal law across a range of modules and one of his key teaching areas is sexual offences. His research and writing interests are in criminal law generally, and specifically in sexual offences law and policy, and the impact of the Sexual Offences Act 2003. He has written numerous articles on criminal law, and was lead author of *Perspectives on sex, crime and society* (2nd edn) (Cavendish, 2001).

Basia Spalek is a professor in conflict transformation within the Department of Therapeutic Practice at the University of Derby, UK. Basia's research interests include peace-building, counter-terrorism, victimisation and trauma. Basia has been a consultant to international and national organisations, including the Office for Security and Cooperation in Europe (OSCE), the Institute for Strategic Dialogue (ISD), the Home Office and the Royal United Services Institute (RUSI). Basia is about to complete a book: *Trauma and victimisation: Theory, policy and practice* (Palgrave Macmillan). Basia is also a British Association for Counselling and Psychotherapy-registered and practising psychotherapist, whose clinical practice is located at www.connect-and-reflect.org.uk

Rachael Steele is a senior lecturer in criminal justice at Liverpool John Moores University, UK. Rachael worked within probation practice for 15 years, carrying out applied research into subjects as diverse as desistance and the impact of cognitive behavioural interventions on reoffending. Research interests include how offenders make decisions to offend, and how criminal justice practice can support rehabilitation and desistance from crime.

Michelle Stoops is a criminologist and an operational manager of SAFE Place Sexual Assault Referral Centre, Liverpool Community Health Trust, UK. Her research interests are in sex work, violence against sex workers, gender-based violence, child sexual exploitation and sexual violence. She has been involved on a national and international level in relation to these subjects, lecturing and advising on policy to a range of audiences. Most recently, she was part of the Steering Group for the National Rape Action Plan for the UK.

Kate Strudwick is senior lecturer and programme leader for criminology at the University of Lincoln, UK. She has researched and published on policing and police complaints, and, more recently, on pedagogic research on student experiences, issues in higher education, the 'student as producer' and employability.

Paul Taylor is a senior lecturer in criminology and deputy head of department in the Department of Social and Political Science at the University of Chester, UK. His research interests include occupational culture in public services, the coronial process and mental health and criminal justice convergence.

Terry Thomas is emeritus professor of criminal justice at Leeds Beckett University, UK. His research areas include sexual offending and police information systems. His most recent books are (with Nicola Groves) *Domestic violence and criminal justice* (Routledge, 2014) and the third edition of his book *Sex crime: Sex offending and society* (Routledge, 2015).

Steve Tombs is professor of criminology at the Open University, UK. He has a long-standing interest in the incidence, nature and regulation of corporate and state crime and harms. Recent publications include *Social protection after the crisis? Regulation without enforcement* (The Policy Press, 2015) and (with David Whyte) *The corporate criminal. Why corporations must be abolished* (Routledge, 2015). He is a trustee and board member of Inquest.

James Treadwell is senior lecturer in criminology at Birmingham City University, UK. His books include *Criminology: The essentials* (Sage, 2013), *Football hooliganism, fan behaviour and crime* (Palgrave MacMillan, 2014) and *Riots and political protest* (Routledge, 2015).

Jo Turner is a senior lecturer in criminology at the University of Chester, UK. She has many research interests, but mainly researches in the broad area of comparative criminology. As a member of the British Crime Historians, Jo is especially interested in crime and criminal justice comparisons with the past. In addition, she has a particular interest in the processes associated with desistence from crime, and women's experiences of the criminal justice system.

Sandra Walklate is Eleanor Rathbone chair of sociology at the University of Liverpool, UK, and adjunct professor at Queensland University of Technology in Brisbane, Australia. Internationally recognised for her work in victimology and research on criminal victimisation, her recent publications include (with Ross McGarry) *Victims: Trauma, testimony, justice* (Routledge, 2015) and (with Gabe Mythen) *The contradictions of terrorism* (Routledge, 2014). She is currently editor in chief of the *British Journal of Criminology*, and in 2014, was given the British Society of Criminology's outstanding achievement award.

Acknowledgements

The editors would like to extend their thanks to Victoria Pittman, Rebecca Tomlinson, the production editor and team, and all the staff at Policy Press for their enthusiasm for the series of Companions and for their support in making them happen. Thanks also to the reviewers, commissioned by Policy Press, who provided positive reviews of the original proposal.

Thanks also go to the authors, who have produced over 100 entries between them. As with the first Companion, *A companion to criminal justice, mental health and risk*, it has been a pleasure to work with colleagues nationally and internationally from a range of backgrounds – many wearing several hats. These include academics, former practitioners, practitioners (legal and otherwise) in the field of victims and victim services, victims' commissioners, policy officers, consultants, advisors, members of steering groups, and members of the World Society of Victimology. Their knowledge is indispensable and we are extremely appreciative of the time that they have given in the context of all their other commitments.

Finally, thanks to those individuals, including students, who have commented verbally and otherwise favourably on the first Companion in this series and who are readily awaiting this *Companion to crime, harm and victimisation*.

Preface

A companion to crime, harm and victimisation is the second Companion in the series, following on from *A companion to criminal justice, mental health and risk*. In keeping with the first Companion, *A companion to crime, harm and victimisation* provides a valuable resource for students, educators, researchers and practitioners interested in crime, criminal justice, victims, victimisation and harm. *A companion to criminal justice, mental health and risk* reflected the current and continuing discursive, policy and practical convergence of criminal justice and mental health. In so doing, it presented succinct explanations of the critical debates and discussions necessitated to present a balanced understanding of the subject. Similarly, *A companion to crime, harm and victimisation* comprises succinct entries written by experts within and outside academia, and is unashamedly victimologically and victim-centred. Collectively, the contributors and contributions exemplify a victimological imagination that can no longer be ignored or regarded as a sub-discipline of criminology or criminal justice. The authors of each entry provide rigorous, evaluative insights into an array of expected, and potentially unexpected, relevant, distinct and connected issues.

The scope of contributions reflects contemporary debates and research in the area; importantly, it also reflects the dynamism of the burgeoning discipline of victimology including its multidisciplinarity and relevance. Globally, there is a public, political and media interest in crime and criminal justice. Within this context, 'victims' are increasingly becoming a key feature. Simultaneously, the discipline of victimology is gathering momentum, and within criminology, victimology and victimisation studies, the focus on crime and victims has been extended to include harms and victimisation beyond the remit of the criminal law. *A companion to crime, harm and victimisation* brings together the areas of crime, harm and victimisation and does so within a victimological, zemiological and human rights framework.

This Companion is significant as it brings together an array of topics and analyses, including victimological theories, key policies and legislation aimed at preventing and/or responding to crime, harm and victimisation, in addition to specialised areas of the field. Key areas such as primary, secondary and tertiary victims and victimisation, blame and victims, criminal justice and victims, compensation, and victims' rights are critically discussed. Furthermore, important victimological theories such as environmental and green victimology, radical victimology, critical victimology, and cultural victimology are provided and critically evaluated.

In addition, this Companion houses an array of unique and somewhat unusual specialised topics. The vast range of topics reflects the growing and diverse nature of current victimological concerns, debates and research. The victims, harms and victimisation incorporated in this Companion range from the conventional focus on victims of crime through to the less conventional, including institutional, environmental, corporate and state harms and victimisation. Some of the harms included in this Companion are harms as a result of an individual's identity, for example, disability hate crime, hate crime based on religion and sex worker hate crime. It includes harm as a result of determining and/or structural contexts, for example: young people and victimisation; elderly victims, gender and victimisation; homelessness and victimisation; and forced displacement. Harms at the hands of the state are also included, for example: the death penalty; miscarriages of justice and wrongful convictions; nuclear experiments; and genocide. So, too, are harms related to corporations, including: corporate manslaughter; fracking; and financial harms. The topics of conflict and war appear at various points within this Companion, with entries such as: criminology and war; music, conflict and torture; and soldiers and victimisation. Many contributions deal with the aftermath of being harmed and victimised, for example: empowerment schemes; restorative justice; victim recovery; and survivorology. Various contributions reflect the significance of human rights to areas of crime, harm and victimisation, and, importantly, the significance of resistance is acknowledged and critically considered. Some of the other topics that are provided are: aversion therapy; iatrogenic harm; night-time economies; victim notoriety; risk management; social abjection; sport; survivor stigmatisation; and visual victimology.

Finally, *A companion to crime, harm and victimisation* showcases the field of victims and victimology, which comprises the ever-developing and expanding victimological imagination and intellectual dialogues within this field. In so doing, it is an indispensable resource to those interested in this area within and beyond academia. It blends theoretical concepts and practicality and it encourages readers to think widely and critically about crime, harm and victimisation. It provides data, theoretical inputs, conceptual frameworks and analyses. Victims, victimisation and victimology are pivotal to the history, theory, policy and practices with regard to criminal justice, penal policy and social control. They are also dynamic areas in their own right, with their future trajectories holding significance in contemporary debates surrounding the injurious effects of individual, collective, state-sanctioned or power-endorsed action or inaction.

Karen Corteen, Sharon Morley, Paul Taylor and Jo Turner
2016

AGE AND VICTIMISATION

It is a well-established and widely cited criminological fact that perpetrating crime and being a victim of crime decreases with age, often referred to as the age–crime curve/distribution. The high prevalence of criminal and deviant behaviour in teenage years is well documented and much of the criminological literature has agreed that offending peaks in the mid- to late teens and decreases thereafter. Similarly, official victimisation surveys, including the Crime Survey for England and Wales, reveal that a much higher proportion of adults aged 16–24 reported being a victim of crime than other age groups; internationally, survey results paint a similar picture. Victimisation sees a particularly steep decrease after the age of 50, with those aged 75 and over reporting the lowest rates of victimisation.

The types of crime that people experience change with age. According to the United Kingdom's Office for National Statistics (2013), in 2011/12, robbery and theft from the person were most common for 16–24 year olds. Violent crimes were also more common for those aged under 24. The statistics are similar elsewhere, particularly in the US. Generally, young men are more at risk of being victimised than young women for the majority or crimes in the public sphere, with domestic and sexual violence being the exceptions. While a useful indication of the rates of victimisation, such statistics have been criticised by scholars such as Muncie (2003) as they do not take into account differential rates of victimisation according to other intersecting variables such as ethnicity or class. Furthermore, such surveys usually exclude participants in institutional settings (eg the secure estate and other environments of detention, residential care, etc), thus ignoring the types of victimisation that may disproportionally affect both young children and the elderly.

Victimology has emerged as a sub-discipline of criminology and is primarily focused on the causes and impacts of crime on victims. However, despite the disproportionate victimisation of younger age groups, age has not received particular attention in the existing work and 'youth victimology' and 'elder victimology' is virtually non-existent. As Muncie (2003) argues, young people are generally stereotyped as deviant and anti-social, and have until recently been absent from victim surveys; thus, they have received little attention as victims – in the UK, it is only since 2009/10 that the Crime Survey for England and Wales has allowed respondents under the age of 16 to take part. Particular gaps are notable in relation to theft, burglary and assault. However, more recently, there has been an increase in attention paid to domestic violence (typically referred to as 'dating violence'), sexual assault involving young victims (particularly sexual exploitation following a number of high-profile cases involving the grooming of young people by groups of adult men) and bullying (particularly cyber-bullying). Young women have received the most attention in relation to domestic and sexual assault, where the majority of campaigns, policy and research focus on those aged 25 and under.

One potential reason for the disproportionate victimisation of younger groups is the vulnerability that is associated with this group due to having significantly less social and financial resources to protect themselves coupled with physical immaturity, which may position them as easy targets of crime. This may be one explanation as to why victimisation decreases with age as people become more independent and physically mature. The dominant criminological explanations are rooted in lifestyles and routine activities theory. Routine activities theory is a core criminological theory developed by Cohen and Felson (1979). The theory attempts to predict who is more or less likely to be a victim of crime. The theory is based on three elements: a motivated offender; a suitable target or victim; and the absence of a capable guardian who might prevent crime from occurring. As young people, particularly young men, are more likely to spend leisure time out in public places, including pubs and nightclubs, and are more likely to be out in public spaces late at night, they are more heavily victimised than other age groups. According to lifestyle/routine activities theories, elderly people are less likely to socialise in nightclubs or public places late at night and so are victimised less, thus explaining their relative low levels of victimisation. However, this theory does not explain domestic violence and sexual violence, which continue to affect high numbers of women throughout their life course, and so-called 'elder abuse', which is usually perpetrated in the home or residential care environments.

There are some notable gaps in the existing literature. First, the experiences of young people who have been victimised and the causes of victimisation have been largely ignored. Second, there is a dearth of research on and scholarly attention to 'older' victims of crime. Older people are routinely ignored as victims of crime or have their victimisation reconceptualised as a welfare issue. Given the limitations of the official statistics and our aging society, the latter warrants particular attention.

HANNAH BOWS

See also: **Child Protection and Children's Rights; Domestic Violence, Victims and Victimisation; Elderly Victims**

Readings

Cohen, L.E. and Felson, M. (1979) 'Social change and crime rate trends: a routine activity approach', *American Sociological Review*, 44(4): 588–608.

Francis, P. (2007) 'Young people, victims and crime', in P. Davies, P. Francis and C. Greer (eds) *Victims, crime and society*. London: Sage, pp 202–33.

Lindesay, J. (1996) 'Elderly people and crime', *Reviews in Clinical Gerontology*, 6(2): 199–204.

Muncie, J. (2003) 'Youth, risk and victimisation', in P. Davies, P. Francis and V. Jupp (eds) *Victimisation theory, research and policy*. Basingstoke: Palgrave.

Office for National Statistics (2013) 'The likelihood of becoming a victim of crime'. Available at: http://webarchive.nationalarchives.gov.uk/20160105160709/ http://www.ons.gov.uk/ons/rel/crime-stats/crime-statistics/period-ending-march-2012/sty-a-victim-of-crime.html

Ulmer, J. and Steffensmeier, D. (2014) 'The age and crime relationship: social variation, social explanations', in K. Beaver, J.C. Barnes and B. Boutwel (eds) *The nurture versus biosocial debate in criminology: On the origins of criminal behaviour and criminality*. California, CA: SAGE, pp 377–97.

ALCOHOL AND HARM

Alcohol consumption is associated with pleasure and sociability; however, it is also linked to a number of health and social harms, including addiction, ill health and injury, crime, (sexual) violence, and anti-social behaviour. Alcohol consumption and its associated outcomes exist not in a vacuum, but within a social, economic and cultural context. Indeed, policy responses to recent concerns about binge drinking ought to be considered with due reference to the relationship between market forces, the state and the alcohol industry. The implicit hypocrisy (Hobbs et al, 2015) in much of the policy concerning alcohol and crime prevention raises important debates around criminality, power and victimisation, especially those involving the state-sanctioned sale and consumption of alcohol, the parallel criminalisation of intoxicated behaviour, and the victimisation of drinkers.

In a drive to stimulate and expand the night-time economy in the UK, there has been a proliferation of licensed leisure venues and policy moves to liberalise the licensing regime (eg the Licensing Act 2003), as well as 'light-touch' self-regulation of the alcohol industry. These policy directions position alcohol firmly as a widespread and available commodity at the heart of sociocultural life in Britain, under the semblance of harm reduction. However, they also increase the alcohol industry's influence in the sale of alcohol and the very nature of British city centres.

While the hope was that the Licensing Act 2003 would stimulate a more continental drinking culture, this has not materialised. Furthermore, there are no clear signs that the abolition of closing time has reduced crime and disorder (Hough and Hunter, 2008). The most recent government alcohol strategy of 2012 welcomes self-regulation of the alcohol industry, suggesting that economic growth and responsibility can coexist well. However, this raises concerns about the 'credibility gap' associated with public health messages promoting moderation and restraint in a cultural context of economic deregulation and excessive consumption (Measham, 2006).

Alongside policy directions enabling the widespread availability and acceptability of alcohol consumption, there has been a parallel suite of civil, criminal and coercive policy tools introduced to deal with the intoxicated behaviour that results from the widespread consumption of alcohol.

These include:

- Penalty notices for disorder (PNDs) (fines for offences such as being drunk and disorderly in a public place).
- Designated Public Place Orders (DPPOs), which give police officers discretionary powers to require a person to stop drinking and to confiscate alcohol in public places.
- The Alcohol Arrest Referral (AAR) scheme, aimed to conduct brief interventions with those who have been arrested for alcohol-related offences in custody suites.
- Drinking Banning Orders (DBOs), which impose a court-ordered period of sobriety, or a tougher criminal punishment, on individuals behaving criminally or disorderly while under the influence of alcohol.
- Alcohol Treatment Requirements (ATRs), which require sentenced offenders to attend group-work programmes in prison, or with an alcohol treatment

provider, and engage with an alcohol reduction or abstinence programme available to the general population.

- Sobriety measures as part of conditional cautions (enforcing abstinence on days that they pose a risk for lower-level offending) and community sentences (which monitor offenders' alcohol consumption using either a breathalyser or electronic 'alcohol tag' for more serious offending), both of which are being piloted at the time of writing.

Such measures focus on managing those deemed to be drinking 'irresponsibly' and appear devoid of any meaningful consideration that individual drinking practices are shaped by cultural tolerance of socially drinking alcohol and the widespread availability of alcohol. They unduly embroil people into the criminal justice system (CJS) for relatively minor offences, breaches and failures to comply – many of which could be avoided by more specifically tailoring interventions to the needs of the individuals at times that they are ready and willing to engage, as well as specifically tackling the relationship *between* alcohol and violence rather than tackling these independently. This is disproportionately the case for the young and the poor (including the homeless), whose drinking is more likely to occur in public places. Moreover, as Broad and Lightowlers (2015) argue, the widespread availability of alcohol and its consumption sets those whose offending is alcohol-related up to fail, drawing them further into the CJS. As such, the successful consumer of alcohol can also be considered the victim of corporate marketing and irresponsible sales (Hobbs et al, 2005).

The aforementioned policy directions highlight the tensions implicit in preserving neoliberal business and market imperatives, governing licensed leisure at the expense of protecting citizens from harm (both health and social) and maintaining their liberty, namely, the liberalisation of regulations governing the sale and consumption of alcohol, and the concurrent criminalisation of intoxication and increased regulation of alcohol-related disorder. This appears particularly conflicted given that reducing availability is still the most promising policy avenue for alcohol harm prevention.

CARLY LIGHTOWLERS

See also: **Anti-Social Behaviour, Harm and Victimisation; Homelessness and Victimisation**

Readings
Broad, R. and Lightowlers, C. (2015) 'Policy and practice tensions in tackling alcohol abuse and violence in probation settings', *Probation Journal*, 62(3): 251–67.
Hobbs, D., Winlow, S., Hadfield, P. and Lister, S. (2005) 'Violent hypocrisy', *European Journal of Criminology*, 2: 161–83.

Hough, M. and Hunter, G. (2008) 'The 2003 Licensing Act's impact on crime and disorder: an evaluation', *Criminology and Criminal Justice*, 8(3): 239–60.

Measham, F. (2006) 'The new policy mix: alcohol, harm minimisation, and determined drunkenness in contemporary society', *International Journal of Drug Policy*, 17: 258–68.

Measham, F. and Moore, K. (2008) 'The criminalisation of intoxication', in P. Squires (ed) *ASBO nation: The criminalisation of nuisance*. Bristol: The Policy Press, pp 273–88.

ANIMAL VICTIMS AND VICTIMISATION

The study of non-human animals as victims of crime and wider social harms has only recently gathered momentum with the parallel development of green criminology. Like criminology, victimology has traditionally been almost exclusively anthropocentric in its outlook. Indeed, even the more recent discussions of environmental victims have largely failed to consider in any depth the victimisation of non-human animals. Beirne and South (2007) argue that given the extension of criminology by green criminologists to *some* environmental harms, this continued anthropocentric bias is unjustified because animals live in environments and their own physical, emotional and psychological well-being is absolutely and intimately linked to the health and good standing of those environments.

In terms of theory, some criminologists have approached the issue as one of animal rights. In discussing this Beirne (2007) has emphasised the utilitarian argument. This gives animals rights on the basis that they are sentient beings who can suffer and feel pain. This perspective is in keeping with the utilitarian philosophy of maximising pleasure while minimising pain; thus, humans should not inflict pain upon them. This is contrasted to the 'animals as moral patients' argument, whereby animals are conceived as 'subjects-of-a-life', and while they are not capable of 'doing right or wrong' themselves, in moral terms, they are equivalent to human infants, the mentally ill and young children by reason of their ability to suffer. It is therefore argued that failing to respect the rights of non-human 'moral patients' while preserving the lives and avoiding harm to 'human moral patients' would be arbitrary and thus unjust.

As a matter of *law* (in most jurisdictions), non-human animals cannot be classed as victims of crime. That said, some crimes exist that involve non-human animals as direct targets, for example: (in the UK) the docking of dogs' tails (Animal Welfare Act 2006, s 6); causing, attending or videoing dog fighting (Animal Welfare Act 2006, s 8); illegal hunting, for example, of foxes under the Hunting

Act 2004; the importation of protected endangered species (Control of Trade in Endangered Species (COTES) (Enforcement) Regulations 1997, as amended by COTES (Enforcement) (Amendment) Regulations 2005 and 2007); killing, injuring or taking a wild bird (Wildlife and Countryside Act 1981, as amended); and sexual intercourse with an animal (Sexual Offences Act 2003, s 69). Other crimes exist that indirectly cause suffering to non-human animals, such as: the discharging of poisonous, noxious or polluting matter into various types of waters (Environmental Permitting (England & Wales) Regulations 2010); illegal logging (through the destruction of habitat); and as part of wider family (domestic) abuse.

All variants of animal rights approaches can be critiqued, and they have proved problematic at best and of little interest to policymakers at worst, particularly within most legal jurisdictions. Even within the 'animal rights' movement, there are significant differences of opinion, notably, between the welfarist/protectionist and abolitionist approaches. The preceding notwithstanding, it is worth emphasising that for non-human victims of (environmental) harm, not all non-human animals are equally ignored by policymakers. In a revealing commentary, Nurse (2013) contends that informal rules embedded in specific practices and nuances might dictate, for example, that in some inner-city police areas, most animal harm (except possibly wildlife crime and the trade in endangered species) is seen as being a low priority for police investigation. Whereas in rural areas (such as Scotland, where rarer birds such as the golden eagle and the osprey are seen as being part of Scotland's heritage, or those parts of the US where California condors or bald eagles hold special cultural significance), considerable police and criminal justice resources may be directed at those offenders who seek to exploit wildlife resources.

Such examples provide a timely reminder that even those seeking to challenge anthropocentricity can fall foul of what may be termed hierarchical speciesism (or differentiation) – the ordering of species by how important, sentient, human-like or even 'cute' they are – those higher in the hierarchy receiving more protective attention. Of course, a similar argument has been applied to public policy in relation to human victims of crime for decades, whereby victims are 'ranked' in terms of their so-called 'ideal' status as innocent, harmed individuals.

MATTHEW HALL

See also: Environmental and Green Victimology; Victim Hierarchy

Readings
Beirne, P. and South, N. (2007) *Issues in green criminology: Confronting harms against environments, humanity and other animals.* Cullompton: Willan Publishing.

Nurse, A. (2013) *Animal harm: Perspectives on why people harm and kill animals.* Farnham: Ashgate.

ANTI-SOCIAL BEHAVIOUR, HARM AND VICTIMISATION

Anti-social behaviour (ASB) is constructed somewhat differently to crime, with *construction* being the operative word. This is because virtually *any* behaviour can be perceived as anti-social if it causes (or is likely to cause) harassment, alarm or distress to the (potential) victim. This all-encompassing definition is useful for victims because it has the ability to capture a broad spectrum of non-criminal behaviours, ranging from persistently barking dogs to problematic drug use. ASB is generally considered to constitute nuisance behaviour; it is often characterised by repetitive behaviours that typically escalate in severity, such as verbal harassment or bullying, which can cause victims significant long-term harm. By contrast, this broad definition can be problematic for those deemed to be committing ASB because by allowing almost any behaviour to be considered anti-social, those exhibiting relatively innocuous behaviour can be brought to the attention of the authorities. Young people are often disproportionately affected in this way, with the teenage pastime of 'hanging around' regularly attracting unfair scrutiny by being perceived as anti-social.

As a result of the flexible definition, counting and measuring incidents of ASB is challenging, making it difficult to accurately assess exactly how much ASB occurs and who suffers harm. Many variations of ASB can affect a number of different people within a community, such as noisy neighbours or vandalism. These incidents may be reported by everyone affected, or the incident may not be reported at all if people are unsure who to report it to (police, local authority or social housing provider) or they are too afraid to report it due to the fear of reprisals. Conversely, the behaviour may not be considered anti-social by anyone at all. Subjective interpretations and tolerance levels towards such behaviours are compounded by local definitions of ASB that were created and tailored to reflect communities' needs.

Despite the difficulties in quantifying ASB, various methods have been employed to assess the harm that ASB causes. In 2003 in the UK, the Home Office conducted a one-day count of all ASB incidents reported to the police and local authorities during a 24-hour period. Despite producing a substantial figure of approximately 65,000 incidents, this method lacks context and fails to recognise the socially constructed nature of ASB. Between 2004 and 2012, *perceptions* of ASB were primarily used to assess the impact of ASB instead of counting incidents, with this constructed proxy measure generated through the British

Crime Survey/Crime Survey for England and Wales. These statistics produced the proportion of residents who perceived there to be high levels of ASB in their local area, which reached a record high of 21% in 2002/03. This suggests that even when perceptions of high levels of ASB were at their greatest, only a relatively small proportion of the population suffered significantly. The data also highlight the societal groups who are *most likely* to perceive ASB as a problem (from which ASB victimisation can be inferred). These include: young people; those who have been victims of crime in the past 12 months; those living in urban areas; and those living in the most deprived areas. Many deprived urban areas comprise social housing estates, where the residual tenure of marginalised groups and challenging tenants that have to live somewhere can combine to create ASB hot spots, an issue stereotypically portrayed by the television drama *Shameless*.

Since 1998, successive governments in England and Wales have attempted to tackle ASB by introducing new legislation, with the most well-known sanction being the Anti-Social Behaviour Order (1999–2015), which was replaced by the (very similar) Civil Injunction in 2015. These civil orders, based on hearsay evidence, prohibit a range of non-criminal behaviours, but are punishable under criminal law upon breach and can attract a prison sentence that may be disproportionate to the ASB being committed. This 'hybrid law' has faced criticism for creating a personalised list of criminal offences for each recipient, making it highly unlikely the authorities will be able to police each order and sanction every breach. These sanctions do not offer instant relief to victims, often taking weeks or months to implement. Victims are often asked to contribute to this process by keeping an incident diary where patterns of persistent ASB can be identified and presented as evidence.

VICKY HEAP

See also: **Policy and Victims in the UK**

Readings
Burney, E. (2009) *Making people behave – Anti-social behaviour, politics and policy* (2nd edn). Cullompton: Willan Publishing.
Duggan, M. and Heap, V. (2014) *Administrating victimization: The politics of anti-social behaviour and hate crime policy*. Basingstoke: Palgrave Macmillan.
Millie, A. (2007) *Anti-social behaviour*. Maidenhead: McGraw-Hill.

APPEALS AGAINST WRONGFUL CONVICTION

It is commonly believed that if an individual is convicted of a criminal offence, they are entitled to appeal if they think that it is wrongful and to have the conviction overturned if the individual is innocent. However, this is not how the criminal appeals system works, nor is being innocent the basis upon which wrongful convictions are overturned. Instead, criminal appeals in England and Wales attempt to determine not whether appellants are factually guilty or factually innocent, but whether convictions are 'safe' or 'unsafe' in law according to the prevailing rules and procedures of the appeal court in question (see Naughton, 2013).

There are two main routes to appeal against a criminal conviction in England and Wales: first, appeals to the Crown Court for convictions given in a magistrates' court for less serious offences, such as motoring offences, minor assaults, theft and handling stolen goods; and, second, appeals to the Court of Appeal (Criminal Division) for convictions given in the Crown Court for more serious offences, such as murder, manslaughter, rape and robbery. Alleged victims of wrongful convictions, whether convicted in a magistrates' court or the Crown Court, can also apply to the Criminal Cases Review Commission (CCRC), the world's first statutory public body that reviews alleged miscarriages of justice that have failed in the normal appeal process, in order to have their convictions referred back to the relevant appeal court for further consideration.

Analysing these in order, those convicted in a magistrates' court have an automatic right to appeal to the Crown Court, whereupon there is a full rehearing of the case. In addition, if alleged victims of wrongful convictions in magistrates' courts fail to obtain an acquittal in an appeal to the Crown Court, the original conviction will be upheld, but the appellant has further appeal rights to the Court of Appeal (Criminal Division).

Despite the extensive appeal rights provided to those convicted in magistrates' courts, there is not an automatic right to an appeal against criminal convictions given in the Crown Court. Rather, those convicted in the Crown Court are only permitted to make a request for leave to appeal to the Court of Appeal (Criminal Division), and this usually has to be done within 28 days from the date of the conviction. Appeals to the Court of Appeal (Criminal Division) against criminal convictions given in the Crown Court also have other stipulations that detract from the lay understanding. For instance, there is a requirement that, except in exceptional circumstances, any evidence to be considered by the Court of Appeal (Criminal Division) is 'fresh' evidence that was not or could not have been made available at the time of the original trial. This means that alleged victims of wrongful convictions who may have evidence of factual innocence that was not made available at the time of the original trial (defence lawyer error or incompetence, for instance) may not have that evidence accepted as grounds of appeal by the Court of Appeal (Criminal Division).

Finally, the CCRC is the last resort for alleged victims of wrongful conviction who fail to have their convictions overturned in the normal appeals system. It was established in response to notorious wrongful conviction cases such as the Guildford Four and Birmingham Six because the previous system for investigating alleged wrongful convictions was apparently failing to refer potentially meritorious cases back to the appeal court for political as opposed to legal reasons (see Naughton, 2009). However, the CCRC has been subjected to much critique (see Naughton and Tan, 2013) in that its claimed independence and ability to assist innocent victims of wrongful convictions is fundamentally undermined by the requirement that it only refer cases back to the appeal courts if it thinks that there is a 'real possibility' that the conviction will be overturned. This literally handcuffs the CCRC to the rules and procedures of the appeal courts, also restricting the cases that it can refer to those in which there is fresh evidence that was not available at the original trial or previous appeal. In consequence, alleged victims of wrongful convictions who may be innocent and who are unable to fulfil this test may not be able to overturn their convictions.

MICHAEL NAUGHTON

See also: **Miscarriage of Justice, Wrongful Conviction and Victims**

Readings
Naughton, M. (2009) 'Introduction', in M. Naughton (ed) *The Criminal Cases Review Commission: Hope for the innocent?* Basingstoke: Palgrave Macmillan, pp 1–14.
Naughton, M. (2013) 'The Court of Appeal (Criminal Division)', in M. Naughton (ed) *The innocent and the criminal justice system.* Basingstoke: Palgrave Macmillan, pp 140–59.
Naughton, M. and Tan, G. (2013) 'Report: Symposium on the Reform of the Criminal Cases Review Commission'. Available at: http://www.innocencenetwork.org.uk/wp-content/uploads/2013/01/CCRC-Symposium-Report.pdf

AUSTERITY, HARM AND VICTIMISATION

In the UK, austerity is the main policy response to the financial crisis that began to unfold in 2007/08 and describes the expansion of a neoliberal economic policy that positions the poor as the main 'debt burden'. It is important to situate discussions of austerity within studies of criminology and victimology because measures of fiscal discipline implemented in the post-crash period have resulted in significant financial, physical and psychological harms experienced by those most affected by it. Within criminology, it is useful to think about the harms of austerity within the context of the 'social harm approach' (Hillyard and Tombs, 2007). As opposed to simply focusing on those harms defined under criminal law, the social harm approach moves beyond those conventional understandings of crime and victimisation and focuses on political programmes that create social problems and produce harmful outcomes, such as inadequate housing and unemployment. The social harm approach, then, is suitably apt for thinking about austerity as a harmful policy response to the financial crisis as it encourages us to engage with the economic, physical and psychological fallout caused by the chain of austerity measures.

Perhaps the first visible victims of the financial crisis were those victims of the 'housing bubble' and housing crisis. When the housing bubble burst in 2007/08, it overwhelmingly and disproportionately affected low-income households with mortgages. In the immediate aftermath, 'empty neighborhoods, depopulated towns' became evident (Rolnik, 2013, p 1058) as banks repossessed hundreds of thousands of homes in North and South America and also across Europe. However, the extent of victimisation caused by austerity is pervasive, affecting even those households without mortgages. From 2010 onwards, governments in those economies most affected by the financial crisis began to implement 'new rounds of fiscal discipline, local government downsizing and privatization' (Peck, 2013, p 3), as well as implementing major welfare cuts and reforming welfare entitlements.

In the UK, the first set of welfare reforms to be made during the post-crash period came into effect in 2011. Since this time, new benefit terms and conditions have made it difficult for welfare recipients to prove that they are eligible for key benefits. Where people are deemed to be eligible, the amount of financial support available has since reduced and the former Coalition government has enforced stricter benefit sanctions for recipients who do not adhere to these new rules. Labelled as 'Britain's secret penal system', Webster (2015) argues that the number of financial penalties imposed as a result of benefit sanctions 'now exceeds the number of fines imposed by the courts'.

Austerity measures have reduced people and households to economic hardship and destitution, where many are left without money for food, gas and electricity. At worst, people have died. In the UK in 2013, a welfare claimant died of acute lack of insulin as a result of not being able to afford the electricity costs to keep his insulin refrigerated. A death inquiry found that he died while serving a benefit sanction and, thus, had no recourse to financial support for his electricity costs. The coroner also confirmed that the individual died with no food in his stomach. In other cases, several people have committed suicide as a result of having their benefit entitlements withdrawn completely. The Department for Work and Pensions (DWP) has carried out 49 peer-reviewed cases of 'benefit-related suicide' (although campaigners argue that many more people have died and/or self-harmed as a result of benefit-related activity). According to the government, benefit-related suicide can be described as suicide or harm that 'is associated with DWP related activity' (House of Commons Work and Pensions Committee, 2015 p 54). In 2013, a victim of benefit-related activity, Stephanie Bottrill, committed suicide by walking into a motorway as a result of having to pay for a spare bedroom – 'the bedroom tax'. The coroner passed a verdict that Stephanie Bottrill committed suicide due to 'stress and anxiety'.

The harmful impact of austerity is not isolated to the UK, but occurring in other countries. In Greece, suicide mortality peaked in 2012, the highest recorded in 30 years, and in Spain, there have been several housing-related suicides as banks repossess homes and homeowners are forced to pay high interest payments on top of their original housing debt.

Almost one decade into the post-crash period, there is a painful awareness of the harms of austerity. Unprecedented levels of suicide mortality, premature death, social inequality and poverty all convey that victims of austerity do not fall within conventional analyses of crime and victimisation, but are victims of a political and economic order – one that fails to protect citizens from the financial, physical and psychological harms of the financial crisis.

VICKIE COOPER

See also: **Financial Harm and Victimisation; Social Harm**

Readings

Hillyard, P. and Tombs, S. (2007) 'From "crime" to social harm?', *Crime, Law and Social Change*, 48: 9–25.

House of Commons Work and Pensions Committee (2015) *Benefit sanctions policy beyond the Oakley Review Fifth Report of Session 2014–15*, London: TSO. Available online at http://www.publications.parliament.uk/pa/cm201415/cmselect/cmworpen/814/814.pdf

Peck, J. (2013) 'Pushing austerity: state failure, municipal bankruptcy and the crises of fiscal federalism in the USA', *Cambridge Journal of Regions, Economy and Society* 7(1): 17–44.

Rolnik, R. (2013) 'Late neoliberalism: the financialization of homeownership and housing rights', *International Journal of Urban and Regional Research*, 37(3): 1058–66.

Webster, D. (2015) 'Benefit sanctions: Britain's secret penal system', Centre for Crime and Justice. Available at: http://www.crimeandjustice.org.uk/resources/benefit-sanctions-britains-secret-penal-system

AVERSION THERAPY, HARM AND VICTIMISATION

Aversion therapy is a form of behavioural conditioning designed to reduce or eliminate unwanted behaviour. Controversially, it was widely deployed in the mid-20th century to treat sexual and social 'deviants', including homosexuals, transsexuals, fetishists and paedophiles. It has also been used to treat alcoholism, drug addiction, obesity, smoking and aggression.

Aversive techniques were derived from Pavlovian conditioning. In aversion therapy, undesirable feelings or behaviours were repeatedly associated with negative stimuli in the hope of inducing an aversion to the undesired feeling or behaviour. Negative stimuli commonly used included electric shocks, nausea-inducing emetics, strong smells or a disapproving clinical gaze. Other aversive reinforcers that have been used include paralytic drugs, noise, the removal of privileges and aversive images. A later development in aversion therapy, covert sensitisation, involves the use of aversive images or imagined negative scenes or scenarios.

Advocates of aversion therapy claimed that it was a quick and effective method for controlling maladaptive behaviour (Tanner, 1973). It was seen as being safer and more humane than alternative psychological treatments, such as those involving the physical restraint of subjects. Additionally, it was argued that the trauma involved in the use of negative stimuli was justified by the benefits experienced by subjects. The rapid control of harmful behaviour, for example, drug abuse, was seen as an ethical good outweighing the application of noxious reinforcers and the potential harms of the therapy (Hadley, 1985).

Even at the height of its popularity, however, aversion therapy was criticised as being unethical and inhumane (Leinwand, 1975/76). Integral to aversion therapy is the infliction of pain and discomfort on the patient. Aversion therapy involving electric shocks could produce serious side effects. Shocks increased anxiety levels in patients, who sometimes responded with aggression. Misapplied electrodes could cause severe skin burns. Aversion therapy involving emetics designed to induce nausea and vomiting led to dehydration and, in at least one case, death. Paralytics used to induce a temporary paralysis produced terror and the sensation of drowning and death. Inducing aversive responses with chemicals proved to be clinically problematic because of difficulties in measuring the timing, onset and duration of the drugs. Synchronising the aversive agent with the deviant behaviour could thus be extremely difficult. Aversive drugs are also particularly unpleasant. It may take a subject too long to recover from their application for the conditioning to be repeated sufficiently frequently for the treatment to be effective.

Aversion therapy was also deployed in the prison system to treat deviant criminal behaviour. Aversion therapy has theoretical sympathies with both retributivist and utilitarian philosophies of justice. They all involve 'punishment' to change a subject's behaviour. The application of aversive therapies in the criminal justice system is seen as problematic because of ethical and clinical concerns. Coercive therapy has been found to be ineffectual and may not be compatible with ethical clinical practice. Depending on the aversant used and the conditions of application, it may constitute cruel and unusual punishment (Leinwand, 1975/76).

The use of aversion therapy in sexual reorientation therapy has also been widely condemned. Aversive techniques have been demonstrated to be effective in producing negative reactions or indifference to sexual stimuli, but they have not been shown to induce a change in sexual orientation. So, while homosexuals, for example, might be conditioned to respond negatively to same-sex sexual stimulation, aversive techniques do not produce corresponding positive responses to heterosexual stimulation where no degree of heterosexual desire or sexual experience was pre-existing. In addition, a range of negative outcomes of sexual reorientation therapy, including long-term sexual dysfunction, suicidal ideation, anxiety, depression, lowered self-esteem and loss of religiosity and family, have been widely reported (Serovich et al, 2008). The use of aversive techniques in sexual reorientation therapy declined dramatically after the removal of homosexuality as a psychiatric disorder from the *Diagnostics Statistical Manual* in 1974.

Aversion therapy practised with electric or chemical aversants would now be considered unethical by professional therapeutic organisations. The milder form of covert sensitisation is still used in treating drug and alcohol addiction, and in some sex offender treatment programmes. Aversive techniques involving a weak aversant (such as snapping an elastic band) may be promoted in self-help programmes.

TIMOTHY W. JONES

See also: **Iatrogenic Harm, 'Crime' and Victimisation; Medicalisation, Harm and Victimisation**

Readings
Hadley, N.H. (1985) *Foundations of aversion therapy*. Dordrecht: Springer Netherlands.

Leinwand, S.N. (1975/76) 'Aversion therapy: punishment as treatment and treatment as cruel and unusual punishment', *Southern California Law Review*, 49: 880–983.

Serovich, J.M., Craft, S.M., Toviessi, P., Gangamma, R., McDowell, T. and Grafsky, E.L. (2008) 'A systematic review of the research base on sexual reorientation therapies', *Journal of Marital and Family Therapy*, 34(2): 227–38.

Tanner, B.A. (1973) 'Aversive shock issues: physical danger, emotional harm, effectiveness, and "dehumanisation"', *Journal of Behavior Therapy and Experimental Psychiatry*, 4(2): 113–15.

B

BLAME AND VICTIMS

The term 'victim blaming' refers to the extent to which a person might be viewed as in some way responsible for the experience that they have suffered. In the context of criminal victimisation, this involves perceptions of how blameworthy or culpable the victim is. This idea is sometimes evident in criminal justice procedures and practice, where, in an effort to divert blame from the offender, blame is attributed to the victim (Davies, 2007). For example, the victim's relationship with the perpetrator might be explored and/or the victim's conduct might be subject to scrutiny, and the ways in which this is done may insinuate that the victim was blameworthy. It is therefore the manner in which the victim as witness is questioned that is crucial. Cross-examination, if insensitively done, can appear to suggest that the victim is partially responsible for bringing the injury upon themselves. The line of questioning in court of the victim-witness can appear to be testing the extent to which they may have contributed to their victimisation (Daly and Bouhours, 2010). These illustrations of 'victim blaming' clearly show that it is an emotively charged term.

'Victim blaming' is closely associated with a range of similarly controversial terms, including 'victim precipitation', 'victim provocation' and 'victim culpability'. Each of these terms has variously been used in an attempt to understand how people become victims of crime (Walklate, 2007). Like the term 'victim blaming', they are emotive and controversial due to the way in which they suggest that the victim might have invited their victimisation or incited the offence and the injury/assault/attack. Examples of the ways in which a victim might contribute to their experience have included what some – including those defending the perpetrator – might view as 'provocative' behaviour before and/or during the criminal event. Alternatively, the victim's conduct might be interpreted as risky if they were taking part in activities that are likely to bring forth harm or increase their own vulnerability. In this way, the victim is seen as the author of their own misfortune, having brought the suffering on themselves. The extent to which crime is 'precipitated' by victim behaviour has been used as a way of explaining criminal homicide, as well as cases of rape, where the assumption that 'she's asking for it' became prevalent. Such explanations encapsulate the concept of victim blaming, where the victim is constructed not as faultless, but as having contributed towards their own victimisation; in the latter example, women are blamed for the serious sexual assault they suffered. The concepts of victim blaming, victim precipitation, victim provocation and victim culpability are employed within victimology to conceptualise the dynamics of victimisation and to illustrate how victimhood is a process.

The 'ideal victim' is a term coined by Christie (1986) to denote the major attributes belonging to a model or ideal-type victim. This term suggests an 'innocent' victim, where the victim has played no part in their own victimisation and fits the stereotyped view of a victim, a worthy victim who deserves help. Such victims tend to have the hallmarks of vulnerability and innocence. They are likely to be incapable of fighting back against an assailant, previously unacquainted with the offender and possess no offending history of their own (Duggan and Heap, 2014). Early writers on victims of crime created a tradition of victim blaming by putting the victims of particular types of crime into a variety of categories according to how innocent or how blameworthy/culpable they appeared to be. They focused on the individual victim's conduct and the victim's relationship with the offender (see, eg, the work of Von Hentig and Mendelsohn, as summarised by Walklate, 2007). These early efforts to differentiate and demarcate victims from non-victims resulted in victim typologies, constructed to help to understand what different types of victims have in common and how they differ from others. However, while identifying and distinguishing between different kinds of victims is a means of generating an understanding of the dynamics of victimisation and, in particular, the victim–offender relationship, it simultaneously creates an impression of a hierarchy of victimisation, with some victims achieving victim status more easily than others. The emotive and controversial aspects of the term 'victim blaming' lie in the suggestion that victims might have invited harm upon themselves by having provoked, contributed or encouraged a response in the offender that increased the victim's likelihood of being criminally victimised. Such victims are 'guilty victims', being less deserving of the label 'victim' due to their own role in the process. In this view, these victims are less worthy victims, they have rendered themselves at greater risk to, or more vulnerable to, victimisation.

PAMELA DAVIES

See also: **Deviant Victims; Victim Hierarchy**

Readings

Christie, N. (1986) 'The ideal victim', in E.A. Fattah (ed) *From crime policy to victim policy: Reorientating the justice system.* Basingstoke: Macmillan Press, pp 17–30.

Daly, K. and Bouhours, B. (2010) 'Rape and attrition in the legal process: a comparative analysis of five countries', *Crime and Justice: An Annual Review of Research*, Vol 39: 565-650, Chicago: University of Chicago Press.

Davies, P. (2007) 'Criminal (In)justice for victims?', in P. Davies, P. Francis and C. Greer (eds) *Victims, crime and society*, London: Sage, pp 251-278.

Duggan, M. and V. Heap (2014) *Administrating victimisation: The politics of anti-social behaviour and hate crime policy*, Basingstoke: Palgrave Macmillan.

Green, S. (2007) 'Crime, victimisation and vulnerability', in S. Walklate (ed) *Handbook of victims and victimology*, Cullompton: Willan Publishing.

Walklate, S. L. (2007) 'Men as victims' in P. Davies, P. Francis and C. Greer (eds) *Victims, crime and society*, London: Sage, pp 142-64.

C

CHILD PROTECTION AND CHILDREN'S RIGHTS

Over many thousands of years, people's notion and awareness of child abuse or neglect has gone through different phases. In ancient times, children were not given special protection; in the Middle Ages, they were looked on as 'little adults' (Aries, 1962). In the mid–1800s, the idea that children ought to be protected first appeared. Beginning in France, for instance, laws first provided limited protection for children in their workplace, then the right for children to be educated and later recognised the status of the child in families. By the beginning of the 1900s, such law was common throughout mainland Europe and also marked the beginning of the transition from children being seen as objects of concern to being subjects of rights; however, another 80 years would pass before the rights of children would become universal.

In places colonised by Britain (eg Australia), early forms of child protection centred initially on concern for vagrant children and, later, on the care of abandoned (including illegitimate) and abused children whose parents were held to be socially inadequate (Swain, 2014). Laws were motivated by a desire to rescue such children and regulate those willing to care for them. Governments, on the one hand, showed a preparedness to hand children over to almost anyone offering to provide for these children while, on the other hand, showed little interest in protecting children from their parents or guardians (Liddell, 1993) or interfering with the sanctity of the family (Fogarty, 2008). Consistent with this, laws were enacted to deter parents 'foisting their children on the state' (Swain, 2014, p 7).

After the First World War, the League of Nations (an early attempt to establish what today is known as the United Nations [UN]) established a committee for child protection, as well as adopting the Declaration of the Rights of the Child, which is the first international treaty concerning children's rights and the responsibilities of adults. Despite its rights orientation, this declaration was predominantly focused on the welfare of children. Next, in the aftermath of the Second World War, the plight of many children was terrible, to say the least. In response, an international fund was set up; this was the United Nations International Children's Emergency Fund (UNICEF), which funds programmes for helping children in, among other things, their education and health.

In the 1940s, the UN adopted the Universal Declaration of Human Rights, which acknowledges that 'motherhood and childhood are entitled to special care and assistance'; in the 1950s, it adopted the Declaration of the Rights of the Child. Although it was 'soft law' that was not endorsed by all UN nation states, the declaration serves as an important step towards the promulgation of the Universal Declaration of Children Rights. It also paved the way for other international law, such as the International Covenant on Economic, Social and Cultural Rights, comprising the right to protection against economic exploitation, the right to be educated and the right to health care. Although progressive, these laws are premised on protecting children as objects rather than as subjects with rights.

In the midst of the Cold War, research on 'battered-child syndrome' (Kempe et al, 1962), which the media highlighted (Tomison, 2001), prompted dramatic changes in child protection. In addition, greater public awareness put pressure on governments to introduce laws and policies to apply to situations where children were seen to be 'at risk'. In the US, for instance, professionally staffed child protection services were set up. Whereas in the US, reliance on the state's coercive powers grew, in Western Europe, nations focused more on their responsibility to provide for children's health and education, as well as to support parents through income support.

During the 1970s, further discourse on children's rights resulted in the International Year of the Child in 1979 and the establishment of a committee to draft a Convention on the Rights of the Child. Then, in 1989, the UN General Assembly unanimously adopted the convention, which encapsulated economic, social and cultural rights of children. These rights go beyond protection to considering children as full subjects of human rights. A decade on, the UN adopted a convention outlawing forms of child labour; just over two decades on, it ratified the optional protocol to the International Charter of Child Rights that prohibits children taking part in armed conflicts. Other declarations and covenants of intergovernmental bodies, such as the Council of Europe, the Organisation of African Unity and the Pan-American Organisation, have reiterated similar concerns to protect children. The 'rights-based' approach now underpins the existence of countless child rights government agencies and non-government organisations.

Following increased awareness of the incidence and impact of child abuse, especially sexual abuse (Council of Europe, 2010), the focus of child protection widened during the 1980s and 1990s to include situations where children were considered at risk not only of abuse, but also of psychological harm and neglect. This has resulted in increased demand on child protection services, which have been found to be wanting in many nations (Scott, 2006). Furthermore, there is a growing acceptance of a public health approach to child protection that provides for: primary interventions universally available to all families; secondary preventive interventions available to families at risk of child abuse or neglect; and tertiary 'protective' interventions for families where child abuse or neglect has happened (Council of Europe, 2010; CFCA, 2014). Yet, as has been the case throughout, children's rights continue to be less about adults' fundamental duties and more about regulating adults' actions.

MICHAEL O'CONNELL and SARAH FLETCHER

See also: **Age and Victimisation; Universal Declaration of Human Rights**

Readings

Aries, P. (1962) *Centuries of children.* New York, NY: Vintage Books.

CFCA (Child Family Community Australia) (2014) *Defining the public health model for the child welfare services context.* Melbourne: Child Family Community Australia & Australian Institute of Family Studies. Available at: www.aifs.gov. au/cfca/publications/defining_public_health_model_child_welfare_servi

Council of Europe (2010) *Protecting children from sexual violence: A comprehensive approach.* Strasburg Cedex: Council of Europe Publishing.

Fogarty, J. (2008) 'Some aspects of the early history of child protection in Australia', *Family Matters,* 78: 52–59. Available at: https://aifs.gov.au/publications/family-matters/issue-78/some-aspects-early-history-child-protection-australia

Kempe, C.H., Silverman, F.N., Steele, B.F., Droegemueller, W. and Silver, H.K. (1962) 'The battered-child syndrome', *Journal of the American Medical Association,* 181: 17–24.

Liddell, M. (1993) 'Child welfare and care in Australia: understanding the past to influence the future', in C.R. Goddard and R. Carew (eds) *Responding to children: Child welfare practice.* Melbourne: Longman Cheshire, pp 28–62.

Scott, D. (2006) 'Towards a public health model of child protection in Australia. Communities', *Children and Families Australia,* 1(1): 9–16.

Swain, S. (2014) *History of child protection legislation.* Sydney: Royal Commission into Institutional Responses to Child Sexual Abuse.

Tomison, A. (2001) 'A history of child protection. Back to the future?', *Family Matters*, 60: 46–57.

CODE OF PRACTICE FOR VICTIMS IN ENGLAND AND WALES

The Victims Code of Practice is a central feature of the principle of 'justice for all' that has informed recent criminal justice policy. It was published as a part of the Domestic Violence, Crime and Victims Act 2004 in October 2005. Effective from April 2006, it codifies all the expectations and obligations that a victim might have of the criminal justice system and sets targets for how and when the criminal justice agencies need to have responded to and/or delivered such services. It therefore pertains to all those services with which any victim of crime might have contact throughout the course of the progress of their case through the criminal justice system.

This code was clarified and enhanced in 2013. That document outlines the minimum standards of service provision that a victim of crime is entitled to expect and outlines enhanced entitlements for particular categories of victims: victims of the most serious crimes; persistently targeted victims; and vulnerable or intimidated victims. This document also outlines the procedures for complaint should these services not be delivered. In assessing the efficacy of the complaints procedure, Manikis (2012, p 169) concludes that the complexity of the process and its associated lack of clarity lends some support to the view that policy responses such as these further illustrate that 'victims can and might be used in the service of system efficiency and system legitimacy' rather than necessarily being a response genuinely motivated by a concern to improve their experiences. Further to this, a less systematic review of the complaints procedure produced by the Victims Commissioner in 2015 remarks on the persistent gap between what is offered by the Code of Practice in terms of the complaints procedure and victims' actual experiences of that system. Nonetheless, the move to codify service delivery in this way constitutes a stronger, more all-embracing approach to sensitising those who work in the criminal justice system to the victims and their experiences of the system than any of the previous victims' charters. This has led some to suggest that these codes moved the victim from being the complainant within the criminal justice system to an equal participant with rights. Indeed, this is a view that appears to be endorsed by the Home Office (2005). However, it should be noted that having claims to rights in law that are thereby enforceable (eg the protection of identity for female victims of rape) is not enshrined within the Victims Code of Practice (Rock, 2004; Criminal Justice Joint Inspection, 2009) or feasible within the structural relationship between complainant and defendant that characterises an adversarial system of justice as in England and Wales (McBarnett, 1988).

So, despite both political and campaign voices that suggest otherwise, victims of crime do not have a general legal claim to rights except in very particular circumstances. Nevertheless, access to a complaints procedure should service delivery fall short of the mark does enhance the role afforded to the victim of crime should they wish to pursue a case in such a process. To what extent the presence of this code makes a real difference to victim/witness experiences is, however, open to debate. It must be remembered that only around 3% of victims of crime actually pursue their case up to the point at which they come into contact with the full range of criminal justice services that are the subject of this code. As a consequence, the conclusion alluded to by Manikis (2012) earlier may be more than justified.

SANDRA WALKLATE

See also: **Human Rights and Victims; Neoliberalism and the Politicisation of the Victim; Policy and Victims in the UK**

Readings

Criminal Justice Joint Inspection (2009) *Report of a joint thematic review of victim witness experiences in the criminal justice system.* London: Home Office HMIC.

Home Office (2005) *Rebuilding lives: Supporting victims.* London: Stationary Office.

Manikis, M. (2012) 'Navigating through an obstacle course: the complaints mechanism for victims of crime in England and Wales', *Criminology and Criminal Justice*, 12(2): 149–74.

McBarnett, D. (1988) 'Victim in the witness box – confronting victimology's stereotype', *Contemporary Crises*, 7: 279–303.

Ministry of Justice (2013) *Code of practice for victims of crime.* London: Ministry of Justice.

Rock, P. (2004) *Constructing victims' rights: The Home Office, New Labour, and victims.* Oxford: Clarendon.

Victims' Commissioner (2015) 'A review of complaints and resolution for victims of crime'. Available at: http://victimscommissioner.org.uk

COMPENSATION

In civil terms, compensation refers to the counterbalancing or neutralising of a condition. This can be achieved by means of remuneration or recompense, by paying back or making amends. Compensation is for the loss or damage done to the injured party. The term 'compensation' is often linked to the term 'restitution'. Restitution in the criminal justice context is commonly recognised as financial recompense to victims of crime where the money that victims get comes from their offender or the state. Thus, both compensation and restitution imply the repayment, often in monetary terms, for loss or injury. In the context of crime and social harm, the pay-back method follows these restorative principles, whereby the injured party receives something in return for the harm that they have suffered. Such methods might include financial compensation but can also include other means of making amends or restoration. Thus, such recompense can be achieved as part of the criminal justice process.

There are many different forms that compensation can take and, consequently, there are a variety of different manifestations of compensatory arrangements and repayment methods. Notwithstanding the variety of forms that compensation can take, and the debates and controversies that these have provoked in the context of crime and victimisation, whatever method of compensation or repayment is used, there is a common underlying philosophy. From the restitutive and reparative perspective, crime represents a breach in the structure of society where the equilibrium has been disrupted. The individual victim has been deprived, disadvantaged or harmed in some way; the offender has estranged him/herself from the community and their victim in particular. Following this philosophy through, the damage done or harm experienced should be counterbalanced by, as far as possible, putting it right or making up for the harm done (Wright, 1982; Harding, 1989). Sanctions are therefore designed to restore the injured party to the state that they were in prior to their victimisation. There is a tangible, often economic, recompense for the victim. Furthermore, within an understanding of compensation as reparative, there is something to be gained by both the victim and their offender. For the offender, there is a direct opportunity for them to reimburse the victim, to make good. Under some schemes, this includes an opportunity to apologise, and for some, this represents a point of re-entry and reintegration into the community, an opportunity for the offender to reinstate their non-criminal status.

There are various routes to compensation, including via civil proceedings. In many countries, criminal justice penalties have compensatory principles enshrined within them (Miers, 2007). The tradition in Britain is such that victims have no right in criminal proceedings to compensation. However, court-ordered compensation has, since the 1980s, been increasingly encouraged as the preferred means of financial penalty used by the courts. Court-ordered compensation is financial recompense to victims of crime where the money that victims get comes directly from the offender. This is achieved by way of a sentence such as a Compensation Order, which can be imposed upon the offender from a criminal court (Davies, 2013). In England and Wales, in all cases involving death or injury, loss, or damage, the court must consider making such an order, which requires the offender to pay compensation to the victim according to their ability to pay.

State compensation refers to financial recompense to victims of crime where the money that victims get comes from the state. Various people and organisations had campaigned for the introduction of compensation arrangements (Mawby and Walklate, 1994), and there was a feeling at the time that too much was being done for offenders, so victims ought to be paid some attention. The state compensation scheme that exists in Britain originated in the 1960s and has since developed into a statutory, tariff-based scheme for victims of unlawful violence. A person may be eligible for an award under this scheme if they sustain a criminal injury that is directly attributable to their being a direct victim of a crime of violence (CICA, 2014). As noted earlier, victims have no right to compensation. Victims who feel that they are eligible must apply and satisfy the eligibility criteria if they are to be awarded compensation from the scheme. The scheme has been modified a number of times since the 1960s partly to ensure that the costs of the scheme are manageable. In comparison with other state compensation schemes across the globe, the scheme in Britain is considered a generous scheme catering for victims of violent crime (Brienen and Hoegen, 2000). However, it does have its critics, who query whether the money might better have been spent on other victim services. Nevertheless, it seems likely to have assisted a good number of victims with the financial costs of dealing with violent and sexual offences. In many cases, this type of compensation may have been a welcome symbolic affirmation of the hardship involved.

PAMELA DAVIES

See also: Victims of Crime

Readings

Brienen, M.E.I. and Hoegen, E.H. (2000) Victims of Crime in 22 European Criminal Justice Systems: The Implementation of Recommendation (85) 11 of the Council of Europe on the Position of the Victim in the Framework of Criminal Law and Procedure, Nijmegen, the Netherlands: University of Tilburg

Criminal Injuries Compensation Authority (2014) *Criminal Injuries Compensation: A guide*, London: Ministry of Justice.

Davies, P. (2013) 'Victims', in K. Hayward, A. Wahidin and E. Wincup (eds) *Criminology* (3rd edn), Oxford: Oxford University Press, pp 453-473.

Harding (1989) 'Reconciling mediation with criminal justice', in M. Wright and B. Galaway (eds) *Mediation and criminal justice: Victims, offenders and community*, London: Sage, pp 27-45.

Mawby, R.I. and Walklate, S. (1994) *Critical victimology*, London: Sage.

Miers, D. (2007) 'Looking beyond Great Britain: the development of criminal injuries compensation', in S. Walklate (ed) *Handbook of victims and victimology*. Cullompton: Willan Publishing, pp 337–62.

Rock, P. (2004) *Constructing victims' rights: The Home Office, New Labour and victims.* Oxford: Oxford University Press.

Wright, M. (1982) *Making good: Punishment and beyond*, London: Unwin Hymen.

CORONERS' INQUESTS AND VICTIMISATION

See: **Primary, Secondary and Tertiary Victims and Victimisation**

CORPORATE MANSLAUGHTER

On 8 December 1994, OLL Ltd became the first company in English legal history to be convicted of homicide after three schoolchildren were killed while canoeing in the 'care' of the company. OLL Ltd was small, so it was relatively easy to find its 'controlling minds', while the risks to which the students were exposed were both serious and obvious, and there was clear evidence that the managing director was aware of these. A handful of such convictions followed, all against small organisations.

The fact that these convictions had all been against very small companies raised the central legal problem in applying the law of manslaughter to a larger corporate entity; the legal test, that of identification, required identifying a company's acts and omissions with those of one or more controlling minds, corporate guilt being dependent on the guilt of one or more senior individuals. There appeared a clear, unjust irony here: while it was easier to apply the law to smaller companies, the very size and complexity of organisations such as P&O, Great Western Trains and Railtrack had not simply been a key factor in producing disasters, but were also the same features that rendered attempts at manslaughter prosecutions almost bound to fail.

In 1996, the Law Commission for England and Wales published a fully developed set of proposals for a new law on corporate manslaughter. The aim was simple: to make it easier for companies to be successfully prosecuted where there was sufficient evidence of serious negligence, in breach of health and safety law, which led to the death of workers or members of the public from work-related activities. However, the path from these proposals to the Corporate Manslaughter and Corporate Homicide Act 2007 (CMCHAct) was full of dead ends, controversies, broken promises and governments succumbing to the lobbying of the Confederation of British Industry, Institute of Directors and other employers and their organisations (Tombs and Whyte, 2007). It is perhaps unsurprising that what came out of a 13-year struggle was something that is 'conservative in form and is unlikely fundamentally to change' an effort to hold corporations legally to account for workplace killing (Almond and Colover, 2012, p 1000).

Successful prosecution under the CMCHAct requires evidence of serious management failure, not of serious individual failures; it includes a clearer test of whether or not the failure is gross ('falling far below what can reasonably be expected in the circumstances'); it sets out a clearer set of factors for juries to consider when determining guilt (related to the seriousness of the breach); and it introduces some element of corporate culture, through reference to the organisation's 'attitudes, policies, systems or accepted practices' (Centre for Corporate Accountability, 2008, p 17). It should also be emphasised that the CMCHAct only allows for the prosecution of organisations – individuals cannot be prosecuted even for contributing to this offence, although the ordinary law of manslaughter continues to apply to them (Centre for Corporate Accountability, 2008).

By the spring of 2015, there had been just 12 successful prosecutions (Tombs, 2015) and scrutiny of these convictions reveals key failings of the law. First, all of the companies successfully prosecuted thus far have been small enterprises that could have been successfully prosecuted under the common law of manslaughter. Thus, the large, complexly owned companies for which the new law was ostensibly designed have so far evaded its reach (Tombs, 2015). Perhaps relatedly, all of the convictions secured to date relate to offences involving a single fatality – while a key intention behind the law was to encompass multiple fatality incidents.

Second, the level of fines passed at sentencing has been relatively low. Following the passage of the CMCHAct, the Sentencing Guidelines Council issued 'definitive' guidance on appropriate levels of penalties following successful prosecution under the Act, with the key rationale for setting the level of fine being the 'seriousness of the offence' and factors contributing to this. Calculated in this way, fines should 'be punitive and sufficient to have an impact on the defendant', so that the 'appropriate fine will seldom be less than £500,000 and may be measured in millions of pounds' (Sentencing Guidelines Council, 2010, p 7). In fact, only *one* fine has so far reached this putative minimum – and this fine of £500,000 was imposed upon a company that at the start of the trial was, in fact, in administration (Sterecycle [Rotherham] Ltd).

Each year in the UK, up to 50,000 workers die from fatal injuries and work-related illnesses, of which a significant but unknown proportion are likely to be the result of legal breaches by their employers. Thus, the rate of convictions under the CMCHAct to date looks like a failure on the part of the Health and Safety Executive, police forces and the Crown Prosecution Service, and it may be that the CMCHAct is another weak, and, at best, symbolic, attempt to hold to account companies that kill.

STEVE TOMBS

See also: **State-Corporate Crime and Harm**

Readings

Almond, P. and Colover, S. (2012) 'Communication and social regulation: the criminalization of work-related death', *British Journal of Criminology*, 52(5): 997–1016.

Centre for Corporate Accountability (2008) *Guidance on the Corporate Manslaughter and Corporate Homicide Act 2007. A comprehensive briefing for the layperson and expert.* London: Centre for Corporate Accountability.

Sentencing Guidelines Council (2010) 'Corporate manslaughter & health and safety offences causing death. Definitive guideline'. Available at: http://www. sentencingcouncil.org.uk/wp-content/uploads/web__guideline_on_corporate_ manslaughter_accessible.pdf

Tombs, S. (2015) 'Corporate killing with impunity', *OU Criminology*. Available at: https://oucriminology.wordpress.com/

Tombs, S. and Whyte, D. (2007) *Safety crimes.* Cullompton: Willan Publishing.

COURTS AND VICTIMS

Courts are rarely victim-friendly places. However, British courts have traditionally been even less victim-oriented than courts abroad. In many countries in continental Europe, there has traditionally been provision for the victim to be involved in the prosecution process, and in the US, court services for victims were radically reformed in the 1970s as part of the Law Enforcement Assistance Administration's attempts to encourage greater victim/witness cooperation. In Britain, court services were somewhat late in arriving. Even now, the UK's system is largely geared towards help for witnesses (many of whom will be victims) in court, while victims' rights in court are limited.

In England and Wales, the need for support for victims in court was identified by research in the 1980s, leading Victim Support to establish a committee to consider the ways in which victims were treated in court. The subsequent report was highly critical of current practices, and made a wide range of recommendations on the information provided for victims/witnesses, the way in which they were treated in court and the layout of court buildings.

A number of initiatives flowed from these findings. First, Victim Support in England and Wales was commissioned to provide support for victims/witnesses in court through a new Witness Service. While, in theory, this involved help for all witnesses, in practice, most clients were victims. By 2002, support services were also established in all courts in England and Wales. Similar arrangements exist in Scotland and Northern Ireland. In 2010/11 in England and Wales, 268,000 witnesses were provided with support; of these, 40,000 witnesses received a pre-trial visit, being shown around the court so that they knew what to expect. Following a review of victim services by the Coalition government in 2012, the Witness Service in England and Wales continues to be administered centrally. However, in 2014, the contract was put out to tender, resulting in it being awarded to the Citizens Advice Bureau, which took over the service in April 2015.

While the development of the Witness Service reflects a UK tradition of involving the voluntary sector in providing support for victims, policies under the New Labour government also illustrated an increased public sector involvement. In England and Wales, but not elsewhere in the UK, Witness Care Units were established, jointly run by the police and Crown Prosecution Service (CPS). Witness Care Units work closely with Victim Support and the Witness Service – they provide a single point of contact for victims in order to allow earlier identification of victim and witness needs and enhanced coordination between the CPS and police. A needs assessment is carried out with all witnesses to identify problems that would prevent the witness attending court to give evidence, such as child-care or transport problems. The witness care officers then coordinate the support offered to the witnesses and manage any referrals to other agencies. They provide updates about the progress of the case, and at the end of the trial, they make sure that witnesses are told about the result and sentencing, and offered further support where appropriate. These systems of support were backed up by changes to the court buildings and pressures on court officials to improve their treatment of victims, as reflected in successive victim and witness charters.

These improvements largely address victims' needs rather than rights. The UK system does not allow victims any right to be involved as active participants in the trial process. They have no right to be heard or to give evidence. Victims do have the right to bring a private prosecution, albeit that this may be stopped in extreme circumstances. The rarity of such cases is largely due to the crippling cost. However, victims' rights have been addressed on two levels. First, following the US usage of Victim Impact Statements, Victim Personal Statements (VPSs) were introduced in 2000 and have been extended by the recent Coalition government. Second, as a result of pressure from within the European Union, victims' rights to challenge the decision not to prosecute have been increased through the Victims' Right to Review scheme, launched in 2013.

In many respects, these changes are to be welcomed. However, extending victims' rights so that victims may influence sentencing raises concerns over justice. While VPSs do not include sentencing recommendations, they do allow victims to describe the impact of the crime on them, which may be unproblematic where offenders are aware of the effects of their crimes on victims that they know to be vulnerable, but more contentious where offenders know little about their victims.

ROB I. MAWBY

See also: **Code of Practice for Victims in England and Wales; Policy and Victims in the UK; Victims of Crime**

Readings

Ministry of Justice (2012) 'Getting it right for victims and witnesses: the government response'. Available at: www.gov.uk/government/publications/getting-it-right-for-victims-and-witnesses-the-government-response
Walklate, S. (ed) (2007) *The handbook of victims and victimology*. Cullompton: Willan Publishing.

CRIME, VICTIMISATION AND VULNERABILITY

Crime is intentional or avoidable harm committed by one party against another. Victimologists study patterns of criminal victimisation and the treatment of victims by the criminal justice system. Using victim surveys, they collect data at the local, national and international levels to find out if some types of people are more likely to become victims than others. Victim surveys convey that the pattern and distribution of victimisation is both varied and complex (Maguire, 2012). In particular, victim surveys have demonstrated that there are many more victims than the official crime rate suggests. The reason for this is that many victims do not report their victimisation to the police, so the crime is never known about or investigated. There are many reasons for this under-reporting and they vary according to the type of victimisation but common reasons include: very minor injury; the belief that the police can do nothing; poor prior experience of criminal justice; social stigma; criminal complicity; desensitisation; or fear of retaliation (Maguire, 2012).

This results in types of 'hidden' victimisation, such as sexual and domestic violence, which are very susceptible to under-reporting because of the combination of powerlessness, stigma, consequences for family life and the sometimes insensitive treatment by criminal justice agencies to these types of intimate violation (Maguire, 2012). Crimes against children and old people living in care homes are also often under-reported because they are comparatively powerless and at the mercy of the staff who are employed to look after them (Davies et al, 2007). Minor physical injuries such as a slap across the face or a very minor financial injury such as having a window broken are also less likely to be reported because of the belief that the crime is so common that the police will not be interested or because the hassle of reporting the crime outweighs any perceived benefit.

Trends in victimisation can also be understood in terms of vulnerability. Vulnerability refers to any aspect of a person's or social group's circumstances that increases the impact of victimisation and is separate from the risk of victimisation. For example, young people are often more likely to be physically assaulted than elderly people but are less likely to be as severely harmed because, in general, they are less physically frail and are quicker to recover (Green, 2007). Elderly people are therefore more vulnerable to physical assault than young people and understandably more fearful of it despite being less at risk of actually being attacked.

As well as age, gender, ethnicity, sexuality and disability are important dynamics in understanding vulnerability. Some social groups, such as women, black and minority ethnic groups, lesbian, gay, bisexual and transgendered people, and disabled people, have less power than others and are subject to discriminatory attitudes such as racism, sexism and homophobia that can lead to forms of systematic victimisation and hate crimes (Chakraborti and Garland, 2015). These prejudicial attitudes can result in material and political vulnerabilities such as not having enough money to buy a decent security system or lacking enough political influence to have your concerns recognised by the relevant authorities. Either way, these structural (rather than individual) vulnerabilities deny less powerful groups the resources necessary to protect themselves from victimisation.

These types of discriminatory attitudes can become so institutionalised that they are not even recognised as forms of victimisation. For instance, minor forms of racial or sexual harassment in the street or workplace have often been seen as an unpleasant but 'normal' part of everyday life rather than crimes that can, and should, be reported. A good example of this type of vulnerability would be the uncovering of historical cases of child sex abuse by some high-profile and public figures during the 1970s and 1980s, when sexual attitudes towards women and young girls were very different and some celebrities took sexual advantage of vulnerable young girls and children. These crimes were not reported to the police at the time precisely because of these prevalent sexist attitudes combined with the relative powerlessness of young girls compared to older male public figures. Contemporarily, public attitudes have begun to change in more recent years and many victims of this type of abuse have come forward as the police and courts seek to investigate and prosecute these crimes. In addition, in the UK and other parts of the world, hate crime legislation has been introduced to prevent and prosecute crimes predicated on the hatred of a particular social, religious or cultural group.

SIMON GREEN

See also: **Official Crime Statistics and Victim Surveys**

Readings

Chakraborti, N. and Garland, J. (eds) (2015) *Hate crime: Impacts, causes and responses* (2nd edn). London: Sage.

Davies, P., Francis, P. and Greer, C. (eds) (2007) *Victims, crime and society*. London: Sage.

Green, S. (2007) 'Crime, victimisation and vulnerability', in S. Walklate (ed) *Handbook of victims and victimology*. Cullompton: Willan Publishing, pp 91–120.

Maguire, M. (2012) 'Criminal statistics and the construction of crime', in M. Maguire, R. Morgan and R. Reiner (eds) *The Oxford handbook of criminology* (4th edn). Oxford: Oxford University Press, pp 205–44.

CRIMINAL INJURIES COMPENSATION AUTHORITY

The Criminal Injuries Compensation Authority (CICA) is the executive agency responsible for the administration of the Criminal Injuries Compensation Scheme (CICS). The CICA is sponsored by the Ministry of Justice and deals with compensation claims from people who have been physically or mentally injured because they were the blameless victim of a violent crime in England, Scotland or Wales. Criminal injuries compensation originated in the 1960s and has since developed into a statutory, tariff-based scheme for victims of unlawful violence. Today, the scheme is overseen by the secretary of state under the Criminal Injuries Compensation Act 1995, having been approved by each House of Parliament (CICA, 2013).

The CICA ultimately decides if a person is eligible to be made an award, and the level of the award. A person may be eligible for an award under this scheme if they sustain a criminal injury that is directly attributable to them being a direct victim of a crime of violence sustaining physical or mental injury. The scheme sets out what the eligibility criteria are, lists and describes the injuries for which an award may be made, and gives tariffs and levels of compensation.

There are several contentious issues related to this form of state compensation. For example, there are concerns connected to key features of the scheme's rules and eligibility criteria. One controversial issue concerns the regard given to the victim's character and history. In so doing, the criteria is linked to applicant biography, which suggests that there are deserving and undeserving victims, and innocent and blameworthy victim applicants. According to the rules and eligibility criteria of the CICS, there are victims who deserve (but do not have a right to) compensation and there are others who can be discriminated against and can be denied their application for a variety of reasons. Some of these reasons are related to keeping down the cost of the scheme (the minimum and maximum payments and the tariff-based approach). The consequences can appear to punish and even re-victimise those who have failed to secure help in the criminal justice process.

In order to qualify for an award, the CICA requires their deserving victims to be blameless and innocent, a worthy or 'ideal-type' victim (see Christie, 1986) who has suffered physical and mental pain and injury due to criminal injury (a physical attack, an assault, wounding or sexual attack, arson, and death of a close relative caused by a criminal act).

Critics suggest that these rules and eligibility criteria, as well as the numerous disentitling conditions (Goodey, 2005), result in an uneven distribution of criminal injuries compensation awards and amount to an exclusive scheme that reinforces the tradition of victims of crime having no rights-based entitlement to compensation (Davies, 2013, 2016). Victims of non-violent crimes are excluded; those with greater financial resources, as well as those with very little economic power, can be subjected to penalty point deductions if they also fall foul of the 'disentitling conditions'. Those whose injuries do not meet the lower threshold of compensation are excluded entirely from the scheme. Under the eligibility criteria for the scheme that the CICA administers, a victim of crime does not qualify if they are considered blameworthy, culpable or partially responsible – if they contributed to the attack/injury, participated in the violence, attracted, incited, precipitated the injury/assault/attack, engaged in 'provocative' behaviour, or were the author of their own misfortune having brought the suffering on their own head. Furthermore, applicants will not qualify if the application is considered fraudulent, that is, the perpetrator is likely to gain from any payment and/or is in collusion with the offender. If no violence was involved or if the victim's behaviour before, during or after the criminal event is considered precipitative, then this will disqualify the application. Similarly, disqualifying factors include whether the victim was involved in excessive risk-taking, failed to cooperate with the authorities, refused to make a statement, refused to go to court, refused or failed to report the incident without delay, refused or failed to

—

cooperate with the police, refused to go on an identity parade, or the injuries were received abroad. Those who do not qualify for the minimum award, have previous (unspent) criminal convictions, have suffered from a minor assault, have suffered from the effects of a non-violent crime or do not know of the existence of the CICS are excluded. Although the scheme was updated in 2001 and 2008, these modifications included additional exclusion criteria and this coincides with victim recourse to the CICA declining.

PAMELA DAVIES

See also: **Compensation; Victims of Crime**

Readings

Christie, N. (1986) 'The ideal victim', in E. Fattah (ed) *From crime policy to victim policy: Reorientating the justice system*, Basingstoke: Macmillan Press, pp 17–30.

CICA (Criminal Injuries Compensation Authority) (2013) *CICA annual report and accounts for 2013 to 2014*. London: HMSO. Available at: https://www.gov.uk/government/organisations/criminal-injuries-compensation-authority

Davies, P. (2013) 'Victims', in K. Hayward, A. Wahidin and E. Wincup (eds) *Criminology* (3rd edn), Oxford: Oxford University Press, pp 453-473.

Davies, P. (2016) 'Victimology' in A. Brisman, E. Carrabine and N. South (eds) *The Routledge Companion to Criminological Theory and Concepts*, London: Routledge.

Goodey, J. (2005) *Victims and victimology: Research, policy and practice*, Harlow: Pearson Education Ltd.

CRIMINAL JUSTICE AND VICTIMS

Criminal justice is often referred to as a system, when, in reality, it is many diverse agencies, often disconnected and even possibly working to differing objectives. Some agencies may be oriented in their objectives to prevent and manage crime, while other agencies may be involved in deliberate attempts to reform those subjected to controls or sanctions. This lack of synergy means that academics refer to criminal justice as a 'process' rather than a 'system' (McConville and Wilson, 2002). The focus of criminal justice is also perpetually changing, excluding past offences that contemporarily can seem ludicrous, such as witchcraft, and criminalising offences whose previous absence seems incomprehensible, such as rape within marriage (Godfrey et al, 2007).

—

The role of victims in contemporary criminal justice is central to established notions of 'justice', and political discourse and resulting policy changes have increasingly sought to improve the service provided to victims. Victims are commonly utilised as the simple ideological counterpart to offenders, and, as such, this oppositional relationship is frequently exploited by those advocating greater rights and resources for victims. Such campaigners claim that victims have been marginalised within criminal justice and that their experiences of victimisation have been neglected. Nonetheless, the fact that victims' rights and concerns do not take primacy is a necessary requirement within the due process of law, often simply referred to as the 'balance' between purportedly competing rights. Redressing that balance is commonly believed to necessitate the expansion of victims' rights and the curtailment of the ostensibly privileged legal position of defendants, who are typically stereotyped as 'criminals'.

Indeed, in the UK, much of the New Labour government's attempt to evidence that they were as 'tough on crime' as the Conservatives is a litany of claims and aspirations to redress the balance in favour of victims of crime and anti-social behaviour. As Edwards (2004, p 969) so accurately summarises: 'Popular discourse about crime and criminal justice, fed and shaped by the media, is dominated by polarized perceptions of criminal and victim, of good and bad, innocent and guilty'. However, in reality, there is little evidence of that alleged imbalance as, certainly since 1979, the vast majority of criminal justice reforms have been regressive in terms of suspects', defendants' and offenders' rights, and, on the contrary, have seen a massive extension in state powers. Victims are likewise exploited and turned into a convenient political weapon with which to attack more liberal and progressive ideas on crime and offenders that are ridiculed as romanticised and/or idealistic (Lea and Young, 1984). Balance 'assumes a duality of positions in diametric opposition' (Edwards, 2004, p 972) wherein the expansion of victims' rights is conditional upon the restriction of suspects' rights. In reality, however, one cannot take rights exclusively from suspects, for example, the right to remain silent without undue inference being drawn, without taking that right from all. Thus, claims that victims must be treated fairly are open to the question 'What does that actually mean?' Even the most superficial longitudinal or cross-cultural gaze will evidence that what is considered 'fair' treatment for victims in criminal justice is historically specific and open to extreme variations in attitudes and practices.

Nevertheless, victims are contemporaneously increasingly allowed to contribute in the criminal justice process, for example, via victim statements in court and parole hearings. Much criminal justice reform has been driven by the ideological exploitation of caricatured victims and offenders and purportedly common-sense solutions exemplified by 'short, sharp shock' punitive regimes. Far from being rebalanced to favour victims, many critical criminologists have observed an increasingly authoritarian and illiberal state propped up and defended by criminal justice agencies left to deal with the inequalities inherent in neoliberal advanced capitalism. Therein, many victims are unacknowledged or their victimisation is obfuscated. The victims of corporate and state crimes are rarely reported and, if so, their deaths and injuries are often portrayed as the result of disasters bereft of criminal responsibility, and/or even victim blaming (Scraton, 2013). Likewise, sexist and racist beliefs can inform attempts to blame or repudiate victims for their behaviour allegedly precipitating their victimisation.

LIAM McCANN

See also: **Blame and Victims; Neoliberalism and the Politicisation of the Victim; State-Corporate Crime and Harm; Victims of Crime**

Readings
Edwards, I. (2004) 'An ambiguous participant: the crime victim and criminal justice decision-making', *British Journal of Criminology*, 44(6): 967–82.
Godfrey, B., Lawrence, P. and Williams, C. (2007) *History and crime: Key approaches to criminology*. London: Sage.
Lea, J. and Young, J. (1984) *What is to be done about law and order? Crisis in the eighties*. Harmondsworth: Penguin.
McConville, M. and Wilson, G. (eds) (2002) *The handbook of the criminal justice process*. Oxford: Oxford University Press.
Scraton, P. (2013) 'The legacy of Hillsborough: liberating truth, challenging power', *Race and Class*, 55(2): 1–27.

CRIMINOLOGY AND WAR

The study of war by criminologists is often attributed to the work of Jamieson (1998) and her suggestion that a 'criminology of war' was important to address the production of mass violence and victimisation. While war can be traced in some of the earliest criminological literatures, it is widely acknowledged that a critical and sustained analysis of the subject of war is a relatively new area of study (Jamieson, 1998; Ruggiero, 2006; Walklate and McGarry, 2015). That is to say, while war was implicit in criminological theorising, it was not until Jamieson's (1998) pivotal chapter 'Towards a criminology of war' that authors were afforded a platform for explorations of war within the discipline.

Historically, criminology has paid sporadic attention to the complexities that connect war and crime. These works tend to be clustered around specific conflicts or specific war crimes and are typically found in the US and the UK. Walklate and McGarry (2015) provide an overview of this engagement and explain the key themes. In the earliest works, wartime crime rates were of interest but warfare was considered a way to identify the state and its ability to engage in *legitimate* violence. Explorations then moved to interrogate the causes of war and claimed that war should only be waged with *just cause* – otherwise, it could be considered a criminal act (or series of acts). For the Chicago School, profiteering from war was considered a corporate crime and it was suggested that this and other corporate deviancy should be treated as a 'war crime'. However, despite these encouraging developments, studies of war within the discipline remained wedded to the legal framework – only discussing those times when behaviours transgressed legal boundaries.

Jamieson's (1998, p 480) purpose was to redress that. She urged students of crime to be more attentive to the material, moral, gendered and emotional complexities that connect war and crime before suggesting a framework in which to conduct further research through a series of critically engaged methods. That framework advised against those debates that overwhelmingly started from the point of legality, advocating instead a focus on the exceptionally damaging and harmful behaviours of warfare and its aftermath. Legitimate behaviours can, of course, cause extreme harm to both people and property. Further to this, Ruggiero (2006) points out that legitimate power creates illegitimate opportunities to maintain that power. There is evidence that this work reached some of the most influential thinkers of the time but it was to be the events of 9/11 that would awaken Western criminological curiosity (Walklate and McGarry, 2015).

The significance of the violence of 9/11 was witnessed in theatres of conflict across the world (and is clearly still being witnessed). Aside from the loss of life and initial declaration of the War on Terror, Guantanamo Bay and Abu Ghraib also revealed many of the limits of juridical power in addressing new and emergent forms of violence. Often referred to as 'states of exception', the response to 9/11 added to the complexities between war and crime by somewhat blurring the lines between war and punishment and the military and policing. The advances in the literature since can be described as moving in four directions: war as inherently criminal or as having criminological properties; the complexities that link military operations with policing functions; war as a site of victimisation; and, lastly, how post-war situations frequently challenge the boundaries of war and domestic criminal justice processes (Murray, 2015).

As criminology continues to contribute to understandings of this new security terrain and offers ways to rethink war and post-war conditions, authors are engaging in a critical exercise. Through their work, they offer a new subject of study to theorists of crime, harm and victimisation. When war is placed within these frameworks, matters concerning victimisation, abuses of political power and human rights, and human rights violations are central to the progress of criminological thought beyond legality.

EMMA MURRAY

See also: **Legal Crimes – Lawful But Awful; Soldiers and Victimisation; Zemiology**

Readings

Green, P. and Ward, T. (2004) *State crime: Governments, violence and corruption.* London: Pluto Press.

Jamieson, R. (1998) 'Towards a criminology of war', in R. Vincenzo, N. South and I. Taylor (eds) *The new European criminology: Crime and social order in Europe.* London: Routledge, pp 480–506.

Murray, E. (2015) 'Can the violent veteran see blurred lines more clearly', in S. Walklate and R. McGarry (eds) *Criminology and war: Transgressing the borders.* London: Routledge.

Ruggiero, V. (2006) *Understanding political violence: A criminological analysis.* Maidenhead: Open University Press.

Walklate, S. and McGarry, R. (eds) (2015) *Criminology and war: Transgressing the borders.* London: Routledge.

CRITICAL VICTIMOLOGY

The roots of critical victimology, indeed, victimology itself, are situated in various approaches to criminology. As the study of crime evolved from positivist attempts to 'solve' the crime problem, to more sophisticated analyses of the social-structural factors that contribute to an understanding of crime and related phenomena, so, too, did considerations and understandings of victim issues.

Early schools of criminology were largely offender-centred, with little or no interest in victims. Most criminologists worked from within positivist frameworks of observing the social world, that is, tools for measuring the social world were adapted from the natural sciences. The aim was to identify the causes of crime (whether they be social, psychological or biological) by comparing criminals to non-criminals, and to develop responses tailored to addressing or eliminating those factors. Positivism, then as now, generally reflects a consensus approach to the social world; what constitutes a crime, what constitutes a criminal, and the neutrality of a benevolent state and its primary agents of social control (police, courts, corrections and judiciary) remain uncontested.

The shift from the focus on offenders to frameworks that accommodated victim-related issues similarly reflected a parallel paradigm rooted in positivism and consensus theory: a comparison of victims to non-victims; the identification of the causes of victimisation (eg lifestyle, risk, victim precipitation) as a route to prevention; and an unexplored relationship between the victim and the neutral state as the guardian of the social good (Walklate, 2007).

'New' or critical criminology emerged in the early 1970s and integrated notions of the unequal distribution of power into our understanding of, and responses to, crime (Taylor et al, 1973). A new set of questions emerged for criminologists that replaced the more mundane considerations of the 'causes' of crime: how 'crime' and 'criminals' were defined and responded to; whether the state and its agents were truly neutral arbiters of the common good; and whose interests were served by a coercive state apparatus such as the criminal justice system (Quinney, 1972; Friedrichs, 1983). The influence of Marxist and feminist thought made explicit the impact of class and gender inequality on both the substance and impact of criminal law, and opened the door to analyses of other social inequalities such as race, age and sexuality (Reiman and Leighton, 2010).

The influence of these new frameworks on victimology was similarly profound. More fundamental questions regarding the influence of power relations and social inequality on what constitutes a 'victim', and the social and political response to victimisation, rose to the forefront of analyses (Christie, 1986; Roach, 1999). Critical victimology could also accommodate considerations of systemic forms of victimisation, such as hate crimes and violence against women, precisely because they reflect social-structural issues of race, class, and gender inequality (Walklate, 2007).

Critical victimology also looks at the role of the state itself in both defining and contributing to victimisation, and encourages a scepticism regarding state-centred responses to *both* crime and victimisation. The framework encourages remedies beyond the punitive and bureaucratic institutional framework of the criminal justice system as the state and its agents (particularly the police and prosecutors) are so regularly 'parties' in victimisations. Alternatives to the 'offender-centred' focus on punishment and deterrence, which generally provides little direct relief to victims, are replaced with more transformative approaches that challenge the underlying processes and inequities that fuel an oppressive and unequal machinery of justice. Transformative approaches have thus provided a bridge between criminology, victimology and other social sciences, and attempt a broader analysis of social and political phenomena such as crime and victimisation.

TAMMY LANDAU

—

See also: **Social Harm; Zemiology**

Readings

Christie, N. (1986) 'The ideal victim', in E. Fattah (ed) *From crime policy to victim policy: Reorienting the justice system.* Basingstoke: MacMillan Press, pp 17–30.
Friedrichs, D. (1983) 'Victimology: a consideration of the radical critique', *Crime and Delinquency*, 29: 283–94.
Quinney, R. (1972) 'Who is the victim?', *Criminology*, 10: 314–23.
Reiman, J. and Leighton, P. (2010) *The rich get richer and the poor get prison: Ideology, class, and criminal justice* (9th edn). Boston, MA: Allyn and Bacon/Pearson.
Roach, K. (1999) *Due process and victims' rights: The new law and politics of criminal justice.* Toronto: University of Toronto Press.
Taylor, I., Walton, P. and Young, J. (1973) *The new criminology: For a social theory of deviance.* London: Routledge and Kegan Paul.
Walklate, S. (2007) *Imagining the victim of crime.* Maidenhead: McGraw Hill and Open University Press.

CULTURAL VICTIMOLOGY

Cultural victimology cannot be understood without addressing cultural criminology as a primary influence on this perspective. Yet, cultural criminology is, in itself, a rather contentious and elastic perspective, and certainly many of the criminologists who are referred to as adopting or exemplifying cultural criminology's methodologies do not refer to themselves as cultural criminologists. Whether it is a genuinely new theoretical perspective and how it differs from similar perspectives like media and cultural studies is queried widely.

The basic and meritorious idea of deploying ethnographic methodologies into criminological research may well be overshadowed at times. The fascination with the intricacies of micro-level subcultures and deviance can lead to a fixation on style, excitement, street life and argot that can obscure the wider socio-political economic and law enforcement factors that are far more determining.

There are copious varieties of cultural criminology and that is part of the problem in trying to define what it is. The most problematic are those who wish to study subcultures as criminogenic and purportedly or actually threatening the existing social order, often evidenced in their resistance to specifically repressive and discriminatory elements of policing. It is important that, herein, the prefacing of culture with 'sub' is done in a pejorative manner designed to marginalise and 'other' those being observed (Williams, 2015). The best 'cultural criminologists attempt to deconstruct the official demonization of various "outsiders" …

to produce alternative understandings of them' (Ferrell, 2013 [1999], p 337). However, importantly, that cultural understanding is empathetic of these others, seeking to know and appreciate, as opposed to wishing to constrain and counter.

This identifies the important social role that the media plays in facilitating the ideological political construction of crime and crime agendas, wherein often relatively insignificant or isolated offending is amplified and caricatured to meet political and law-and-order agendas. Herein, cultural criminology's foci upon image and style and political and media representations of ascribed meanings and significance is central to cultural victimology. How this focus impacts upon the social, political and cultural creation or denial of victimisation and victimhood is crucial. It is the significance of difference, real or ascribed, between cultures that delineates the legitimacy of victims. Thus, complex and dynamic socio-economic and political factors impact on not just cultures, but also their acceptance or rejection; thus, much more than merely meaning is found in their representation.

Cultural victimology explores diverse and contested notions of alleged cultural differences and purportedly 'natural' cultural antagonisms that drive conflicts and facilitate victimisation in many forms. These are most significant, but not exclusively, in relation to victimisation linked to hate crimes, around sex and sexuality, 'race' and racism, and, increasingly, xenophobia and Islamaphobic ideologies adopted by some mainstream political parties. This is exemplified by claims that some alleged cultural values are at odds with an idealised uniform 'British culture' threatened by these caricatured 'alien others'.

It is therefore the language and images used to construct the persona around the 'victim' that signify their social legitimacy or not. Political and media discourses prefaced with key value-laden words that entice our empathy – 'innocent', 'honest' and 'hard-working' – and those inviting our animosity – 'savage', 'brutal' and 'feral' – typify such. Likewise, some cultural forms are claimed to deviate from and offend homogeneous traditional morals and values so much so that they are claimed to precipitate their victimisation.

LIAM McCANN

See also: Hate Crime and Victimisation; Xenophobia

Readings
Ferrell, J. (2013 [1999]) 'Cultural criminology', in E. McLaughlin and J. Muncie (eds) *Criminological perspectives: Essential readings*. London: Sage, pp 330–44.
Gelder, K. and Thornton, S. (eds) (1997) *The subcultures reader*. London: Routledge.

Gilroy, P. (1987) *There ain't no Black in the Union Jack: The cultural politics of race and nation.* London: Routledge.

Williams, P. (2015) 'Criminalising the Other: challenging the race–gang nexus', *Race & Class*, 56(3): 18–35.

Young, J. (2003) 'Merton with energy, Katz with structure: the sociology of vindictiveness and the criminology of transgression', *Theoretical Criminology*, 7(3): 388–414.

CULTURE AND VICTIMISATION

At an individual, group and societal level, wider social, political, religious and other cultural frameworks of understanding will impact upon experiences and understandings of, and responses to, victimisation.

In Western liberal democracies, victimisation attracts considerable media and public policy attention. While suffering has always been a part of human experience, in Western societies today, increasing numbers of people are attaching the label of 'victim' to themselves in order to understand their experiences. This might be as a result of a wider 'culture of complaint', in that people are seeking financial compensation for their harmful experiences (Furedi, 2004). This may also be part of a marketisation of victim experiences. There are many books, newspaper articles and social media forums written by and about victims. A common theme within these outputs seems to be that victims have survived their horrific experiences to become stronger and better people, to become survivors. This may be because a victimising experience can cause a great deal of distress not only to the people directly involved, but also to the wider audience who become aware of the terrible event as this brings into the open the vulnerability of human beings and the disorder that can engulf their lives. The contemporary fascination with victimisation may be partly explained as a societal search for meaning, a way of understanding why there is suffering (Spalek, 2016 [2006]).

Political cultures can mediate victimisation. Where there is ongoing conflict between different ethnic, political, religious and other groups, then there may be competition over claims of victimisation. Each group will be engaged in claiming that they are the real victims, that what has happened to them is far worse than to other people and groups. Terrorist movements like Al Qaeda and ISIS can use victimisation as a way of trying to justify violent acts, and individuals engaged in violence can themselves justify their acts as a result of their own or their group's historical and/or current victimisation. Al Qaeda and ISIS have both evoked powerful emotions within targeted populations in order to try to attract people to their cause.

—

Culture in relation to 'race'/ethnicity, faith and other aspects of diversity can also influence victimisation. Within some minority ethnic groups, there may be an increased focus upon extended families, who may or may not be supportive of family members who are being victimised. Honour and shame, and language barriers, may mean that victims do not seek help from wider society and so may remain within their abusive environments, particularly in cases of domestic and sexual violence. Dominant stereotypes of particular minority groups may impact upon how victimisation is experienced by individuals. For example, black women may be less likely to disclose experiences of sexual assault than white women as a result of expecting to be judged negatively by wider society due to racism and sexism. 'Race' and other diversity factors may impact upon recovery from victimisation. Cultural attributions about why individuals believe that they have been victimised will impact upon their responses to victimisation.

When studying the victimising experiences of minority ethnic women, critical black feminists have introduced the concept of 'spirit injury' or 'spirit murder' in order to explain and to try to understand the full impact of victimisation in relation to racism and sexism. The continual, daily harassment that black women can experience as a result of their race and gender might mean that to understand their victimisation, it is important to go beyond traditional understandings of the impacts of crime (Davis, 1997). Black women's victimisation might go beyond the psychological, emotional, behavioural and physical impacts of crime, as documented by social scientists (Davis, 1997; Neville et al, 2004), because their victimisation goes beyond single incident events. The notion of 'spirit injury' perhaps helps to capture the ongoing nature of some black women's victimisation. Within the notion of 'spirit injury' is an understanding that everyday and common experiences of racist and sexist abuse amount to a brutalisation of an individual's self-identity and dignity. Wider social structures that help to maintain racism and sexism can therefore victimise people at the level of their individual and group identities (Mama, 2000; Neville et al, 2004).

BASIA SPALEK

See also: **Compensation; Honour-Based Victimisation; Terrorism and Victimisation**

Readings
Davis, D. (1997) 'The harm that has no name: street harassment, embodiment and African American women', in A. Wing (ed) *Critical race feminism: A reader*. New York, NY: New York University Press, pp 192–202.
Furedi, F. (2004) *Therapy culture*. London: Routledge.
Mama, A. (2000) 'Woman abuse in London's black communities', in K. Owusu (ed) *Black British culture and society: A text reader*. London: Routledge, pp 89–110.

Neville, H., Oh, E., Spanierman, L., Heppner, M. and Clark, M. (2004) 'General and culturally specific factors influencing black and white rape survivors' self-esteem', *Psychology of Women Quarterly*, 28: 83–94.

Spalek, B. (2016 [2006]) *Crime victims: Theory, policy and practice.* Hampshire: Palgrave Macmillan.

D

DEATH PENALTY, HARM AND VICTIMISATION

The death penalty is literally judicial punishment by death. It is carried out in many parts of the world, particularly those adhering to Koranic law (ie those countries in which the public and some private aspects of life are regulated by Islam). Over 60% of the world's population live in countries where executions still take place – namely, China, India, Indonesia and the US – four of the world's most populous countries (UN, 2014). It has been practised by most societies at some point in their history, often accompanied by torture and often carried out in public. Methods range from beheading, stoning and hanging, to the use of an 'electric chair' or drugs. Despite its long existence, the recent trend in Western societies in particular is towards abolition. The continued use of the death penalty in some parts of the US is the exception, which Garland (2010, p 11) has called 'a peculiar institution', an 'anomaly'.

Defining the death penalty as a human rights issue is something resisted by retentionist countries, but it is useful for considering the harm related to it. As a matter of human rights, it sits in an uncomfortable position (O'Byrne, 2003). It is permitted by international law and therefore, in international law, does not by itself necessarily constitute cruel, inhuman or unusual punishment or torture. However, it may become an arbitrary violation of the right to life if imposed in circumstances that breach other rights – including the right to a fair trial and the prohibition on torture. It is particularly important that those facing the death penalty should be afforded special protection and guarantees to ensure a fair trial above and beyond those afforded in cases not carrying the death penalty. The

—
47

reality is that prevailing law and practice in many retentionist countries across the Caribbean, Africa and Asia do not provide the level of protection required in capital cases (UN, 2014). For example, in many of these cases, individuals who are sentenced to death have subsequently been found to be suffering from mental illness and/or an intellectual disability that affected the safety and lawfulness of their convictions and death sentences. Failure to follow agreed procedural safeguards in relation to trial in capital cases also extends to the right to appeal. However, in some countries such as North and South Korea, Japan, and parts of Pakistan, for example, there is no automatic right to appeal and the sentence is carried out swiftly (UN, 2014).

Conversely, the expensive and harm-inducing delay between trial and execution in the US to allow for appeals leads to lengthy stays on 'death row' and to a situation whereby more people on 'death row' die from natural causes than they do from execution (Garland, 2010). However, this delay between sentence and execution has allowed a series of victims of wrongful conviction to come to light, especially when DNA evidence has been found subsequent to the trial. Thus, the recent concern in the US about the death penalty is mainly concerned with the process by which it is applied and with the limits of what is constitutional under the Eighth Amendment's ban on 'cruel and unusual punishment', rather than with the morality of the sentence. In general, the death penalty is imposed upon the poorest, most powerless, most marginalised people in society, and in the US, can be considered a vestige of slavery and racial oppression (Lynch, 2013). Philips (2009) argues that due to suspects' poverty, they are often assigned lawyers who lack the skills and resources to represent them capably. While the biased imposition of the death penalty in the US remains, there is a general (Western) trend towards abolition. In 2010, the United Nations General Assembly made its most recent call for a global moratorium on executions. Despite such factors, Unnever (2010) argues that global support for the death penalty remains high, and remains particularly elevated in the US.

JO TURNER

See also: **Universal Declaration of Human Rights**

Readings

Garland, D. (2010) *A peculiar institution: America's death penalty in an age of abolition.* New York, NY: Oxford University Press.

Lynch, M. (2013) 'Institutionalising bias: the death penalty, federal drug prosecutions, and mechanisms of disparate punishment', *American Journal of Criminal Law*, 41(1): 91–131.

O'Byrne, D. (2003) *Human rights: An introduction.* Harlow: Pearson Education Limited.

—

Phillips, S. (2009) 'Criminology: legal disparities in the capital of capital punishment', *Journal of Criminal Law & Criminology*, 99(3): 717–55.

UN (United Nations) (2014) 'Moving away from the death penalty: arguments, trends and perspectives'. Available at: http://www.ohchr.org/Lists/MeetingsNY/Attachments/52/Moving-Away-from-the-Death-Penalty.pdf

Unnever, J. (2010) 'Global support for the death penalty', *Punishment & Society*, 12(4): 463–84.

DEVIANT VICTIMS

The concept of deviant victims is premised on the notion that 'deviance' is a label for characteristics and/or behaviour that a person or group attributes or imputes to another person or group, rather than anything inherent in the characteristics or behaviour. Deviance arises from the violation of norms that are always socially constructed and the product of social interaction and social processes. Similarly, as a label, 'victim' can be thought of as a meaning that gets attached to people, rather than something that can be taken for granted or assumed. Like deviance, it is an attribution and depends upon the norms in a given society. If a person cannot meet the normative expectations for a victim identity that operate in a particular historical period within a specific culture or subculture, important social actors such as victim advocates, law enforcement personnel, the public and even their friends may decide that they are a *deviant victim* (Dunn, 2010).

In the US in particular, these normative expectations are very similar to the 'feeling rules' governing sympathy. Ordinarily, sympathy is directed towards people whom are felt to be not at all responsible for their misfortune, whether their circumstance is financial, societal, medical or criminal victimisation. If a person gambles away their life savings, drinks to excess and develops cirrhosis of the liver, or is robbed while trying to purchase cocaine, less sympathy is felt for them than if their employer stole their pension, they have an illness due to environmental toxins or they are 'innocent bystanders' injured in the course of others' criminal activity. Sympathy is felt for the latter group, and they are the people most likely to be thought of as victims (whether the victimisation is criminal or not). The gambler, the drunk and the drug addict are going to have more trouble establishing their credibility as victims. Rather, people will think of them as deviant victims (although some may try to excuse their responsibility, referring to the casino industry, a genetic predisposition towards alcoholism and drug addiction, or terrible poverty as explanations).

To the degree that a person appears innocent of responsibility for victimisation, or that blame can be deflected towards some other cause, that person will conform to the ideal of the 'true' or 'real' victim. Alternatively, a person who looks to be in any way accountable for what has happened to them will face labelling as deviant, and the more people blame them, the more deviant the label and the less sympathy society imagines they deserve. One can think of this as a kind of continuum: as a case becomes more ambiguous, the label moves towards the 'blame' (and 'deviant victim') pole; when a person is clearly not at fault, or at least we label them as such, they appear blameless, and they earn the 'innocent victim' label at the other pole. As a consequence, the innocent victim is deemed deserving of help and sympathy, while the deviant victim is not.

Labelling people as deviant victims has many effects. In criminal justice systems, police officers are less likely to report crimes and to make arrests when victims do not meet their expectations of the 'normal victim' (unless mandated to do so). Prosecutors may pursue fewer or lesser charges, or decide not to prosecute at all. If a case does go to trial, the judge or jury may dismiss the charges, or find the perpetrators innocent. In a courtroom, a 'victim contest' may take place, wherein prosecutors and defence attorneys advance competing claims of blame and innocence. As the cost of losing such a contest is high for the prosecutor, many cases with even slightly deviant victims will be negotiated out of court (eg plea bargaining in some legal jurisdictions), despite what actually happened.

Unfortunately, normative expectations for innocent victims, like feeling rules for sympathy, are often highly gendered. In cases of intimate partner violence, women who do not appear feminine enough, or dependent enough, may look too 'tough' to be real victims. Rape victims who have been sexually active might be labelled as 'asking for it' in a culture in which women's virtue is more highly policed than the behaviours of sexual predators. The race, class and sexuality of victims may also play a role in a person being labelled as deviant, regardless of its relevance to the case.

Scholarly and campaigning opposition to culturally derived sentiments and practices that create identities of victims of less eligibility does exist. Indeed, the work of social movements such as those campaigning against rape and domestic abuse advocate against such 'victim blaming'. Despite this, labelling continues to be a problem.

JENNIFER L. DUNN

See also: **Blame and Victims; Courts and Victims; Victim Hierarchy**

Readings
Christie, N. (1986) 'The ideal victim', in E.A. Fattah (ed) *From crime policy to victim policy: Reorientating the justice system.* Basingstoke: Macmillan Press, pp 17–30.

Dunn, J.L. (2010) '"Vocabularies of victimization": toward explaining the deviant victim', *Deviant Behavior*, 31(2): 159–83.

Holstein, J.A. and Miller, G. (1990) 'Rethinking victimization: an interactional approach to victimology', *Symbolic Interaction*, 13(1): 103–22.

DISABILITY HATE CRIME

Disability hate crime was first recognised in the US in 1969 but was not formally acknowledged in the UK until April 2005 with the introduction of section 146 of the Criminal Justice Act 2003 (CJA). Hate crime laws are designed to target crimes motivated by hate and give increased sentences to perpetrators of crime that demonstrate violence, hostility or prejudice to people because of their race, gender identity, sexuality, religion or faith, or perceived or actual disability. Such legislation, and the various initiatives and policies that followed, focused on putting the victims first and obtaining 'fair' sentences for people committing these crimes. In the UK, the focus on disability hate crime can also arguably be attributed to some high-profile media reporting of cases of such crime, not least the tragic death of Fiona Pilkington, which, following an independent report, highlighted the failure of the criminal justice system (CJS) to appropriately identify, respond to and react to disability hate crime (Independent Police Complaints Commission, 2009). Furthermore, a report written in 2013 stated that there is a lack of clarity within the CJS (including police officers, the Crown Prosecution Service and Probation Trusts) and among the public as to what constitutes a disability hate crime. This influences whether or not cases are reported at all, whether they are reported as hate crimes, and the way in which they are dealt with once they are reported (Criminal Justice Joint Inspection Board, 2013).

Disability hate crime has increased over a number of years within England and Wales. In 2013/14, disability hate crime made up 4% of all hate crimes reported, with a total of 1,985 reported cases (an 8% increase on the previous year) (Creese and Lader, 2014). This increase could partially be explained through improved identification of and recording procedures for hate crime, although genuine increases in the actual rates of disability hate crime are also likely, especially considering the various attacks upon disabled people by mainstream media coverage and political rhetoric. Compared to other types of hate crime (eg race hate crimes, where 37,484 cases were reported in 2013/14), disability hate crime figures may appear relatively low. The Criminal Justice Joint Inspection Board (2013, p 4), however, make it clear that the low numbers should not indicate that the issue is any less serious as these are more likely to 'relate to the inability of the criminal justice system to combat prevalent social attitudes and to deal effectively with cases that can have inherent complexities'.

Within the CJA's 2003 framework of defining criminality and deciding on the most appropriate punitive action lie various ableist assumptions that serve to 'other' the disabled victim (as well as the perpetrator). The victim can be with or without impairment (but has been perceived to have a disability) and must be able to recognise that a hate crime has been committed against them. The victim has to therefore enter the category of 'other' and vulnerable for a crime to be identified. Assuming that the CJS continues to respond to its own internal critiques and begins to deal with disability hate crime in the manner that it deems appropriate, the desired end result will only ever be the (most harsh) persecution of a single perpetrator or group of perpetrators, who, after all, are merely acting upon the numerous damaging discourses that exist to denigrate, belittle and distrust disabled people. Section 146 of the CJA does nothing to re-educate and refocus the misguided hate or ideas surrounding disability. Some academics have nevertheless turned their attention to highlighting the problematic regimes of normalising discourses that render disabled people 'other' and 'inferior', and suggest that this is the place requiring attention if the causes of disability hate crime are ever to be abolished (Taylor et al, 2012).

Although disability hate crime legislation can help make an example of those who explicitly act on hate towards disabled people, contradictions exist in a society where some contemporary political rhetoric encourages suspicion and hatred towards disabled people (while justifying consistent attacks on disabled people's right to welfare). Without an interrogation and critique of neoliberal, normalising discourses, disabled people will struggle to escape the stereotype of dependent, vulnerable and disempowered victim. Governments need to stop investing solely in legislation that serves to fire-fight the symptoms of a society that refuses to acknowledge difference as positive, and interdependence as a necessary part of everyday life, and instead take steps to reduce the instances of disability hate crime in the first place.

CASSANDRA A. OGDEN

See also: **Hate Crime and Victimisation; Racist Hate Crime**

Readings
Creese, B. and Lader, D. (2014) *Hate crimes, England and Wales, 2013/14*. London: Home Office Statistical Bulletin. Available at: https://www.gov.uk/government/uploads/system/uploads/attachment_data/file/364198/hosb0214.pdf

Criminal Justice Joint Inspection Board (2013) 'Living in a different world: joint review of disability hate crime', HMCPSI, HMIC, HMI Probation, Crown copyright. Available at: https://www.justiceinspectorates.gov.uk/hmic/media/a-joint-review-of-disability-hate-crime-living-in-a-different-world-20130321.pdf

Independent Police Complaints Commission (2009) 'IPCC report into the contact between Fiona Pilkington and Leicestershire Constabulary 2004–2007', IPCC Reference: 2009/016872. Available at: http://www.ipcc.gov.uk/sites/default/files/Documents/investigation_commissioner_reports/pilkington_report_2_040511.pdf

Taylor, P., Corteen, K., Ogden, C. and Morley, S. (2012) '"Standing" by: disability hate crime and the police in England', *Criminal Justice Matters*, 87(1): 46–7.

DISASTERS AND VICTIMISATION

The early study of victimisation led by Mendelsohn began in 1937 and evolved to its zenith in 1976 with his concept of 'General Victimology'. This last victim classification clearly included those victimised by disasters (Hoffman, 1992). Since victimology emerged from criminology, the focus on non-crime victimisations has not developed much. However, in recent decades, interest in disasters has grown with regard to humanitarian responses and research (Freedy et al, 1992).

Although the definition of disasters varies according to organisations, the traditional definition has been: 'a sudden event affecting a focused area that produces great loss of life and property caused either by nature, by humans or by wars' (Webster's, 1971). The two key elements are: the force and speed of the event; and the presence of vulnerable people, especially children and elders. A disaster results when vulnerable people and property are exposed to a major force to the extent that the survival of their community is at significant risk. Today, by legislatively, economically and politically reforming prevention strategies, the role of humankind has been recognised as having the ability to significantly ameliorate the extent of death, injury and damage (International Federation of Red Cross and Red Crescent Societies and the Centre for Research on the Epidemiology of Disasters, 1993).

The most remarkable feature of a disaster that separates it from other forms of victimisation is its character as a sudden concentrated major force and the magnitude of its harm and damage: the number of deaths and injury, and the extent and cost of property damage. Another unique feature of disasters is the unexpected and blatant way that it exposes vulnerable persons and property, not only in the negligence to prevent or reduce the number of helpless people, but also in the inadequacies of the response to immediately rescue victims, to facilitate their recovery as soon as possible and to maintain treatment until recovery is achieved (Alexander, 2005). Perhaps the one country that exercises the most extensive prevention and response resources, especially with regard to earthquakes, mudslides and tsunamis, is Japan, one of the most developed and seismically active countries in the world. At the opposite end of the spectrum are countries that suffer greatly when experiencing disasters due to the extent of abject poverty, as with Bangladesh, one of the least developed and most densely populated countries in the world. These unique extremes in the availability of resources directly influence the ability of a country to cope and treat victims in the aftermath of massive victimisation.

Trying to match inadequate resources with overwhelming needs to treat many people is one of the significant challenges of developing countries that experience frequent disasters. These are countries that, under normal circumstances, struggle with poor governance, problematic economic conditions, poor public health and inadequate medical services. Despite understanding the severe risks faced by much of the population, these countries usually do not devote adequate resources to reducing vulnerability and increasing response preparedness. Especially noticeable is the paucity of full-time psychosocial professionals who could serve as the cadre of volunteer responders. In the aftermath of a disaster, the situation becomes exacerbated by the dire need for importing resources into an already disorganised environment. Most major disasters generate responses from foreign nations, which usually focus on the search and rescue mission during the first months, then they mostly depart. Few foreign resources are available to provide psychosocial treatment when it is needed after the search and rescue phase. In those countries where there are adequate mental health-care providers, the lion's share of disaster response comes from them: they are available, speak the local language and are able to remain for longer periods.

One of the ideal times to suggest reforms is during the aftermath, when the society and government officials are acutely aware of its shortcomings. This is the time to take advantage of the receptive audiences to suggest changes and lobby for legislative reforms. Some nations, such as the US, Japan and Indonesia, have developed model disaster legislation worthy of emulating.

JOHN P.J. DUSSICH

See also: **Victim Recovery**

Readings
Alexander, D.A. (2005) 'Early mental health intervention after disasters', *Advances in Psychiatric Treatment*, 11: 12–18.
Freedy, J.R., Resnick, H.S. and Kilpatrick, D.G. (1992) 'Conceptual framework for evaluating disaster impact: implications for clinical intervention', in L.S. Austin (ed) *Responding to disasters: A guide for mental health professionals*. Washington, DC: American Psychiatric Press, pp 2–33.

Hoffman, H. (1992) 'What did Mendelsohn really say?', in S. Ben David and G.F. Kirchhoff (eds) *International faces of victimology*. Mönchengladbach: WSV Publishing, pp 89–104.

International Federation of Red Cross and Red Crescent Societies and the Centre for Research on the Epidemiology of Disasters (1993) *World disasters report*. Norwell, MA: Kluwer Academic Publishers.

Webster's (1971) *Webster's third new international dictionary of the English language unabridged*. Springfield, MA: G. & C. Merriam Company, Publishers.

DISPLACEMENT, CRIME, HARM AND VICTIMISATION

Displacement has been defined as occurring 'when a person or group has been forced or obliged to flee or to leave their homes or places of habitual residence', and can be both internal, within a state's border, or external, where state borders are crossed (Duthie, 2012, p 13). The legal framework continues to distinguish between refugees, who have fled across state borders, and internally displaced persons (IDPs), who remain within their own state. Refugees are defined under the Refugee Convention of 1951 as persons fleeing persecution, which in more recent legal documents has been extended to include persons fleeing armed conflict, violence and human rights violations. Under the 1998 Guiding Principles on Internal Displacement, the definition of IDPs is broader and also includes displacement due to natural or human-made disasters. Nevertheless, there are clear similarities in the experiences of refugees and IDPs.

Displacement is predominantly caused by armed conflict and mass human rights violations. There has been a sharp escalation in the number of displaced persons globally, with an estimated 59.5 million people forcibly displaced at the end of 2014 compared with 37.5 million in 2004 (UNHCR, 2015). While the conflict in Syria partly accounts for the rise since 2011, there is an increased prevalence of displacement across many regions. Conflicts and situations of political repression in countries in Africa, Asia, the Middle East and Europe (Ukraine) have forced increasing numbers of people to flee their homes (UNHCR, 2015). Armed conflict has always driven displacement as civilians have fled the inevitable dangers of war. However, the increased targeting of civilians in contemporary armed conflict is a significant factor in the current figures. Displacement may be used not only to undermine the enemy, but also to 'ethnically cleanse' a particular territory of certain civilian populations, as witnessed in the conflict in the former Yugoslavia (Jacques, 2012).

Three branches of international law regulate the treatment of displaced persons: international humanitarian law (IHL), human rights law and international refugee law. While international refugee law does not encompass IDPs, the Guiding Principles constitute non-binding, but nevertheless significant, principles that address the treatment of IDPs. Under IHL, the forcible transfer and deportation of civilians in situations of occupation is prohibited and forced displacement is proscribed in non-international armed conflict (unless the security of civilians or imperative military reasons so demand). Moreover, IHL clearly prohibits the deliberate targeting of, and attacks on, civilians, such as rape, pillage, collective punishment and other acts aimed at terrorizing the civilian population, which may precipitate displacement. Under international criminal law, forcible or unlawful transfer or deportation may amount to war crimes or crimes against humanity and may be prosecuted in international or domestic tribunals. Related attacks on civilians, such as murder, rape and torture, also constitute international crimes.

The harms of displacement are manifold, including harms directly related to displacement and the harms that refugees and IDPs are exposed to as a result of displacement. Interdisciplinary insights have prompted understandings of the complex physical and psychological harms of displacement and the need for various forms of redress (Duthie, 2012; Bradley, 2013). There is also increasing recognition that displacement may be experienced differently according to gender, and that children, the elderly and disabled persons are particularly vulnerable (Hovil, 2012).

Displacement may be precipitated by extreme forms of violence and human rights violations, such as torture, sexual violence and the destruction of homes and livelihoods. Following displacement, refugees and IDPs are vulnerable to further violence as a result of unstable living conditions and the lack of family, community and state protection. Displaced persons may experience victimisation, discrimination and violence from host communities, as well as violence from other refugees and IDPs. In particular, there are clear linkages between the perpetration of sexual violence and displacement. Continued insecurity and violence may prevent return, meaning that the loss of home and prior community structures may be permanent. However, it is important to recognise both the multiple forms of victimisation experienced by displaced persons and the agency of refugees and IDPs and the strategies that they employ to survive and to rebuild their lives.

DIANA SANKEY

See also: **Criminology and War; Genocide, Harm and Victimisation**

Readings

Bradley, M. (2013) *Refugee repatriation: Justice, responsibility and redress*. Cambridge: Cambridge University Press.
Duthie, R. (ed) (2012) *Displacement and transitional justice*. New York, NY: SSRC.

—

Hovil, L. (2012) *Gender, transitional justice and displacement: Challenges in Africa's Great Lakes Region*. New York, NY: ICTJ.

Jacques, M. (2012) *Armed conflict and displacement: The protection of refugees and displaced persons under international humanitarian law*. Cambridge: Cambridge University Press.

UNHCR (United Nations High Commissioner for Refugees) (2015) *Global trends: Forced displacement in 2014*. Geneva: UNHCR.

DOMESTIC VIOLENCE, CRIME AND VICTIMS ACT 2004

The Domestic Violence, Crime and Victims Act 2004 (DVCVA) is an Act of the UK Parliament that received Royal Assent on 15 November 2004, applying to England, Wales and, in part, Northern Ireland. The DVCVA comprises three parts and contains provisions of major significance relating to victims of crime and, specifically, victims of domestic violence.

Part I of the DVCVA heralded what was viewed by the Home Office (2005) as the 'biggest overhaul of the law on domestic violence in the last 30 years' and was intended to improve and extend extant protections for victims. The Act aimed to achieve this by altering what had become crucial elements in responses to victims of domestic violence: non-molestation orders and occupation orders. Non-molestation orders were introduced by section 42 of the Family Law Act 1996 (FLA) and prohibited individuals from molesting an 'associated person', and/or prohibited the molestation of a 'relevant child' (s 62). Occupation orders (ss 31–41 FLA) often provided a means for excluding perpetrators of domestic violence from the family home and/or surrounding areas.

Notwithstanding that non-molestation and occupation orders represented a lynchpin in the protection of victims of domestic violence, there were various problems in their practical application that Part I of the DVCVA sought to address. First, section 1 of the DVCVA made breach of a non-molestation order a criminal offence, punishable by up to five years' imprisonment. Prior to this, while it was possible to attach a power of arrest to non-molestation orders, such orders remained under the governance of civil law via the family court and breaches were only punishable via the law of contempt, carrying a maximum sentence of two years. Second, sections 3–4 of the DVCVA enabled the courts to apply orders in cases involving same-sex couples and couples who had never cohabited or married by changing the FLA definition of 'associated persons'. Finally, section 2 of the DVCVA repealed section 41 of the FLA, which required courts to take into account decisions to cohabitate, rather than marry, when considering the nature or parties' relationships for the purpose of occupation orders. At the time, this was rightly seen to discriminate against same-sex couples. Section 2, however, did retain the need for courts to consider 'the level of commitment' involved in the relationship when making determinations.

In addition to the notable changes to the protections of the FLA, Part I of the DVCVA also addressed issues of domestic homicide. Section 5 created the new offence of 'causing or allowing the death of a child or a vulnerable adult', later amended to 'causing or allowing serious physical harm' by the Domestic Violence, Crime and Victims (Amendment) Act 2012. This was provided as a remedy in situations where it was clear that one or other of a child's parents had been responsible for their death but there was not sufficient evidence to demonstrate which one. The presence of such ambiguity presents as a 'loophole' in extant law. Section 9 originally established the procedure for domestic homicide reviews, though this provision was not brought into force until 2011 and further statutory guidance has followed.

Part I of the Act received mixed reactions. Many of the extensions in protection, such as that to same-sex couples, were seen as long overdue and welcomed (Home Office, 2003b). Other aspects of the Act were more controversial, such as the 'blurring of criminal and civil law' presented by section 1 (Liberty, 2003) and the impact that criminalisation has on the autonomy of survivors. Early evaluation of the DVCVA largely reflected the mixed initial reaction, showing a 'limited' and 'unclear' impact (Hester et al, 2008). The introduction of domestic violence protection orders post-2011 arguably makes it yet more difficult to assess the significance of the DVCVA provisions.

Part II of the DVCVA made various alterations to criminal procedure, including the extended availability of restraining orders (ss 12–13). Particularly significant are sections 22–25, which relate to the determination of defendants' fitness to plead and the disposals available to the court in these circumstances, and where the defendant is found not guilty by reason of insanity.

Part III of the DVCVA contained provisions of significance for victims more generally, namely, giving statutory recognition to the 'Code for Victims' and establishing the 'Commissioner for Victims' (s 48), who is responsible for promoting the interests of victims and witnesses. Sections 35–46 create rights of victims to receive information about, and make representations relative to, the release and discharge of those found to have committed sexual or violent offences.

KATHRYN DUTTON

See also: **Code of Practice for Victims in England and Wales; Domestic Violence, Victims and Victimisation**

Readings

Hester, M., Westmarland, N., Pearce, J. and Williamson, E. (2008) *Early evaluation of the Domestic Violence, Crime and Victims Act 2004*. London: Home Office.

Home Office (2003a) *Safety and justice: The government's proposals on domestic violence*, Cm5847. London: The Stationery Office.

Home Office (2003b) *Summary of responses to Safety and justice: The government's proposals on domestic violence*. London: The Stationery Office.

Home Office (2005) 'Correspondence: The Domestic Violence Crime and Victims Act'. Available at https://www.gov.uk/government/publications/the-domestic-violence-crime-and-victims-act-2004

Lawson, E., Johnson, M., Adams, L., Lamb, J. and Field, S. (2005) *Blackstone's guide to the Domestic Violence, Crime and Victims Act (2004)*. Oxford: Oxford University Press.

Liberty (2003) *Liberty's second reading briefing on the Domestic Violence, Crime and Victims Bill in the House of Lords*. London: Liberty.

DOMESTIC VIOLENCE, VICTIMS AND VICTIMISATION

'Domestic violence' is a phrase in everyday usage, but in a manner that often belies the difficulties associated with the term. 'Domestic violence' is not a simple denotation, but rather a term with multiple potential connotations, and one that may be viewed as ideologically loaded. In the US, for example, distinct differences in perspective and position were identified by the differentiation of feminist scholarship on violence against women and that produced by 'family violence' scholars (Johnson, 1995). Indeed, the World Health Organisation (WHO) largely eschews the term 'domestic violence' and, instead, has definitions of 'violence against women' and 'intimate partner violence'.

Debates over terminology are exacerbated by the fact that, despite common misconceptions, 'domestic violence' is not a discrete criminal offence and has neither a statutory nor common law definition. Rather, the phrase operates as an umbrella term encompassing a wide (and frequently disputed) variety of behaviours – many prohibited explicitly in the criminal law but others not so. For example, the term may include physical violence but it may also be seen to encompass more subtle behaviours, such as emotional control and financial abuse. Clearly, the term is not defined in law, or by a particular behaviour, or even by the locus of the behaviour; rather, it takes its meaning from the relationship between the individuals exhibiting, and those subject to, the behaviours. Classically, this was viewed as intimate partnership but, more recently, use of 'domestic violence' has expanded to recognise acts that can take place in a much broader variety of family relationships – such as between parent and child.

In the UK, statutory definition of the term was mooted during the genesis of the Domestic Violence, Crime and Victims Act 2004. Women's Aid, for example, called for a definition that mirrored that contained in the New Zealand Domestic Violence Act 1996 (Broadbridge et al, 2004). Proponents of this approach generally contended that a statutory definition would not only raise awareness, but also assist interagency collaboration in addressing the problem (Home Office, 2003). While the government of the day recognised the potential efficacy of a single definition, they rejected calls for this to be statutory, arguing that such an approach carried dangers of restrictiveness and inflexibility (Broadbridge et al, 2004). Thus, in 2004, a non-statutory 'cross-governmental' definition of domestic violence was introduced, intended to inform policy and practice across the public sector. It provided a broad definition of domestic violence: 'Any incident of threatening behaviour, violence or abuse [psychological, physical, sexual, financial or emotional] between adults who are or have been intimate partners or family members, regardless of gender or sexuality' (Home Office, 2005). Following consultation, this definition was further widened in March 2013 to include 16–17 year olds and behaviours characterised as 'coercive control'. Under this definition, domestic violence is:

> any incident or pattern of incidents of controlling, coercive, threatening behaviour, violence or abuse between those aged 16 or over who are, or have been, intimate partners or family members regardless of gender or sexuality. The abuse can encompass, but is not limited to:
>
> • psychological
> • physical
> • sexual
> • financial
> • emotional. (Home Office, 2013)

The 'expansion' of the meaning of 'domestic violence' is not unproblematic or uncontested. While some have welcomed the recognition that domestic violence may affect all genders and sexualities, others (and feminist commentators in particular) have noted the danger of a widened definition to potentially render the concept meaningless (Reece, 2006). Accordingly, there are still strong calls for a statutory definition, or specific criminal offence, that recognises the unique, 'pattern-based nature of the wrong' (Youngs, 2015, p 55).

Given that the terms 'victims of domestic violence' or 'domestic violence victimisation' are derivative and dependent on the definition of domestic violence, they too carry some of the difficulties outlined earlier. Indeed, difficulties are exacerbated in relation to these terms because of the link with the term 'victim', which is recognised as problematic in itself. Prima facie, a 'victim of domestic violence' is an individual who may have suffered a variety of abusive behaviours from, most commonly, an intimate partner but also another family member. Again, however, the word 'victim' has no legal significance; the criminal justice system merely recognises 'complainants'. Moreover, the use of the term 'victim' has been strongly contested by feminists in particular, who have objected to the implicit attributions of passivity and powerlessness (Walklate, 2014). As issues of 'domestic violence' only achieved any initial social recognition due to the work of feminist activists and scholars, this makes the use of the term 'victim of domestic violence' particularly problematic. Many, therefore, prefer the use of the term 'survivor'.

KATHRYN DUTTON

See also: **Domestic Violence, Crime and Victims Act 2004**

Readings

Broadbridge, S., Strickland, P. and Berman, G. (2004) *The Domestic Violence, Crime and Victims Bill [HL]: Domestic violence provisions*, Research Paper 04/44. London: House of Commons.

Home Office (2003) *Summary of responses to Safety and justice: The government's proposals on domestic violence.* London: The Stationery Office.

Home Office (2005) *Domestic violence: A national report.* London: The Stationery Office.

Home Office (2013) 'Guidance: domestic violence and abuse'. Available at: https://www.gov.uk/domestic-violence-and-abuse

Johnson, M. (1995) 'Patriarchal terrorism and common couple violence: two forms of violence against women', *Journal of Marriage and the Family*, 57: 283.

Reece, H. (2006) 'The end of domestic violence', *Modern Law Review*, 69(5): 770.

Walklate, S. (2014) 'Victims of crime', in P. Taylor, K. Corteen and S. Morley (eds) *A companion to criminal justice, mental health and risk*. Bristol: The Policy Press.

Youngs, J. (2015) 'Domestic violence and the criminal law: reconceptualising reform', *Journal of Criminal Law*, 79(1): 55.

E

ELDERLY VICTIMS

When focusing on elderly victims, there is a need to critically identify age as a socially constructed and evolving concept that has an impact on how those defined as 'elderly' victims are understood, responded to and defined. What is meant by 'elder', 'older' and 'old' has been discussed by Powell and Wahidin (2006), who argue that criminologists and victimologists could look to 'critical gerontology' to inform their disciplines from an 'age-aware perspective'. Rypi (2012, p 167) argues that these terms can complicate research as such 'cultural discourses' present 'dualistic notions ... of agency within old age'. Thus, common notions of the dependent 'elderly' needing care are juxtaposed against active, independent senior citizens who are very much in control of their lives. Green (2007) also argues that while there are some trends relating to age and victimisation, age alone cannot totally explain these, with risks also being related to race, gender and socio-economic status.

Elderly people are believed to be disproportionately fearful of crime, despite official statistics and victim surveys like the Crime Survey of England and Wales (CSEW) suggesting that they are least likely to become victims of crime. Research suggests that age is a close second to gender in relation to the fear of victimisation, but it may reflect the fear of crimes that predominantly target women, such as rape, sexual assault and harassment, a significant amount of which are not officially reported or recorded. Pain (1995, cited in Goodey, 2005) suggests that elderly women's heightened fear may be explained by a lifetime of victimisation, threat and fear, and that, in reality, domestic violence against elderly people is more prevalent than is acknowledged. Important factors relating to fear of crime are previous experience of victimisation, perceived risk of victimisation and personal vulnerability (Goodey, 2005), although the high-fear/low-risk equation (victim fear paradox) has been challenged as simplistic. This is because the official picture of elderly victimisation does not necessarily represent the reality of people's lives and it is interesting to note that the CSEW does not survey people in institutional care, such as care homes.

Elderly people's fear tends to be seen as rational as they are perceived to be less resilient and more vulnerable to the residual harms of victimisation (Pain, 1995, cited in Rypi, 2012). The elderly, women and the poor are more likely to feel unable to protect themselves, both physically and financially, and may take longer to recover from physical or material injuries (Hale, 1996, cited in Green, 2007). There are, however, dangers of labelling certain crime victims as weak and vulnerable as this can shape state responses to victimisation (Fattah, 1986, cited in Green, 2007). It has been found that some of the harms that the elderly are most likely to suffer have become redefined as 'welfare issues', rather than 'crimes'. Brogden and Nijhar (2000, cited in Green, 2007) argue that this might be because of the difficulties that some victims have in accessing the authorities to report harms, but it might also be about a 'wider cultural distaste' about confronting harms in the family or care setting, which are widely believed to be places of care and protection.

Although not a homogeneous group, elderly people may be defined as the 'ideal victim' as they are predominantly seen as 'weak, respectable and blameless'; however, the power to establish an identity as the 'ideal victim' is also important (Christie, 1986). This power may be lacking for those in institutional care situations, which may mean that both the crimes against them and their experience of victimisation are rendered invisible, challenging the victim fear paradox. Rypi (2012) argues that the concept of the 'crime victim' is also an ambivalent one maintained through a process of negotiation, and while the elderly are typically portrayed as weak, vulnerable and fearful, some elderly individuals both resist the assumption that they should fear crime and see the victim label as a threat in itself.

JILL JAMESON and KATE STRUDWICK

See also: Age and Victimisation; Victims of Crime

Readings

Christie, N. (1986) 'The ideal victim', in E. Fattah (ed) *From crime policy to victim policy: Reorientating the justice system*. Basingstoke: Macmillan Press, pp 17–30.
Goodey, J. (2005) *Victims and victimology: Research, policy and practice*. Harlow: Pearson Education Ltd.

Green, S. (2007) 'Crime, victimisation and vulnerability', in S. Walklate (ed) *Handbook of victims and victimology*. Cullompton: Willan Publishing, pp 91–118.

Powell, J. and Wahidin, A. (2006) 'Rethinking criminology: the case of "ageing studies"', in A. Wahidin and M. Cain (eds) *Ageing, crime and society*. Cullompton: Willan, pp 17–34.

Rypi, A. (2012) 'Not afraid at all? Dominant and alternative interpretive repertoires of discourses of the elderly on fear of crime', *Journal of Scandinavian Studies in Criminology and Crime Prevention*, 13: 66–180.

EMPOWERMENT SCHEMES AND VICTIMS

Policy moves in the Western world towards the (alleged) empowerment of victims of crime may be conceptualised in terms of three distinct waves. The *first wave* was characterised by a growth of academic interest in victims. The *second wave* saw the development of non-governmental victim assistance organisations in many jurisdictions. The *third wave* corresponds to the acceptance of victims as the topic of mainstream policymaking and legal reform in the criminal justice systems of such jurisdictions. Potentially, one might characterise the increased debate on and use of restorative justice in many jurisdictions as something of a *fourth wave*. Such third-wave (and fourth-wave) developments are demonstrated by the publication of service standards for victims of crime in many jurisdictions and, in most cases, the enactment of primary legislation.

In most jurisdictions, much of the victim reform agenda has been to address secondary victimisation. This is the notion that poor treatment at the hands of a criminal justice system re-victimises the victims. In England and Wales, one of the most visible examples of such reform has been the rollout of mechanisms to reduce the impact of adversarial evidential procedures. For example, 'Special Measures' under the Youth Justice and Criminal Evidence Act 1999 allow victims and other witnesses to give evidence from behind screens, via video-link or even via pre-recorded testimony. Similarly, the rollout of the volunteer 'Witness Service' (run by the charity Victim Support) in Crown and Magistrates' courts, and joint Crown Prosecution Service–Police Witness Care Units in England and Wales, has gone some way to supporting victims that give evidence. There is a clear criticism to be made, however, in that the majority of victims of crime will never report this victimisation to the criminal justice system. This adds to the impression that much of this agenda is focused on 'ideal victims' (Christie, 1986).

The provision of 'rights' to victims is controversial. Commentators have debated the degree to which victims can be permitted to influence decision-making within a criminal justice system while still safeguarding defendants' right to due process. A common distinction is that drawn by Ashworth (2000) between 'service rights' and 'procedural rights'. The service rights that Ashworth has in mind include: respectful and sympathetic treatment; support; information; the provision of facilities at court; and compensation from the offender or state. Procedural rights afford victims the ability to make a practical contribution to the criminal justice process, most often in relation to sentencing. In this latter case, the use of 'Victim Impact Statements' in many jurisdictions has been heralded by some as a significant empowerment tool, although Sanders et al (2001, p 44) famously dismissed them with the comment 'don't work, can't work'. In a more recent development in England and Wales, victims can now request reviews of prosecutors' decisions to drop cases.

State (publicly funded) compensation for victims of crime has equally been an important factor in the development of the international victims' movement. Rock (2004) cites compensation as a key influence on the development of victim policymaking in England and Wales, and Canada specifically. In this respect, there is a trend whereby governments have moved from state compensation to the introduction of offender-based compensation or 'restitution' schemes and the establishment of victims' funds financed by surcharges imposed on offenders. Recently, many jurisdictions have experimented with various forms of restorative justice as a means of affording redress to victims of crime. State compensation schemes tend to be relatively restrictive in terms of the scope of victimisation and the impacts of crime they cover. They are usually aimed at victims of *violent* crime suffering *physical* injury. It is also significant that these schemes tend to judge the victim as well as the victimisation. Many schemes exclude victims who have previously had criminal convictions or were not entirely 'innocent' in their victimisation.

Challenging the assumption that victims are being 'empowered' in many jurisdictions, critical commentators have argued that much of this policy movement, in fact, represents an exploitation of victims to further political goals and drive increased punitive responses to offenders. Such arguments have been made by Rock (2004) and, most recently, Duggan and Heap (2014).

MATTHEW HALL

See also: **Compensation; Policy and Victims in the UK; Victims of Crime**

Readings
Ashworth, A. (2000) 'Victims' rights, defendants' rights and criminal procedure', in A. Crawford and J. Goodey (eds) *Integrating a victims' perspective within criminal justice: International debates.* Farnham: Ashgate.

Christie, N. (1986) 'The ideal victim', in E.A. Fattah (ed) *From crime policy to victim policy: Reorientating the justice system*. Basingstoke: Macmillan Press, pp 17–30.

Duggan, M. and Heap, V. (2014) *Administrating victimization: The politics of anti-social behaviour and hate crime policy*. Basingstoke: Palgrave Macmillan.

Hall, M. (2009) *Victims of crime: Policy and practice in criminal justice*. Cullompton: Willan Publishing.

Rock, P. (2004) *Constructing victims' rights: The Home Office, New Labour, and victims*. Oxford: Oxford University Press.

Sanders, A., Hoyle, C., Morgan, R. and Cape, E. (2001) 'Victim impact statements: Don't work, can't work', *Criminal Law Review*, 447–58.

ENVIRONMENTAL AND GREEN VICTIMOLOGY

As with criminology, almost all the work carried out by victimologists on the impact of victimisation, its causes and the way in which societies respond to it has focused on human victims, more specifically, human victims of officially recognised criminal offences. As such, the critique levied at criminology for focusing too narrowly on official notions of criminality can equally be applied to victimology.

Even among the critical school of victimology, victims of environmental harms have been overlooked in the literature, although the first call for the development of what was then termed 'environmental victimology' came as early as 1996 in an article by Williams. Williams (1996) begins by addressing environmental victimisation and notes the obvious need for social justice to parallel formal legal processes. Williams (1996) calls for a move away from prevailing concepts of 'environmental justice', which he criticises both for its subjectiveness and because, for him, this is overly swayed by activism. It is clear that further development of victimological study in this area has been slow to progress from this point, even as green criminology as a whole has gathered pace. Skinnider (2011) emphasised the need for such specific research given the difficulties of applying broad-brush victim reforms to environmental harm. Notwithstanding such arguments, there are isolated exceptions to the general proposition that something 'more', or at least 'different', is needed for environmental victims over and above that which is already being provided for victims of crime: the most significant of which being the application of the US Crime Victims' Rights Act 2004 (CVRA) to victims of environmental crime.

The victimological literature on environmental harms has remained scarce until quite recently. Thus, when South and Beirne (2006) compiled one of the first collections of writing on green criminology in 2006, Williams' (1996) work was still the only piece specifically focused on the victims of environmental crimes.

The collection by South and Beirne (2006) also contained a section entitled 'Rights, Victims and Regulation', which included another important intervening contribution from Lynch and Stretesky (2006 [2001]) on toxic crimes and what they called 'corporate victimisation'. The authors present evidence of the significant health effects (mainly to humans) of corporate practices (specifically the production of pesticides), leading them to conclude that relevant corporations show a blatant disregard for the effects of their products and by-products on human and animal populations.

Following South and Bierne's (2006) edited collection, progress towards understanding environmental crime/harm from a victimological perspective continued to stall. Thus, in White's (2009) reader on environmental crime, three years later, the only chapter dedicated to victimisation was another reprint of Williams' (1996) paper. A further edited collection from White in 2010 (White, 2010) had no specific chapter on victimisation, although, in that volume, South (2010) reflected upon the unequal impact of climate change on various groups of (usually poor) victims, and the possibility that some 'environmental rights' are being breached. This discussion contradicts one of Williams' (1996) views that the impacts of environmental harm are more evenly spread between rich and poor. White (2011) has more recently dedicated a chapter to environmental victims in which he emphasises the sociocultural context of understanding and responding to environmental harm, arguing that a social-constructivist approach should be adopted by green criminologists and green victimologists. More recently, in 2013, Spencer and Fitzgerald (2013) offered fresh insight into environmental victims by essentially taking the argument beyond its (predominantly, they argue) Marxist roots to apply more post-structuralist thinking. In particular, they employ Guattari's critique of what he called integrated world capitalism by applying his three 'ecologies of transversity' to the question of corporate environmental offending and subsequent victimisation, using the 2010 BP Oil spill in the Gulf of Mexico as a case study. Thus, Spencer and Fitzgerald (2013) argue, this victimisation event can be understood in terms of environmental, social and mental ecologies. In so doing, the authors expose the complex and multifaceted nature of such victimisation itself both in human terms and in terms of the environment and non-human animals. Finally, another recent chapter by Bisschop and Van de Walle (2013) discusses (human) victims of illicit e-waste transportation practices, calling, in particular, for the involvement of local stakeholders in addressing these problems in line with concepts of environmental justice.

MATTHEW HALL

See also: **Environmental Harm and Victimisation; Victims of Crime**

Readings

Bisschop, L. and Van de Walle, G. (2013) 'Environmental victimization and conflict resolution: a case study of e-waste', in R. Walters, D. Westerhuisand and T. Wyatt (eds) *Emerging issues in green criminology: Exploring power, justice and harm*. Basingstoke: Palgrave Macmillan, pp 34–56.

Hall, M. (2013) *Victims of environmental harm: Rights, recognition and redress under national and international law*. London: Routledge.

Lynch, M.J. and Stretesky, P. (2006 [2001]) 'Toxic crimes: examining corporate victimization of the general public employing medical and epidemiological evidence', in N. South and P. Beirne (eds) *Green criminology*. Farnham: Ashgate.

Skinnider, E. (2011) *Victims of environmental crime – mapping the issues*. Vancouver: The International Centre for Criminal Law Reform and Criminal Justice Policy.

South, N. and Beirne, P. (eds) (2006) *Green criminology*. Farnham: Ashgate.

South, N. (2010) 'The ecocidal tendencies of late modernity: Transnational crime, social exclusion, victims and rights, in R. White (ed) *Global environmental harm: Criminological perspectives*, Cullompton: Willan Publishing, pp 228-247.

Spencer, D. and Fitzgerald, A. (2013) 'Three ecologies, transversality and victimization: the case of the British Petroleum oil spill', *Crime, Law and Social Change*, 59(3): 209–23.

White, R. (ed) (2009) *Environmental crime: A reader*. Cullompton: Willan Publishing.

White, R. (ed) (2010) *Global environmental harm: Criminological perspectives*. Cullompton: Willan Publishing.

White, R. (2011) *Transnational environmental crime: Towards an eco-global criminology*. Abingdon: Routledge Publishing.

Williams, C. (1996) 'An environmental victimology', *Social Science*, 3(4): 16–40.

ENVIRONMENTAL HARM AND VICTIMISATION

Environmental degradation often falls within legally grey areas or, as Passas (2005) has argued, may be 'lawful but awful'. Building on critical and radical criminological perspectives, many green criminologists therefore speak in terms of 'environmental harm' rather than 'environmental crime'. Looking beyond criminology, Hillyard et al (2004) argue that focusing on 'harm' rather than crime has several advantages, a number of which seem to have particular resonance with the impacts of environmental pollution and climate change. Focusing on harm has the potential to include the often legally ambiguous activities that foster environmental damage, as well as those that are already covered by civil and administrative systems. Indeed, even when such activities are criminal in the strict legal sense, focusing on harm allows an ability to account for such activities in cases where whatever mechanisms of justice that are available (at the national and international levels) fail to adequately prosecute such transgressions. The social harms approach also allows for the consideration of 'mass harms'. Again, this chimes well with the problems inherent in environmental degradation, where the effects may spiral out to include great swathes of animal, plant and human life. Traditional criminology (like traditional criminal justice), on the other hand, has struggled to fully embrace the concept of mass victimisation (certainly in relation to non-humans) and, with the exception of limited inroads into the fields of state crime and corporate crime, has largely remained focused on the individual.

White (2008) offers four key 'considerations of environmental harms'. The first of these considerations is that of *identifying* the victims of such harm. Criticising more mainstream criminological notions, White (2008) makes the important point that victims of environmental harm include the biosphere and non-human animals. Again, it follows that a further advantage of applying the social harms approach in this field is that it allows commentators to explore the non-human consequences of environmental degradation beyond the highly anthropocentric concept of 'criminal victimisation'.

The second of White's (2008) considerations is geographical, encapsulating the fact that environmental harm is often a regional, national, international or even global problem. In a similar vein, White (2008) distinguishes geographical considerations from considerations of 'place', by which he means the different types of harm experienced in urban, built-up centres of human habitation, compared with the harm caused to natural environments such as oceans, wilderness areas and deserts. Finally, White (2008) conceives environmental harm in terms of temporal considerations, meaning that the impact of environmental damage may be short-, medium- or long-term and may have immediate and/or lasting social impacts. There is a key link to be made here with more mainstream discussions of criminal victimisation and the growing acceptance that the impacts of individualistic harms (in this case, crimes) vary considerably over time (as well as between individuals), and with it, the support needs of those victimised. For White (2008), it is important for commentators, especially those concerned with green issues, to move beyond *defining* harm and onto *debating* harm because only the latter can lead to real-life, operational developments. Of course, such a view presents real difficulties for those seeking to develop *legal* systems for addressing environmental harms as such a system must ultimately be based on concrete and predictable definitions. This apparent conflict between predictable legal rules and flexible notions of environmental harm is a pervading issue in green victimology and criminology.

MATTHEW HALL

See also: **Environmental and Green Victimology; Legal Crimes –
Lawful But Awful; Social Harm**

Readings

Beirne, P. (2007) 'Animal rights, animal abuse and green criminology', in P. Beirne
and N. South (eds) *Issues in green criminology: Confronting harms against environments,
humanity and other animals.* Cullompton: Willan Publishing, pp 55–86.

Hillyard, P., Pantazis, P., Tombs, S. and Gordon, D. (2004) *Beyond criminology:
Taking harm seriously.* London: Pluto Press.

Passas, N. (2005) '"Lawful but awful": legal corporate crimes', *Journal of Socio-
Economics,* 24: 771–86.

White, R. (2008) *Crimes against nature: Environmental criminology and ecological
justice.* Cullompton: Willan Publishing.

ETHICS AND METHODS IN VICTIM RESEARCH

Theory and practice in victim research are inextricably linked. The different
theoretical strands within victimology (positive, radical, critical and emerging
cultural) lead the research agenda and the question of researching victims of harm
in quite different directions.

However, by its very nature, all research with victims has a heightened likelihood
of collecting data on sensitive issues from participants that might be described
as 'vulnerable'. In such cases, researchers should make every effort to respect
the rights of those they study, and their interests, sensitivities and privacy. To
help facilitate this, academic disciplines provide a code or statement of ethics
(see, eg, the 'Statement of ethics' of the British Society of Criminology, 2015)
intended as a frame of reference to encourage responsible ethical practice in
research. However, such ethical codes are often considered administrative; what
might be termed *procedural* ethics. Ethical codes typically describe professional
standards to which researchers should adhere in order to ensure that they produce
high-quality and methodologically sound research. Ethical codes and guidelines
have been developed to express the core values, principles and procedures of a
particular discipline. These are highly socially normative in that they constitute
what that professional group agrees are acceptable standards of conduct. Codes and
principles are also culturally bound and require sensitivity in their interpretation.
However, a sound knowledge of the main principles and relevant codes makes a
good starting point for ethical thinking and discussion.

In real-world research, ethics are not fixed. The reality of active research with
those who have been labelled, or perceive themselves, as 'victims' may lead

—

to contradictory principles coming into play. A researcher employs 'ethics in practice' that they consider to be acceptable according to real-time situations that are often challenging, complex and unpredictable (Lumsden and Winter, 2014). This is not achieved by simply reading and signing up to a statement of ethical practice. Researchers working with victims of harm as a result of crime or otherwise need to give full consideration to the potential situations that they may find themselves in and reflect on how to respond. Importantly, academics need to be more honest when writing about their methodological approach about what they actually did (Farrimond, 2013). In this sense, research ethics is a *practice*. It is something that social researchers think about and do; it is the actions that are taken (or not taken) during their everyday research life, not simply an intellectual exercise in the abstract.

Contemporarily, it is more common for some researchers to engage reflexively with the research process, acknowledging knowledge production as situated, partial and emotional. Less commonly expressed is reflexivity regarding the ethics of particular studies, acknowledging how the implementation of ethical safeguards is sometimes compromised in the field (a fine example of which is the chapter by Armstrong et al, in Lumsden and Winter, 2014). This is particularly heightened around research with 'vulnerable' populations, where such precautions can sometimes inhibit research that aims to encounter these individuals within the (risky) realities of their lives. In some ways, reflexive perspectives on research aim to take the reader to the underside of the research process (Gelsthorpe, 2007) in order to expose the ethical vulnerabilities and thereby deliver a more accurate reflection of the ethical rigour of the research described. It is here that research ethics can have a significant impact on how research is conducted, controlled and facilitated.

There are different approaches to researching victims of crime. The development of the criminal victimisation survey constituted the first substantial and influential research conducted on victims of crime, where victims themselves were asked about their experiences. Previous to this, there had been a rather heavy reliance by early victimologists upon statistics and case records compiled by criminal justice agencies. Research from the victim perspective occurred both in the form of victim surveys (local, national and international) and in a change of approach towards more qualitative research methods. Thus, victimology began to embrace both large-scale empirical work, which made an important contribution to the patterning and regularity of most conventional forms of criminal victimisation, and simultaneously smaller-scale qualitative work, which tried to listen to and understand particular victims' experiences.

More recently, there is an increasing diversity of methodological approaches to research with victims that represent a foregrounding of the 'ethical imperative'. Under the broad umbrella of 'social justice research', approaches such as 'transformative research', in particular, focus on the resilience and capabilities that already exist within research participants, rather than taking a 'problem-oriented' approach, which may be deficit-focused. It is here that we can see the ethical imperative, where research becomes ethical through its purpose.

NICOLA O'LEARY

See also: **Crime, Victimisation** *and Vulnerability; Knowledge-Power Nexus;* **Victims of Crime**

Readings
British Society of Criminology (2015) 'Statement of Ethics'. Available at: http://www.britsoccrim.org/new/?q=node/22
Farrimond, H. (2013) *Doing ethical research*. Basingstoke: Palgrave Macmillan.
Gelsthorpe, L. (2007) 'The Jack Roller: telling a story?', *Theoretical Criminology*, 11: 515–42.
Lumsden, K. and Winter, A. (eds) (2014) *Reflexivity in criminological research: Experiences with the powerful and powerless*. Basingstoke: Palgrave Macmillan.

ETHNIC MINORITIES AND VICTIMISATION

The term 'ethnic minority' is often used to refer to a group who are usually of immigrant heritage and of different national or cultural background to others in a given country. Often, its members share an identity and sense of belonging based on claims to a (real or imagined) common descent. In this sense, the term is more about political power and representation as opposed to being solely about numbers, for instance, in Apartheid South Africa, black Africans were the numerical majority, but the ethnic minority.

Non-white ethnic minority groups are far more likely to be victims of hate crimes, in particular, racially or religiously aggravated offences – including verbal abuse, harassment and physical attacks. A hate crime is a criminal act motivated by hostility or prejudice based on actual or perceived race, ethnicity, gender, religion or other variables. A hate crime may be direct or indirect or, in drawing on Connolly and Keenan's (2001, p 2) distinction, 'hot' – where the initial motivation to harass is non-racial or non-religious, but the result is nevertheless racial or religious harassment – or 'cold' – where the perpetrator's desire from the outset is to behave in a cold and hostile manner based on racial or religious hatred.

In comparison to one another, different ethnic minority groups experience different types and levels of victimisation. These differences are framed by historical, social and political context, for example, since the 9/11 terrorist attacks in the US and ensuing anti-Muslim hostility, there has been an increase in Islamaphobic and racist hate crimes. The concept of 'intersectionality' is useful here. This refers to how there are different outcomes when different structures of inequality, for instance, race, class and gender, intersect in order to determine victimisation experience (Hill-Collins, 2000).

Following the view of critical race theory (Ugwudike, 2015) that racism is dangerously ordinary, it can be suggested that hate crimes against ethnic minority groups are also common and 'ordinary', and that they remain largely under-reported and non-recorded. This is true more so for some ethnic minority groups than others, for example, research conveys that Gypsies and Travellers experience high rates of victimisation, especially in relation to anti-social behaviour and harassment, yet levels of reporting are very low. Research also reveals that ethnic minorities are also more likely to experience victimisation within criminal justice organisations, such as the police and courts. This may be in the form of enhanced monitoring and victimisation, for instance, by police officers undertaking stop and search, or in the form of secondary victimisation, for instance, by courtroom officials carrying out the cross-examination of victims.

In keeping with Von Hentig's (1948) argument that certain groups may be victim-prone, later work by other criminologists began to consider the enhanced victimisation status of particular ethnic minority groups, for example, in the UK, there was a focus on the victimisation of those of black African, Caribbean or Asian background. More recently, this body of work has found that such groups do not passively accept their victimisation (or proneness to being a victim). Rather, they actively resist potential victimisation and challenge those bodies whose support and justice processes are considered to be insufficient and/or as resulting in additional victimisation.

Advocacy groups and pressure groups have sought to encourage the reporting of hate crimes against ethnic minority groups in an attempt to deliver justice, as well as making the true extent of such victimisation visible. In the UK, this has been supported by various legislative measures, such as: offences that are racially or religiously aggravated under section 28 of the Crime and Disorder Act 1998 (as amended); the incitement to racial hatred under Part III of the Public Order Act 1986; and the stirring up of religious hatred under the Racial and Religious Hatred Act 2006.

TINA PATEL

See also: **Hate Crime and Victimisation; Xenophobia**

Readings

Connolly, P. and Keenan, M. (2001) *The hidden truth: Racial harassment in Northern Ireland*. Belfast: Northern Ireland Statistics and Research Agency.

Hill-Collins, P. (2000) *Black feminist thought* (2nd edn). London: Routledge.

Spalek, B. (2008) *Ethnicity and crime: A reader*. Berkshire: Open University Press.

Ugwudike, P. (2015) *An introduction to critical race theory*. Bristol: The Policy Press.

Von Hentig, H. (1948) *The criminal and his victim: Studies in the sociobiology of crime*. Hamden, CT: Archon Books.

F

FEMALE GENITAL MUTILATION

The term 'female genital mutilation' (FGM) (also termed 'female genital cutting') is defined as 'all procedures involving partial or complete removal of the external female genitalia or other injury to the female genital organs, whether for cultural or any other non-therapeutic reasons' (WHO, 1997, p 1). There are several forms of FGM; however, they fall broadly into three main forms: Type 1, clitoridectomy, where all or part of the clitoris is removed; Type 2, excision, where all or part of the clitoris *and* labia are removed; and Type 3, which consists of infibulation with excision. The World Health Organisation (WHO) reports that Types 1 and 2 are the most common forms of FGM globally, with current estimates suggesting that around 90% of FGM cases include Types 1 and 2.

FGM is a practice usually performed by untrained 'midwives' who lack the requisite medical expertise to deal with complications. It is a procedure that is commonly performed in unsanitary conditions with unsterilised instruments, many of which are non-medical instruments such as glass, blades and other sharp or sharpened objects. In some cases, the practice is performed by medical professionals under sanitary conditions; however, this is usually in cases where the girls and young women come from wealthy families. It is a common practice in regions of Africa, Asia and the Middle East, with an estimated 100 million to 140 million girls and women being victims of FGM (WHO, 2008). Although FGM is traditionally practised in these countries, the WHO (2008) declared that the practice by immigrants has made it a public health issue in Europe, Canada, Australia and the US.

The rationale and justifications for practising FGM are multifaceted and include reasons of superstition, perceptions of gender roles, beliefs regarding health and cleanliness, and religious customs. Despite this, there is little or no evidence to support these justifications. For example, with regard to the latter, there is no mandate in the Koran or the Bible that girls and young women should undergo the practice of FGM. However, as a practice rooted in religious as well as cultural and social factors going back centuries (primarily in order to safeguard virginity, and also as a rite of passage into womanhood), it is difficult to eradicate. As a result of the numerous harmful and medical implications for girls and women, in the short and long term, many countries, predominantly developed countries, regard the practice as barbaric. The physical and emotional effects of FGM on those subject to it are numerous and long-lasting. They include death through haemorrhaging or sepsis through the use of unsterilised instruments, painful sexual experiences, menstrual problems, urination problems, and risks during pregnancy for the mother and during birth for both the mother and child. There are also psychological harms associated with FGM.

It is without doubt that FGM is a complex and controversial practice that extends into the terms used to describe it. For example, some commentators prefer to use the term 'female genital circumcision'. However, some argue that this term does not capture the severity of the harm inflicted on girls and young women who, in the majority of cases, are forced to undergo the practice, which can include the cutting of the genitalia. 'Female genital cutting' has been proposed as the most appropriate term to use as it acknowledges the harm inflicted. Many commentators, however, prefer to use the term 'female genital mutilation' as it is better able to capture the harm and violence inflicted on girls and young women. In spite of this, it is regarded as a loaded term, carrying negative connotations and being linked with barbaric practices carried out by 'uncivilised' and/or 'underdeveloped' countries.

Some feminist thought (eg Hosken, 1993; Monagan, 2010) contends that FGM is a patriarchal practice that subordinates girls and women and is part of a continuum of control that includes controlling their sexual behaviour. They highlight how there is pressure to conform to the social order and that it is a practice performed in preparation for marriage. These factors and deeply held beliefs about gender roles and sexuality contribute to the perpetuation of the practice of FGM. Hence, some feminists argue that FGM is often practised by women on girls and young women for the benefit of men (Monagan, 2010), consequently disempowering women through, for example, constraining their sexual pleasure while, at the same time, enhancing men's sexual pleasure. Additionally, the 2009 United Nations International Children's Emergency Fund (UNICEF) report titled *UN agencies unite against female genital mutilation* argues that FGM 'is a manifestation of unequal relations between women and men with roots in deeply entrenched social, economic and political conventions' (UNICEF, 2009).

Indeed, FGM is considered to be a violation of the human rights of women and an act of violence (1979 Convention on the Elimination of All Forms of Discrimination Against Women [CEDAW]), and a form of child abuse (1989 Convention of the Rights of the Child [CRC]). In 1993, the United Nations created the 'Declaration on the Elimination of Violence against Women'. In addition to these conventions and declarations, legislation has been introduced to eradicate the practice of FGM and protect victims. For example, the Female Genital Mutilation Act 2003 in England, Wales and Northern Ireland was introduced, while in Scotland, there is the Prohibition of Female Genital Mutilation Act 2005, and, more recently, the Serious Crime Act 2015 includes a protection order. An order can include the withdrawal of the child's passport and place restrictions on travel. A child's contact with specific family members can also be stopped. A breach of an FGM protection order is a criminal offence with a maximum of five years' imprisonment. Also, under these Acts of Parliament, it is illegal to arrange for a UK national to be taken overseas to undergo FGM.

As discussed, legislation has been introduced in many developed countries, with France prosecuting the largest number of perpetrators. France has strict laws tracking and prosecuting practitioners and consenting parents of FGM victims, and requiring medical professionals to report incidents of FGM. Many countries have implemented legislation that covers cases where the practice is conducted outside the country of residence. Despite current legislation, girls and young women are being sent to their native countries to have FGM performed. This is due to the difficulty of identifying cases, reporting cases, finding evidence and protecting girls at risk (Leye et al, 2007).

More recently, countries where FGM is practised have also introduced legislation to eradicate the practice, including Kenya, Nigeria and the Gambia. The introduction of legislation in these countries is regarded as a major move in the eradication of FGM. However, despite this, it could be counterproductive in that there could be misunderstandings of what is being legislated against. Indeed, it could drive FGM underground, resulting in less skilled 'midwives' and 'practitioners' performing the practice. Moreover, it could result in women being fearful of seeking medical attention. Therefore, it could be more productive to address traditional cultural beliefs. While this may be a constructive way forward, it could prove to be more difficult than the implementation of legislation as cultural beliefs are deeply rooted. Action to tackle cultural beliefs and to break down the stigma associated with FGM include REPLACE, a project funded by the European Union to support and motivate influential people in FGM-prevalent communities to engage others in working to implement actions and eradicate the practice of FGM.

SHARON MORLEY

—

See also: **Gender and Victimisation**

Readings

Hosken, F. (1993) *The Hosken report: Genital and sexual mutilation of females* (4th edn). Lexington, MA: Women's International Network News.

Leye, E., Deblonde, J., Garcia-Anon, J., Johnsdotter, S., Kwateng-Kluvitse, A., Weil-Curiel, L. and Temmerman, M. (2007) 'An analysis of the implementation of laws with regard to female genital mutilation in Europe', *Crime, Law, Social Change*, 47: 1–31.

Monagan, S.L. (2010) 'Patriarchy: perpetuating the practice of female genital mutilation', *Journal of Alternative Perspectives in the Social Sciences*, 2(1): 160–81.

UNICEF (United Nations International Children's Emergency Fund) (2009) 'UN Agencies unite against female genital mutilation'. Available at: http://www.unicef.org/media/media_42998.html

WHO (World Health Organisation) (1997) *Female genital mutilation, fact sheet n 153*. Geneva: World Health Organisation.

WHO (2001) *Female genital mutilation: A student manual*. Geneva: World Health Organisation.

WHO (2008) *Eliminating female genital mutilation: An interagency statement*. Geneva: World Health Organisation.

FINANCIAL HARM AND VICTIMISATION

In the past 30 years, consumers of financial services firms have been victims of three major waves of offences in the UK. First, the gradual withdrawal of the Conservative government from pension provision, coupled with deregulation of the retail financial services sector in the latter half of the 1980s, created the conditions for a wave of pensions mis-selling. Companies launched into a hard sell, wrongly advising many clients to cash in their existing pensions contributions and transfer them to new, private schemes about which they received false information. One survey conducted by the Securities and Investments Board found that only 9% of pensions companies had complied with legal requirements when originally advising on these pensions transfers. Meanwhile, although breaches had first been uncovered in 1990, a KPMG survey of pensions advice given during 1991–93 revealed that in 'four out of five cases', pensions companies were still giving advice short of legal standards (Slapper and Tombs, 1999, p 63). Early in 1998, the then new regulatory body, the Financial Services Authority (since 2012, the Financial Conduct Authority), estimated the final costs of mis-selling as around £11 billion, with some 2.4 million victims.

At the end of the 1990s, evidence of widespread mis-selling of endowment mortgages also began to emerge. Following the end of state house-building and government encouragement to buy their homes, millions of such policies had been sold through the 1980s and 1990s based on the claim that on maturity of the endowment policy, the sum returned to an investor would pay off the costs of their homes, a claim that often proved to be false. About 5 million people were victimised (Fooks, 2003). The saga is uncannily similar to that of pensions mis-selling. First, the list of companies involved in each is very similar. Second, the endowment mortgage scandal was characterised by long-term obduracy on the part of companies in the sector initially to admit any wrongdoing, then subsequently to compensate victims.

A virtually identical sequencing of events then unfolded with respect to Personal Payment Protection Insurance (PPPI). PPPI policies were widely marketed and sold at the start of this century, at the height of the credit boom. Financial services firms targeted customers with debts such as mortgages, credit cards or loans with insurance against any future inability to meet repayments. However, again, these products were often sold when unnecessary, or without customers' knowledge, or, indeed, were to prove invalid in the event of customers claiming against them. In 2005, the Citizens Advice Bureau filed a 'super-complaint' relating to PPPI mis-selling to the Office of Fair Trading. Yet, this did not stop companies continuing to engage in a business that they knew to be illegal: some 16 million PPPI policies have been sold *since* 2005. Moreover, the companies embroiled in the mis-selling of PPPI included many of the, by now, 'usual suspects' involved in the previous 'crime and harm' waves.

These will not be the last 'scandal' associated with the retail financial services sector and its direct targeting of individual consumers – quite apart from the wider allegations of crime and harm such as those associated with the fixing of LIBOR and FOREX, sanctions busting, money laundering, cartelisation, and insider trading. In combination, such phenomena are likely to generate greater media and popular, if not political and regulatory, scrutiny of the sector, and this, in turn, will bring to light further categories of mis-selling. Any further such harms will involve more or less the same companies and will affect millions of people in ways that are diffuse, exacerbating now well-established processes of victimisation and social harms, which have had many dimensions.

First, these products and their markets were regulated – albeit not adequately – but state expenditures were consumed in the various stages of this regulatory process, expenditures sourced from general taxation. Second, while millions of individuals did receive compensation, this cannot take account of any emotional or psychological costs that they or their families may have incurred in the process, not least where claims for compensation across each form of mis-selling were, routinely and falsely, denied and denied again. Third, new market opportunities for businesses have emerged around these waves of mis-selling, markets in 'claims management', where private companies pursue claims on behalf of individuals on the basis of a percentage of the settlement; thus, private profits were created out of victims' compensation. Fourth, the costs incurred by financial services companies in compensation must be offset elsewhere, through raising charges for other products – so the costs of offending are dispersed to existing and future customers (Tombs, 2015).

Perhaps most significantly of all, taking these waves and layers of harms together, a combined effect of them may be to generate popular anger, anxiety or apathy. The routine and seemingly endless production of harms may inure people to their malevolence as the population becomes anaesthetised to such harm. Thus, perhaps the most pernicious effect is that harm and crime become virtually normalised, part of what 'banks' do, seemingly inevitable and unstoppable, thus destroying social trust in banking, a basic and a necessary social function.

STEVE TOMBS

See also: **State-Corporate Crime and Harm; Zemiology**

Readings
Fooks, G. (2003) 'In the valley of the blind the one eyed man is king: corporate crime and the myopia of financial regulation', in S. Tombs and D. Whyte (eds) *Unmasking the crimes of the powerful.* New York, NY: Peter Lang, pp 105–25.
Slapper, G. and Tombs, S. (1999) *Corporate crime.* London: Longman.
Tombs, S. (2015) 'Corporate theft and fraud: crime and impunity in the retail financial services sector', in D. Whyte (ed) *How corrupt is Britain?* London: Pluto, pp 168–76.

FRACKING, HARM AND VICTIMISATION

In brief, hydraulic fracturing or 'fracking' is a technique that involves drilling into the earth before directing large amounts of water (together with sand and chemicals) at shale rock under high pressure in order to release natural gas. This method of unconventional gas extraction (UCG) is highly debated: both praised as an answer to energy and job security, as well as a significant benefit to local communities by industry (Cuadrilla Resources, 2015) and government; and simultaneously condemned as a practice that cannot be undertaken without threatening human health (CHPNY, 2015).

In order to explore the harm and victimisation associated with 'fracking', it is important to address the discourses associated with it, and, in particular, there is a need to explore notions of power tied up with it. According to eminent theorists such as Foucault (1980), for something to be established as true, other equally valid statements must be discredited and denied. Thus, where information comes from must be acknowledged and who has the 'expertise' to speak 'truths' has to be considered. This can be evidenced in the discursive debate surrounding the issue of fracking.

The Concerned Health Professionals of NY (CHPNY, 2014) detail a plethora of concerns, including (but not limited to): air pollution; water contamination; occupational health and safety hazards; public health effects; noise and light pollution and stress; seismic activity; threats to agriculture and property values; inaccurate job claims; inflated estimates of oil and gas reserves and profitability; and increased crime rates. Moreover, such concerns are more real than imagined given the accumulation of supporting evidence.

Despite this and many similar concerns from numerous countries where moratoria on 'fracking' have either been called for or are in place, the UK Coalition government's Prime Minister David Cameron pledged in 2014 to 'go all out for shale', and a leaked letter from Chancellor George Osborne has raised questions regarding relationships between the government and the unpopular industry (Carrington, 2015).

In January 2015, a UK cross–party Environment Audit Committee report calling for an indefinite hold on fracking amid huge concerns regarding water supplies, air quality and public health was dismissed as 'total rubbish' by government sources (Gosden, 2015). Hence, while one government body asserts pro-fracking 'truths', another warns against it; therefore, who is to be believed, or trusted, is questionable.

At the time of writing (March 2015), the UK has yet to experience the 'shale boom' industry that has hit the US and Australia, but evidence of negative health, environmental and economic impacts from communities in both countries has become widely circulated via social media and the Internet, for example, the documentaries *Gasland* (2010) and *Fractured Country* (2014). This kind of discourse is informing people, and, as a result, a social movement opposing the industry is rapidly growing across Britain (see, eg, frack-off.org). This movement is not just made up of concerned members of the public (and their many professions), numerous non-governmental organisations (NGOs) have also taken an anti-fracking stance. These include Greenpeace, WWF and Friends of the Earth to name but a few. It can be seen, therefore, that social media allows widespread broadcast of this kind of discourse, yet the question remains, does it have the power to be understood as 'true'?

—

Other contested truths are evidenced in that dominant official discourse assures the UK will avoid dangers experienced by other countries via 'Gold standard' regulations. For example the Royal Society & Royal Academy of Engineering (2012) made ten recommendations in order that this be achieved, but such assurances are contested by Friends of the Earth (2014) who warn, that much regulation is inadequate, flawed or ineffectively applied.

BETH McJURY

See also: Environmental and Green Victimology; Environmental Harm and Victimisation; State-Corporate Crime and Harm

Readings

Carrington, D. (2015) 'George Osborne urges ministers to fast-track fracking measures in leaked letter', *The Guardian*, 26 January. Available at: http://www.theguardian.com/environment/2015/jan/26/george-osborne-ministers-fast-track-fracking

CHPNY (Concerned Health Professionals of NY) (2014) *Compendium of scientific, medical, and media findings demonstrating risks and harms of fracking (unconventional gas and oil extraction)* (2nd edn), 11 December. Available at: http://concernedhealthny.org/wp-content/uploads/2012/11/PSR-CHPNY-Compendium-3.0.pdf

Cuadrilla Resources (2016) 'Benefits', available at: http://www.cuadrillaresources.com/

Foucault, M. (1980) *Power/knowledge: Selected interviews and other writings 1972–1977* (ed C. Gordon). New York, NY: Pantheon Books.

Friends of the Earth (2014) 'Executive summary: all that glitters.... Is the regulation of unconventional gas and oil exploration in England really "gold standard"?' Available at: www.foe.co.uk

Gosden, E. (2015) 'Fracking: MPs demanding ban "listened to ill-informed green groups not science"', *The Telegraph*, 26 January. Available at: http://www.telegraph.co.uk/news/earth/energy/fracking/11368632/Fracking-MPs-demanding-ban-listened-to-green-campaigners-not-science.html

The Royal Society and The Royal Academy of Engineering (2012) *Shale Gas Extraction in the UK: A review of hydraulic fracturing*, The Royal Society & The Royal Academy of Engineering: London. Available at: https://royalsociety.org/topics-policy/projects/shale-gas-extraction/

G

GENDER AND VICTIMISATION

There are key differences in the victimisation profiles of males and females. Males are predominantly the victims of homicide, robbery and non-domestic physical assault (Bureau of Justice Statistics, no date; Australian Bureau of Statistics, 2015; Office for National Statistics, 2015). Females are predominantly the victims of sexual assault and related violence. However, females also experience much higher rates of intimate-partner violence (homicide and domestic/family violence) than males, and are more likely to be victimised in a domestic setting and experience sustained violent abuse. Males are generally more likely to be victimised by a stranger or friend/acquaintance as part of an isolated incident of violence and more commonly in a public location.

The notion that a valid relationship exists between gender and the type, frequency and impact of victimisation from crime emerged with the second-wave feminist movement of the 1970s and 1980s (see Walklate, 2007; Davies, 2011). Of specific influence were the radical feminist literature and the anointing of patriarchy as fundamental in the experiences of women and girls, including their victimisation from crime. This work challenged the authority of the positivist framework of victimology, which referred to typologies, lifestyle and victim precipitation as affecting differences in victimisation. Instead, female victimisation was distinct and created by those factors that predetermined the subordinate position of women in society.

Thus, the types of crime primarily experienced by women and girls (sexual and domestic violence), the gender of those who predominantly victimised them (males) and the location that they were mostly victimised in (the home or the private domain) were a consequence of the pervasiveness of patriarchal control. The recognition of a form of victimisation specific to females led to the creation of the phrase 'gender-based violence', which encapsulates crimes mostly or only experienced by women and girls. These include domestic and family violence, sexual assault, female genital mutilation, stalking and trafficking into the sex industry.

The recognition of gender-based (female) victimisation substantiated the observation that men were the primary perpetrators of crime but it also had two inadvertent outcomes (Walklate, 2007). The first was to tie femininity with victimhood and risk consolidating women and girls as the ideal victim. The second was to conceal the experiences of men as victims of crime. Theoretical considerations of masculinity – normative heterosexuality and hegemonic masculinity – that were used to explain male proclivities towards criminal behaviour were subsequently employed to consider the relationship between the masculine gender, crime *and* victimisation. Rather than establish a male-centric form of victimisation, these considerations explored how victimisation is articulated and felt in reference to individual and societal notions of masculinity.

Three potential misapprehensions have arisen with the examination of gender-based victimisation. First, victimisation studies have tended (in the past) to conflate sex (a biological construct) with gender (a social construct), resulting in the (mis) assignment of sex-based correlates of victimisation to the effects of gender. Where gender is accurately applied there has been the occasional temptation to assign all effects to this factor alone. Second, Davies (2007, p 188), in her appraisal of the 'salience' of gender, notes both the 'conceptual tensions' identified by Walklate (2003) in her evaluation of feminist victimology and the literature that demonstrates the equivalent importance of other factors in defining victimisation risk and experience. Factors of age, ethnicity, socio-economic status and sexuality all exhibit differential and combinational effects with gender.

Finally, there is the issue of the homogenisation of gender (Davies, 2007), which suggests that any gendered experience, such as victimisation, is based on a uniform experience of masculinity and femininity. Homogenisation reinforces habitual concepts of male and female roles in crime perpetration and victimisation. It also assumes a uniform experience of masculinity or femininity, rather than acknowledging the existence of masculin*ities* and feminin*ities*, and how these (and other salient factors) shape the victimisation experience. Victimology research from the last two decades has both reinforced and challenged these habitual concepts.

SAMANTHA BRICKNELL

See also: **Domestic Violence, Victims and Victimisation; Male Victims of Violence; Sexual Violence**

Readings

Australian Bureau of Statistics (2015) *Recorded crimes – victims, Australia 2014*, Catalogue no 4510.0. Canberra: ABS.

Bureau of Justice Statistics (no date) 'NCVS victimization analysis tool (NVAT)'. Available at: http://www.bjs.gov/index.cfm?ty=nvat

Davies, P. (2007) 'Lessons from the gender agenda', in S. Walklate (ed) *Handbook of victims and victimology*. Cullompton: Willan Publishing, pp 175–202.

Davies, P. (2011) *Gender, crime and victimisation*. London: Sage.

Office for National Statistics (2015) *Crime statistics – focus on violent crime and sexual offences, 2013/14*. London: ONS.

Walklate, S. (2003) 'Can there be a feminist victimology?', in P. Davies, P. Francis and V. Jupp (eds) *Victimisation: Theory, research and policy*. London: Palgrave, pp 28–45.

Walklate, S. (2007) 'Men, victims and crime', in P. Davies, P. Francis and C. Greer (eds) *Victims, crime and society*. London: Sage, pp 142–64.

GENOCIDE, HARM AND VICTIMISATION

Proclamations of *never again* following the liberation of the Nazi concentration and death camps after the Second World War led to the 1948 United Nations Convention on the Prevention and Punishment of the Crime of Genocide. The Convention defined genocide as 'acts committed with the intent to destroy, in whole or in part, a national, ethnical, racial, or religious group'. Combining the Greek *genos* for kin, race or tribe and the Latin suffix *-cide* for to kill or murder, Lemkin (a Polish lawyer of Jewish origin) in 1944 coined the term 'genocide' for a practice that has arguably been perpetrated through the ages. However, it is no longer the historical occurrence of genocide that preoccupies social scientists, but rather its disturbing recurrence in recent times despite the preceding and other international conventions drawn up to protect human rights.

Although genocide is a crime under international law, it has only recently been the subject of the criminological gaze, and, more recently still, the subject of the victimological gaze (see Rafter and Walklate, 2012). Rafter and Walklate (2012) relate this, in part, to the problems of avoiding charges of victim blaming, whereby some people (or groups) are either seen to be more prone to victimisation than others or to have some culpability in their victimhood. However, this is simply not the nature of genocide victimhood; rather, genocide is fundamentally connected to concepts of difference and otherness. Bauman (1995, p 203) demonstrates this well:

> In every genocide, the victims are killed not for what they have done, but for what they are; more precisely still, for what they, being what they are, may yet become; or for what they, they being what they are, may not become. Nothing the appointed victims may or may not do affects the sentence of death – and that includes their choice between submissiveness or militancy, surrender or resistance.

The crimes, harm and victimisation suffered by those subject to genocide is patent. Although death of members of the group is the ultimate intention, there are recognised processes or common elements that lead up to the final act. Stanton (2013) has identified 10 stages that genocides go through (with harms occurring at every stage). In the lead-up to the Holocaust, Jewish people were subject to discrimination before being dehumanised and their property violently targeted in pogroms. Such processes can be seen in previous and subsequent genocides. For example, just as Jewish people were equated with vermin and disease in the middle of the 20th century, so too had the Armenian people at the beginning of the century, and so were the Tutsis in the Rwandan genocide towards the end of it. Harm can also be inflicted in other ways. 'Destroying' a group can be achieved through murdering the male population of the group, or certain males in the group, and raping and infecting the females with fatal infections, as occurred in the Rwandan genocide, or by forcing the females, children and old men on marches whereby they die through starvation and exhaustion, as occurred in the Armenian genocide.

For the survivors of genocide, the lasting victimisation and harm is undeniably immeasurable. Those who survive genocide can and do bear witness to their experiences of humiliation, loss and pain. Oral testimonies can allow an unshielded truth to emerge (see Langer, 1991), and autobiographical novels written by survivors can provide such testimonies through imagery and style (see Levi, 1947; Delbo, 1968). For some, the guilt at surviving and the traumatic experiences are too much to bear. Levi (1947) claimed that he could not be a true witness to the horrors of the Nazi death camps as only those who had, those who had faced the *Gorgon* and not returned, could truly bear witness. Despite surviving Auschwitz,

Levi took his own life many years later. The crimes, harms and victimisation of past and present genocides continue to resonate.

JO TURNER

See also: **Universal Declaration of Human Rights**

Readings

Bauman, Z. (1995) *Life in fragments: Essays in postmodern morality*. Oxford: Blackwell Publishers.

Delbo, C. (1968) *None of us will return*. New York, NY: Grove Press.

Langer, L.L. (1991) *Holocaust testimonies: The ruins of memory*. New Haven, CT: Yale University Press.

Levi, P. (1947) *If this is a man*. London: Abacus.

Rafter, N. and Walklate, S. (2012) 'Genocide and the dynamics of victimization: some observations on Armenia', *European Journal of Criminology*, 9(5): 514–26.

Stanton, G.H. (2013) 'The ten stages of genocide'. Available at: http://genocidewatch.org/genocide/tenstagesofgenocide.html

Totten, S. and Bartrop, P.R. (eds) (2009) *The genocide studies reader*. New York, NY: Routledge.

HATE CRIME AND VICTIMISATION

The term 'hate crime' is used to encompass an increasing range of crimes motivated by hate or what can also be described as 'bias-motivated' crime. While hate crime has been traditionally understood as encompassing racism, xenophobia and religious intolerance – in the aftermath of the Holocaust and reflecting developments in the 1960s concerning civil rights and non-discrimination – its scope has recently broadened to include crimes such as homophobia, transphobia, anti-Roma crime and hate crime against persons with disabilities (UK Equality and Human Rights Commission, 2011). In addition, gender-based violence – which disproportionately impacts on women – is also being recognised as a potential form of hate crime. It can also include crimes against persons who are incorrectly identified as belonging to certain groups, or who are victimised because of their connection with certain groups (such as the 'white' wife of a 'black' husband) (FRA, 2012a). Hate crime can manifest itself in relation to both interpersonal crime and property crime, and also encroaches into the realm of freedom of expression when it incites hatred and violence. In this regard, the Internet is increasingly recognised as a medium that warrants monitoring and action to combat and punish hate-related offences, so-called 'cyber-hate' or online 'trolling'.

The recognition of and responses to hate crime differs widely between countries, and can be partially understood when looked at alongside each country's history as it relates to slavery, colonialism, immigration and dictatorship, among other factors; for example, both German and Austrian legislation, policing and criminal justice data collection have focused on combating right-wing extremism and anti-

Semitism in the aftermath of the Second World War. Contemporary events also shape how the state responds to hate crime; for example, in England and Wales, the Macpherson inquiry into the investigation of Stephen Lawrence's murder served as a catalyst to reforming the policing of racist crime (Macpherson, 1999).

At a regional level, across the 28 member states of the European Union (EU), Council Framework Decision 2008/913/JHA – on combating certain forms and expressions of racism and xenophobia – set out to ensure that certain behaviour constitutes a criminal offence and results in similar penalties across the EU. Whereas this 2008 legislation is limited to race, colour, religion, descent or national or ethnic origin, a number of member states' laws now encompass additional grounds under hate crime. This development reflects the broader range of grounds covered under non-discrimination law – namely, Article 14 of the European Convention on Human Rights and Article 21 of the Charter of Fundamental Rights of the European Union. Reflecting this, the EU Victims' Directive 2012/29/EU, which EU member states have to transpose into national law by the end of November 2015, refers to 'victims who have suffered a crime committed with a bias or discriminatory motive which could, in particular, be related to their personal characteristics' and also refers directly to victims of 'hate crime'. In this regard, hate crime – encompassing a broad range of victims – is increasingly being recognised at the level of EU and member state law.

Whereas the law is changing to recognise a range of hate crimes, it remains the case that hate crime is under-reported in many member states. Criminal victimisation surveys at the national level (such as the Crime Survey for England and Wales), alongside EU-wide surveys on hate crime by the European Union Agency for Fundamental Rights (FRA, 2012b, 2014), consistently indicate the disparity between the extent of hate crime victimisation that people experience and what they report to the police. Reflecting this, official data collection on a range of hate crimes – which the FRA systematically documents in its annual reports – can only be classified as 'comprehensive' in a handful of EU member states, namely, Finland, the Netherlands, Sweden and the UK. Herein, non-governmental organisations and the media continue to play an important role in many countries in documenting hate crime, which is particularly valuable when official statistics cannot be relied on to record the extent and nature of abuses.

Finally, the impact of hate crime victimisation goes beyond the individual victim, intimidating entire groups in society. It serves to distinguish between 'us' and 'them' and, in this regard, it warrants recognition and action as a particularly damaging form of crime.

JO GOODEY

Note

The views expressed are those of the author and do not necessarily reflect the views or official position of the European Union Agency for Fundamental Rights.

See also: **Racist Hate Crime; Sex Work, Hate Crime and Victimisation**

Readings

FRA (Agency for Fundamental Rights) (2012a) *Making hate crime visible in the European Union: Acknowledging victims' rights*. Luxembourg: Publications Office of the European Union. Available at: http://fra.europa.eu/en/publication/2012/making-hate-crime-visible-european-union-acknowledging-victims-rights

FRA (2012b) *EU-MIDIS data in focus report 6: Minorities as victims of crime*. Luxembourg: Publications Office of the European Union. Available at: http://fra.europa.eu/en/publication/2012/eu-midis-data-focus-report-6-minorities-victims-crime

FRA (2014) *EU LGBT survey: European Union lesbian, gay, bisexual and transgender survey – main results*. Luxembourg: Publications Office of the European Union. Available at: http://fra.europa.eu/en/publication/2014/eu-lgbt-survey-european-union-lesbian-gay-bisexual-and-transgender-survey-main

Macpherson, W. (1999) *The Stephen Lawrence inquiry: Report of an inquiry by Sir William Macpherson of Cluny (Cm 4262)*. London: The Stationary Office.

UK Equality and Human Rights Commission (2011) 'Hidden in plain sight – inquiry into disability-related harassment'. Available at: http://www.equalityhumanrights.com/publication/hidden-plain-sight-inquiry-disability-related-harassment

HISTORICAL PERSPECTIVES ON VICTIMS

The role and visibility of victims of crime in a criminal justice system varies according to jurisdictions. This role and visibility has also varied over time within jurisdictions. These variations reflect the historical evolution of legal concepts, as well as diverse approaches to the interpretation of such notions as that of individual responsibility. While it is true that the victim of a crime plays, and has always played, a central role in Western criminal justice systems, that role today is much more passive, less visible and arguably less important than it was in the past (Kirchengast, 2006; Godfrey and Lawrence, 2014).

The 11th-century British crime victim occupied a central position in common law, being responsible for the apprehension, charge and prosecution of offenders. However, the law at this time was feudal in character, with little distinction between civil and criminal jurisdictions, and mainly served to protect the property of the landed gentry. Kirchengast (2006) argues that the growth of the state out of feudal relations is central to the relocation of the victim in criminal law and justice. Thus, the role of the victim began to be weakened from the 12th century onwards, mainly due to the rise of the jury, the rise of the constable and other policing methods, and the collective and individual obligation of citizens to keep the King's peace. The 14th century saw the Crown and state taking an increasingly active role in managing and regulating civil society, such that they solely began to define what constituted 'crime'. This rise of the early state also saw discipline being consciously planned, designed, implemented and imposed on the population. By the 17th century, criminal justice, along with poor relief and public order law, had become the way to control society.

In Western societies, the relationship between the offender, the offended and criminal justice significantly altered during the period spanning roughly 1750 to 1950, but this change was due as much to broad changes in society as to the expansion of the remit of the state (Godfrey and Lawrence, 2014). There was no single turning point, but, for example, developments over the 19th century in English and Welsh policing certainly had a great effect. These changes in policing were part of changing attitudes to violence. Weiner (2004) has shown that levels of interpersonal violence that would never be accepted today were accepted previously, and given the cost of bringing a prosecution, many violent cases were settled by the offender and the victim outside the court. For example, particularly in working-class communities, 'fair fights' were a common way for working men (and sometimes women) to settle their disagreements. This continued through the 19th century and into the 20th as the New Police tended to 'look the other way' rather than interfere in a 'fair fight'. Other systems of informal justice were also accepted. Offences could have been dealt with by community action on behalf of or by the victim, such as ducking the offender in rivers and ponds; others still would have been dealt with by 'rough music' – public shaming rituals – often used for adulterous couples or henpecked men (Banks, 2014).

Ironically, then, changes in policing and increasing societal intolerance of violence have increased the *visibility* of the victim in the criminal justice process as more cases came to court. However, the *role* of the victim diminished. Hay (1989) has shown that during the period 1750–1850, victims (or someone acting on behalf of the victim) brought 80% of all criminal cases to court rather than an agent of national or local government. However, by about 1950, the police, and since 1986 the Crown Prosecution Service, had more or less assumed responsibility for prosecuting a case in court.

The state therefore continues to be the power restricting the victim's access to the courts and ultimately the criminal trial. However, there have been attempts recently to redress this imbalance. In Britain, one such measure – the 2013 Code of Practice for Victims of Crime – states that extra support should be given to victims of the most serious crime, those persistently targeted and vulnerable or intimidated victims. It includes new sections aimed at businesses and young victims of crime. The Code also allows victims to choose to make a Victim Personal Statement and to read it out in court if the defendant is found guilty. Along with enhanced victim services generally in Britain and elsewhere these changes go some way to restoring the role and visibility of the victim of crime in the criminal justice system.

JO TURNER

See also: **Code of Practice for Victims in England and Wales; Victim Impact Statements**

Readings
Banks, S. (2014) *Informal justice in England and Wales, 1760–1914: The courts of popular opinion*. Woodbridge: Boydell and Brewer.
Godfrey, B. and Lawrence, P. (2014) *Crime and justice, 1750–1950*. Abingdon: Routledge.
Hay, D. (1989) 'Using the criminal law, 1750–1850: policing, private prosecution, and the state', in D. Hay and F. Snyder (eds) *Policing and private prosecution in Britain 1750–1850*. Oxford: Clarendon Press.
Kirchengast, T. (2006) *The victim in criminal law and justice*. Basingstoke: Palgrave Macmillan.
Weiner, M. (2004) *Men of blood. Violence, manliness and criminal justice in Victorian England*. Cambridge: Cambridge University Press.

HOMELESSNESS AND VICTIMISATION

What is officially known about the victimisation of hard-to-reach and marginal groups whose lives are conditioned by and structured around primary, secondary and multiple experiences of victimisation is inaccurate and incomplete. In criminal justice policy and in broader social policy, homelessness is governed and administered by local authority agencies and service providers as a 'criminogenic situation', where 'participation in crime increases with homelessness' (McCarthy and Hagan, 1991, p 397). Consequently, these dominant policy discourses concentrate their attention on homeless populations as perpetrators of crime, rather than as victims of crime.

There is a rich body of literature that focuses upon homelessness and victimisation, both in homelessness and criminology studies. These studies overwhelmingly show that homeless people are exposed to extreme and persistent violence (Rock and Newburn, 2005), where they encounter multiple experiences of victimisation (Wardhaugh, 2000; Jasinski et al, 2010). Studies reveal that prior to becoming homeless, young people often encounter their first traumatic experience of victimisation within the home setting, where they may be subject to violence, abuse and/or neglect (Wardhaugh, 2000). Equally, feminist analyses of violence (McWilliams, 1998; Jasinski et al, 2010) situate the role of domestic violence as a substantial contributing factor to female homelessness, where women leave the home to end cycles of violence. Therefore, victimisation within the home is an important starting point for analyses of homelessness. 'Homeless at home' (Wardhaugh, 1999) is a concept that is used to describe the common scenario where men, women and children have a home but, due to structural damage and/or ongoing experiences of violence and victimisation, they do not feel that they can return there. The notion of 'homeless at home' challenges the assumption that 'there is less of a sense of violation' when an act of violence occurs within one's own 'sanctuary' (McWilliams, 1998, p 130) and rejects the commonly held view that the home is a place of sanctuary and emotional harmony. By turning this happy ideology of the home on its head (Wardhaugh, 1999), studies in victimisation and homelessness confront the home as possibly the most significant and traumatic site of crime, harm, violence and victimisation that will later come to shape the lives of homeless individuals.

Yet, the most compelling factor in thinking about homelessness and victimisation is not where victimisation starts, but where it ends: victimisation is rarely a one-off experience for homeless individuals. Homeless people experience much greater levels of crime than the general population (Rock and Newburn, 2005) and everyday experiences of homelessness, whether it be street homelessness or living in temporary shelter, is underpinned by multiple experiences of victimisation. Homeless individuals are frequently subject to violence, theft and harassment from both strangers and within the homeless community (Scurfield et al, 2009; Huey, 2012). From within the homeless community, men are more likely to be at risk of physical assault and theft, and women are more likely to be at risk sexual violence and harassment (Scurfield et al, 2009). Young homeless people can be subject to a whole range of crimes as a result of their relative inexperience of homeless street culture (Wardhaugh, 2000).

'Othered' for their poverty and, by extension, for transgressing conventional norms associated with housing, homeless individuals can be subject to much hostility in mainstream society and are often subject to 'hate crimes'. Common experiences of hate crime include being harassed by the general public (Rock and Newburn 2005; Scurfield et al, 2009), with the most violent experiences involving being set on fire (Millward, 2014) or beaten to death in random violent attacks (*The*

Guardian, 2013). However, such aggressive responses to homeless groups are not merely contained at the individual level. Countries such as Hungary, the US and the UK all enforce 'anti-begging' laws that criminalise homeless activities and, what is more, permit corporations to erect 'defensive architecture' – such as anti-homeless spikes and anti-homeless benches – to prevent homeless people from using key public spaces.

Despite the extent of victimisation in the lives of homeless people, research within and beyond criminology shows that crimes against the homeless are grossly under-reported (Scurfield et al, 2009) and thus their experiences of victimisation remain under the radar. There are several reasons why homeless individuals do not report their crime, but perhaps the most significant reason – one that contributes more generally to key debates around the politics of victimisation (Elias, 1986) – is that homeless individuals do not assume 'the ideal victim' status (Christie, 1986). By virtue of their poverty and, by extension, their transgression of meanings of the home, homeless individuals are often blamed for triggering the very crime perpetrated against them.

Such victim-blaming responses effectively deter homeless individuals from reporting crimes to the police. As a result, police-recorded data fail to provide a clear indication of the extent of victimisation among homeless populations. Another insufficient source of knowledge when evaluating victimisation among homeless populations is the Crime Survey for England and Wales. This survey takes an arbitrary and isolated selection of 50,000 households to ask about people's experience of crime in the past year. By focusing only on those experiences of individuals and families living in households, the Crime Survey therefore fails to include homeless populations. The exclusion of homeless populations in the national data on victimisation, first, renders them invisible victims of crime and, second, produces a knowledge and political reality about victimisation that is wholly inaccurate.

In summary, then, in England and Wales, official knowledge and understanding of homeless individuals as victims of crime is, at best, sketchy. This is primarily due to the fact that homeless individuals fall outside of 'ideal victim' typologies, are more likely to be blamed for their own victimisation and, consequently, are more likely than the general population to avoid reporting a crime to official authorities.

VICKIE COOPER

See also: **Hate Crime and Victimisation; Official Crime Statistics and Victim Surveys**

Readings

Christie, N. (1986) 'The ideal victim', in E.A Fattah (ed) *From crime policy to victim policy: Reorientating the justice system*. Basingstoke: MacMillan Press, pp 17–30.

Elias, R. (1986) *The politics of victimization: Victims, victimology and human rights*. Oxford: Oxford University Press.

Huey, L. (2012) *Invisible victims: Homelessness and the growing security gap*. Toronto: University of Toronto Press.

Jasinski, L.J., Wesley, D.J., Wright, K.J. and Mustaine, E.E. (2010) *Hard lives, mean streets: Violence in the lives of homeless women*. Lebanon: Northeastern University Press.

McWilliams, M. (1992) 'Violence against women in societies under stress', in R.E. Dobash and R.P. Dobash (eds) *Rethinking violence against women*. London: Sage, pp 111-140.

McCarthy, B. and Hagan, J. (1991) 'Homelessness: a criminogenic situation?', *British Journal of Criminology*, 31(4): 393–410.

Millward, D. (2014) 'Teenager to be sentenced for setting homeless man on fire'. Available at: http://www.getreading.co.uk/news/local-news/teenager-sentenced-setting-homeless-man-6730305

Rock, P. and Newburn, T. (2005) *Living in fear. Violence and the victimization in the lives of single homeless people*. London: Crisis. Available at: http://www.crisis.org.uk/data/files/publications/LivingInFear_prelim%5B1%5D.pdf

Scurfield, J., Rees, P. and Norman, P. (2009) 'Criminal victimisation of the homeless: an investigation of Big Issue vendors in Leeds', *Radical Statistics*, 99: 3–11.

The Guardian (2013) 'Three teenagers sentenced for homeless man's murder', 15 April. Available at: http://www.theguardian.com/uk/2013/apr/15/three-sentenced-homeless-man-murder

Wardhaugh, J. (1999) 'The unaccommodated woman: home, homelessness and identity', *The Sociological Review*, 47(1): 91–109.

Wardhaugh, J. (2000) *Subcity: Young people, homelessness and crime*. Aldershot: Ashgate.

HOMOPHOBIC HATE CRIME AND VICTIMISATION

See: **Hate Crime and Victimisation**

HONOUR-BASED VICTIMISATION

'Honour-based victimisation', most commonly referred to as 'honour-based violence' (HBV), is an umbrella term used to describe a range of offences or practices that are used to control victims and/or to protect cultural beliefs and 'honour'. Honour is a fluid concept with varying meanings across different contexts; however, in the present context, it is used to describe a range of cultural beliefs and practices that are based on respect, value and status. Leading scholars in the area, such as Gill and Anitha (2011) and Gill, Strange and Roberts (2014), have highlighted the lack of an appropriate and cross-culturally relevant definition of HBV.

Many scholars and practitioners prefer the term 'so-called honour-based violence' to reflect the fact that these behaviours are actually contradictory to the normal definitions and understandings of 'honour'. There is no single offence of honour-based crime in the UK; however, a number of behaviours that are linked to HBV have been made criminal, including forced marriage.

The majority of victims of HBV are women and it is thus generally viewed as a form of violence against women. However, in some ways, HBV differs from other types of violence against women, for example, domestic violence, because it is typically perpetrated by more than one individual from the victim's family, partner or husband's family, and/or the wider community. In contrast, domestic violence is typically perpetrated by a partner, former partner or other family member on an individual basis and is hidden from the wider community. HBV is not confined to any one particular religion or culture, despite strong societal perceptions that it is rooted in South and West Asian religious and cultural practices.

At a national and international level, there are either no or few available statistics on the prevalence of HBV as it is not separated in the official statistics from other forms of violence and there is no single crime that can be recorded by the police. HBV is a hidden phenomenon and is known to be severely unreported. Furthermore, many crimes that are committed in the context of HBV may not be recognised as such by authorities, thus leading to under-recording. The available statistics are mostly published by charities, for example, the Iranian and Kurdish Women's Rights Organisation (IKWRO) found that, in 2008, there had been 2,800 incidents of HBV reported to police forces across the UK in the previous year. The UK Home Office suggests there are around 12 recorded killings a year defined as honour killings; however, the true number is likely to be significantly higher.

The two forms of HBV that have seen some of the biggest developments in terms of legislation and policy are forced marriage and female genital mutilation

(FGM) (sometimes called 'female genital cutting'), which are the only two forms of HBV to be made into specific criminal offences in the UK and elsewhere. Forced marriage is defined in the UK as a marriage where one or both people cannot or do not consent and pressure or abuse is used. Such pressure can be physical, emotional or financial. Forced marriage was made a criminal offence by the Anti-social Behaviour, Crime and Policing Act 2014 and carries a maximum seven-year prison sentence. National statistics published by the UK Home Office in 2014 report that the Forced Marriage Unit gave advice or support related to 1,267 cases of possible forced marriage. The vast majority involved young female victims, typically aged between 16 and 30 and from the Indian subcontinent. However, the true extent is likely to be significantly higher than this.

FGM is the practice of intentionally altering or causing injury to the female genital organs for non-medical reasons and is thus a gender-specific practice, affecting girls and women exclusively. The practice can be carried out by men or women and is prevalent across Africa and the Middle East, although it also occurs in Western countries. Religious or cultural reasons are cited for FGM, based on the control over women's sexuality and as a ritual initiation into adulthood. A study conducted by Dorkenoo, Morison and Macfarlane (2007) estimated that more than 20,000 girls under the age of 15 are at risk of FGM in the UK. In the UK, FGM was made a criminal act under the Female Genital Mutilation Act 2003 and carries a maximum 14-year prison sentence. Elsewhere, for example, in the US, FGM has been criminalised since the 1990s; however, the maximum prison sentence is five years (and/or a fine). In Australia, the maximum sentence has recently been increased from seven years' to 21 years' imprisonment.

There is a lack of theory underpinning the current research and literature around HBV. Feminist theories recognise the gendered nature of HBV and position it within a wider patriarchal society that oppresses women and where women are seen as sexual commodities to be controlled and enjoyed by men. However, while the majority of victims of different forms of HBV are girls and women, there are known male victims of forced marriage, assaults and killings that are not explained by feminist theory. Furthermore, there is a lack of empirical or theoretical publications relating to FGM; the existing literature is dominated by health and medical frameworks and is primarily focused on the physiological implications of FGM rather than the causes of this practice.

HANNAH BOWS

See also: Culture and Victimisation; Female Genital Mutilation; Gender and Victimisation

Readings

Dorkenoo, E., Morison, L. and Macfarlane, A. (2007) *A statistical study to estimate the prevalence of female genital mutilation in England and Wales*. London: Forward.

Gill, A. and Anitha, S. (2011) *Forced marriage: Introducing a social justice and human rights perspective*. London: Zed Books.

Gill, A., Strange, C. and Roberts, K. (2014) *'Honour' killing and violence: Theory, policy and practice*. London: Palgrave Macmillan.

Home Office (no date) *Female genital mutilation, the facts*. London: Home Office.

HUMAN RIGHTS AND VICTIMS

Human rights have variously addressed 'victims' or 'victimhood' through the lens of large-scale or group victimisation (most notably, the Holocaust), or when looking to highlight the abuse of individuals (such as journalists and political prisoners) in countries where rights such as freedom of expression and freedom of assembly are curtailed. The United Nations (UN) and regional human rights entities, such as the Council of Europe, have been at the forefront of highlighting these human rights abuses, and have been greatly aided in this by non-governmental organisations like Amnesty International and Human Rights Watch. Here, the focus has been on victimisation against groups and individuals *by the state*. Against this backdrop, it is only recently that victims of *crime* – which is not committed by the state – have been mainstreamed within the human rights field.

The right to a fair trial and the right of defence are central pillars of human rights law – as set out in articles 10 and 11 of the 1948 Universal Declaration of Human Rights; article 6 of the 1950 European Convention on Human Rights; and, most recently, articles 47 and 48 of the Charter of Fundamental Rights of the European Union (EU), which entered into force in 2009. What these various articles focus on is the defendant and his/her rights – because it is the defendant, rather than the victim, who is seen as having everything to lose if not given a fair trial and, as a result, incorrectly found guilty. Reflecting this, in common law jurisdictions, such as England and Wales, the victim has traditionally been constructed as the 'alleged victim', or witness, and has had few rights in law. Other jurisdictions have given victims more legal rights to actively participate in a trial or hearing – for example, in France as a 'partie civile' and in Germany as a 'Nebenkläger' (joint plaintiff) – though it is often the case that these rights exist on paper more than they are exercised in practice (FRA, 2015).

Only relatively recently – when compared with the long history of defendants' rights – has consideration been given to the fact that the victim also has much to lose if a defendant is incorrectly found innocent (General Assembly of the

United Nations, 1985). Also, growing recognition of the 'secondary victimisation' that policing and criminal justice can cause victims if they are poorly treated has served to increase recognition of victims' needs – and latterly their rights – in practice (Crawford and Goodey, 2000), for example, with increased provision of victim support services. Traditional concerns that enhancing victims' rights would serve to jeopardise defendants' rights have now given way to increased recognition of victims' rights as being part of human rights, for example, to be treated with dignity and respect, and to be free from discrimination – as a victim – on different grounds, such as gender and race.

At the regional level of the EU, the EU's 2012 Victims' Directive, which replaced the 2001 Framework Decision on the Standing of Victims in Criminal Proceedings – which was poorly implemented in practice at EU member state level – has set a new benchmark for enhancing victims' rights. The preamble to the Directive states that 'This Directive respects fundamental rights and observes the principles recognised by the Charter of Fundamental Rights of the European Union' (European Parliament and Council, 2012, para 66). To this end, the Directive covers a broad swathe of rights – from the right to information and support, through to the right to be heard in criminal proceedings. An important element in the Directive is its reference to the individual assessment of victims – to be able to assess their needs – while, at the same time, recognition is given at different points in the Directive to vulnerable victims, such as victims of gender-based violence, hate crime and child victims.

Finally, criminal victimisation surveys have recently been given a new lease of life in some human rights quarters as a means of measuring the extent of victimisation against specific groups, including data on reporting to the police and other services. Notably, the EU Agency for Fundamental Rights (FRA) and the UN's Office of the High Commissioner for Human Rights have promoted the use of 'outcome' indicators as a means of assessing how people experience rights on the ground. The FRA's large-scale victim surveys – ranging from a survey of 42,000 women's experiences of violence across the EU's 28 member states, through to another survey on 23,500 minority ethnic groups' and immigrants' experiences of hate crime – currently present some of the largest transnational data sets that allow for the comparison of human rights norms and policies on paper with victims' experiences in practice.

JO GOODEY

Note

The views expressed are those of the author and do not necessarily reflect the views or official position of the European Union Agency for Fundamental Rights.

See also: **United Nations Declaration of the Basic Principles of Justice for Victims of Crime and Abuse of Power; Universal Declaration of Human Rights**

Readings

Crawford, A. and Goodey, J. (2000) *Integrating a victim perspective within criminal justice: International debates*. Aldershot: Ashgate.

European Parliament and Council (2012) 'Directive 2012/29/EU of the European Parliament and of the Council of 25 October 2012 establishing minimum standards on the rights, support and protection of victims of crime, and replacing Council Framework Decision 2001/220/JHA'. Available at: http://eur-lex. europa.eu/legal-content/EN/TXT/?uri=CELEX:32012L0029

FRA (Agency for Fundamental Rights) (2015) *Victims of crime in the EU: The extent and nature of support for victims*. Luxembourg: Publications Office of the European Union. Available at: http://fra.europa.eu/en/publication/2014/ victims-crime-eu-extent-and-nature-support-victims

General Assembly of the United Nations (1985) 'Declaration of basic principles of justice for victims of crime and abuse of power'. Available at: http://www. un.org/documents/ga/res/40/a40r034.htm

HUMAN TRAFFICKING AND VICTIMISATION

Human trafficking is often referred to as 'modern-day slavery'. Examples of human trafficking include people who are willingly recruited to work abroad but who find themselves being victimised by their traffickers, and the persons they end up working for, through the use of violence, threats and coercion – as well as other means of exploitation. Herein, human smuggling – where someone typically pays a fee to a smuggler to be taken from place A to B – becomes human trafficking once a person is exploited and controlled to the extent encompassed by anti-trafficking legislation and relevant case law.

In the last two decades, international attention has increasingly been paid to trafficking in human beings. The 2000 United Nations Convention on Transnational Organised Crime and its accompanying protocols on trafficking and smuggling served to highlight the problem of trafficking as a global phenomenon. In addition, the following are just two regional instruments that have served to address trafficking: first, in Europe, the 2005 Council of Europe Convention on Action against Trafficking in Human Beings, which is accompanied by an evaluation mechanism in the form of the Group of Experts on Action against Trafficking in Human Beings (GRETA); and second, the more recent 2011 European Union (EU) Directive on Preventing and Combating Trafficking in Human Beings. Within the EU, the position of an EU Anti-Trafficking Coordinator was established alongside the Directive to try and ensure coordinated action at EU and member state level to address trafficking. This development is mirrored in the establishment of national anti-trafficking coordinators and offices in a number of EU member states.

The renewed attention on trafficking in the 1990s and early 2000s was led by a number of civil society organisations, such as 'La Strada' Poland, which initially focused on the sexual exploitation of women and girls who were being transported from economically disadvantaged and unstable regions to be exploited elsewhere. More recently, attention has shifted to include a more comprehensive reading of trafficking that includes men, women and children who are trafficked for purposes other than sexual exploitation. As a result, a number of studies – which are frequently accompanied by media reports – have emerged in recent years to document the extent and nature of different forms of trafficking, particularly in relation to severe forms of labour exploitation in areas such as agriculture, fishing, construction and domestic work (UNODC, 2014; FRA, 2015; US Department of State, 2015). At the same time, trafficking is now recognised as encompassing the exploitation of persons within a country, and is not confined to the movement and exploitation of persons across international borders.

The various 'push' and 'pull' factors influencing patterns of trafficking have been documented, focusing in the main on victims' economic circumstances and recruiters' ability to exploit them, which includes the demand for cheap goods and services on a global scale, be this in relation to agriculture or the sex industry. The response to trafficking has traditionally focused on what was termed the three 'Ps', namely: prevention (of trafficking); prosecution (of offenders); and protection (of victims) (see, eg, the website of the United Nations Office on Drugs and Crime). A fourth 'P' was added in reference to 'partnership' between different actors that seek to address the problem of trafficking, for example, the police working in partnership with National Rapporteurs on Trafficking.

The plight of trafficking victims has given rise to laws and policies that seek to ensure that their victimisation is recognised and effectively responded to. However, the provision of services for trafficking victims – such as access to victim support services and a residence permit (where needed) – has often gone hand-in-hand with the requirement that they cooperate with the authorities in their investigation of trafficking cases. Herein, the line between a trafficking victim being an 'illegal' immigrant and a victim who has rights regardless of their immigration status is often blurred.

The continued relatively low number of prosecutions against trafficking, in comparison with estimates of the scale of trafficking, is an indication that the needs of trafficking victims are not being met and that traffickers continue to act with relative impunity in many jurisdictions. At the same time, it should be noted that it is notoriously difficult to accurately assess the scale of trafficking (Goodey, 2008). The cross-border nature of trafficking also serves to add to the challenges faced when trying to combat these crimes. Ongoing loss of life in the Mediterranean, which received widespread political and public attention in the period 2013–15, has pointed to the continued abuses of human smuggling, which can so often become human trafficking, in the 21st century. This is a situation that is compounded by the lack of political agreement over how to respond to this problem in the framework of a human rights and a migration context.

JO GOODEY

Note

The views expressed are those of the author and do not necessarily reflect the views or official position of the European Union Agency for Fundamental Rights.

See also: **Gender and Victimisation; Victim Services**

Readings

FRA (Agency for Fundamental Rights) (2015) *Severe labour exploitation: Workers moving within or into the European Union.* Luxembourg: Publications Office of the European Union. Available at: http://fra.europa.eu/en/publication/2015/severe-labour-exploitation-workers-moving-within-or-european-union

Goodey, J. (2008) 'Human trafficking: sketchy data and policy responses', *Criminology and Criminal Justice*, 8(4): 421–42.

UNODC (United Nations Office on Drugs and Crime) (2014) *Global report on trafficking in persons.* Vienna: UNODC. Available at: https://www.unodc.org/unodc/en/human-trafficking/publications.html#Reports

US Department of State (2015) 'Trafficking in persons report 2015'. Available at: http://www.state.gov/j/tip/rls/tiprpt/

I

IATROGENIC HARM, 'CRIME' AND VICTIMISATION

An iatrogenic harm refers to the injury, hurt or damage generated by an institutional practice that is justified on the basis of helping, assisting or healing individuals with problems requiring remedy. In other words, it is a direct consequence of an intervention by a state agency that rather than curing an individual or making a set of affairs better, makes things worse. Iatrogenesis is said to occur when schools create ignorance, hospitals create ill-health, asylums create madness, social control creates 'crime' or policing creates victimisation.

The term 'iatrogenesis' was first introduced by the radical social critic Illich (1974). In his classic text, Illich (1974) defined iatrogenesis on three conceptual levels: clinical, social and cultural. Clinical iatrogenesis refers to the direct harms suffered by people through the ineffective, unsafe or erroneous treatment by state agents. Illich (1974) explored the concept of 'clinical iatrogenesis' with specific reference to the medical profession, but such direct harms are now often referred to as 'institutional iatrogenesis'. Social iatrogenesis deals with the vested interests of corporations and businesses in promoting particular forms of responses to human problems. For Illich (1974), unnecessary 'human needs' are generated by private companies in the relentless pursuit of profits and new markets. At the same time, social problems and structural inequalities are obfuscated. Cultural iatrogenesis refers to the colonisation of the lifeworld and subsequent destruction of alternative ways of handling conflicts. Not only is cultural iatrogenesis counterproductive to human well-being, but it also fosters new forms of dependency on state bureaucracies and new opportunities for capitalist exploitation.

In his early writings, Illich (1971) explored the ineffectual nature of state education. Although his first book, *Deschooling society* (Illich, 1971), did not explicitly refer to iatrogenesis, the term can be retrospectively applied. Illich (1971) argued that formal education systems served the interests of elites rather than the people. Useful and specialised knowledges are restricted, while state schooling focuses upon discipline, repression and disimagination: the vast majority of people are taught how *not to think* and to suppress their natural imagination. Institutionalised education restricts progress, creates ignorance and robs people of basic skills and practical knowledge. Illich (1974) also explained how medicalisation creates illness. He evidenced not only how medicine was negligible to good health – in reality, the product of socio-economic circumstances conducive to human well-being – but also that such interventions had terrible and long-lasting side effects. Rather than 'cure' people, medicalisation creates 'sickness'. For example, benzodiazepine tranquillisers, which were initially prescribed as a quick fix for depression, were later discovered to have harmful side effects, including panic attacks, palpitations, sleeplessness, cold sweats and uncontrollable shaking. Medicalisation can be stigmatising, produce patient dependency and distract attention away from the real sources of illness – social inequalities.

A number of the preceding arguments are reflected in critical criminological analysis of detention, social control and policing. Foucault (1967) maintained that asylums were invented as a way of 'imprisoning madness' rather than reflecting humanitarian progress, whereas for Goffman (1963), 'total institutions', such as the asylum, stripped individuals of their human identity. This led to 'institutionalisation' and 'disculturalisation'. Saturated in conflict and antagonistic stereotypes undermining potential 'therapeutic alliances', total institutions like the asylum damage mental health rather than provide places of sanctuary or healing. Foucault (1977) and Cohen (1985) apply these insights to prisons and other machinery of social control. Cohen (1985) vividly illustrates how practices of social control generate 'crime', while Foucault (1977) explores how classification techniques create 'delinquency', a critique bringing into question the very legitimacy of criminological knowledge. Finally, there is considerable evidence that policing creates victimisation. This is especially so in the policing of marginalised and impoverished black and minority ethnic (BME) communities. Victimisation manifests itself in terms of: disproportionate police stop and searches; the inferior treatment of black victims of sexual and racist violence ('racially aggravated hate crime'); and the large number of BME deaths – 137 of nearly 1,000 – in police custody from 1991 to 2014. Iatrogenic policing is thus closely intertwined with state racism.

DAVID SCOTT

See also: **Aversion Therapy, Harm and Victimisation; Iatrogenic Harms and the Prison**

Readings

Cohen, S. (1985) *Visions of social control*. Cambridge: Polity.

Foucault, M. (1967) *Madness and civilisation*. London: Routledge.

Foucault, M. (1977) *Discipline and punish*. Harmondsworth: Penguin.

Goffman, E. (1963) *Asylums*. Harmondsworth: Penguin.

Illich, I. (1971) *Deschooling society*. London: Marion Boyars Publishers Ltd.

Illich, I. (1974) *Limits to medicine: Medical nemesis – the expropriation of health*. London: Marion Boyars Publishers Ltd.

IATROGENIC HARMS AND THE PRISON

Iatrogenic harms refer to the injury, hurt or damage generated by institutions that instead of facilitating positive outcomes, deliberately manufacture the opposite. Iatrogenesis can occur when criminal processes directly create 'crime' and other problems, leading to an escalation, rather than reduction, of illegalities, social harms and human suffering.

The term 'iatrogenesis' was first introduced by Illich (1974), and penal abolitionists have developed this concept when exploring the damaging consequences of imprisonment (Cohen, 1985; Christie, 2000; Scott and Codd, 2010). There are three forms of penal iatrogenesis: institutional iatrogenesis, which refers to the intended or unintended harms directly generated by the counterproductive nature of the prison place; social iatrogenesis, which captures the ulterior motive of punishing for the pursuit of profit; and cultural iatrogenesis, which focuses on the destruction of traditional non-punitive means of conflict handling. Each will be covered in turn.

The term 'institutional iatrogenesis' can be used to refer to the harms experienced by prisoners as a direct result of the ineffective, unsafe and violent nature of penal confinement. Despite rhetoric of 'reform' and 'rehabilitation', pain infliction is the overarching rationale of the prison place and a number of scholars have identified the inherent harms and damage reeked by imprisonment on individuals and society. For Foucault (1977), institutional iatrogenesis was, in fact, a hidden aim of imprisonment, for the prison was a machine that deliberately manufactured dysfunctional individuals who could be subsequently blamed for societal ills. In a similar vein, Mathiesen (1990) argues that prisons have always been more likely to 'dehabilitate' rather than 'rehabilitate' offenders, while Goffman (1963) identifies how 'total institutions', such as the prison, socially produce 'mortification', 'institutionalisation' and 'disculturalisation', all of which hinder the ability of those confined to later cope in wider society.

The focus of Scott and Codd (2010) is on the consequences of the prison place for human well-being. Prisons harm rather than help: boredom creates a need for substance usage; isolation and degradation exacerbates mental health problems; and the institutionally structured pains of imprisonment generate suicidal ideation and death. Scott and Codd (2010) also chart penal iatrogenesis through the unintended side effects of imprisonment, most notably, on prisoner families and the children of prisoners, who, despite having done nothing wrong, can experience trauma, stigmatisation and financial hardship if a parent or carer is sent to prison.

Christie (2000) utilises the writings of Illich to investigate the rapid rise in global prison populations since the 1970s, especially in Russia and the US. Christie (2000) locates the causes of this 'social iatrogenesis' within: a dismantling of welfare provision; growing social and economic inequalities and the associated weakening of social solidarities and attachment; the creation of a 'dangerous', substance-using 'surplus population' who have been criminalised and need to be contained; and, most significantly, the privatisation of the crime control apparatus. 'Punishment for profits' now means that corporations have a vested interest in promoting punishment, thus filling prisons with 'social junk' and other 'suitable enemies'. For Christie (2000), there are no 'natural limits' to crime controls, whereas private vested interests obfuscate social problems and neglect, which are the harmful consequences of structural inequalities.

Cohen (1985) also explored the logic of penal expansionism. Like Christie (2000), Cohen (1985) explores how penal expansion is driven by the creation of new categories of deviance and the redefining of social problems within the logic of an elitist and self-serving 'crime control industry'. However, for Cohen (1985), social iatrogenesis is closely conjoined with 'cultural iatrogenesis' – the colonisation of the lifeworld by the punitive rationale and the subsequent destruction of alternative ways of dealing with individual troubles and social problems. Cohen (1985) famously described this process through the metaphor of 'fishing nets'. Net widening resulted from the penetration of 'control talk', new classificationary systems and the normalisation of state power, discipline and surveillance within the family, school and wider community. As a result, a new disciplinary vision of social organisation is embedded in our culture while state practices, ironically, are legitimated by iatrogenesis – or, rather, attempts to 'mop up the casualties created by its own operations' (Cohen, 1985, p 170).

DAVID SCOTT

See also: **Iatrogenic Harm, 'Crime' and Victimisation**

Readings

Christie, N. (2000) *Crime control as industry*. London: Routledge.

Cohen, S. (1985) *Visions of social control*. Cambridge: Polity.

Foucault, M. (1977) *Discipline and punish*. Harmondsworth: Penguin.

Goffman, E. (1963) *Asylums*. Harmondsworth: Penguin.

Illich, I. (1974) *Limits to medicine: Medical nemesis − the expropriation of health*. London: Marion Boyars Publishers.

Mathiesen, T. (1990) *Prison on trial*. London: Sage.

Scott, D. and Codd, H. (2010) *Controversial issues in prisons*. Buckingham: Open University Press.

J

JUSTICE AND VICTIMS

Justice for victims is the desire to achieve the ideal state of fairness, equality and respect via the atonement for wrongs and harms caused to them. Justice in relation to victims cannot be understood if it is abstracted from interrelated concepts and practices of criminal justice, due process, social justice and fairness. Yet, those concepts and practices are often ambiguous, contested and dynamic, and open to political and ideological adulteration. The principled and ethical appropriateness of decisions and practices relating to 'deserving' victims must unequivocally atone for their victimisation in order to secure what is claimed to be 'proper' justice. Attempts to secure justice for victims of crimes and harms are not exclusive to the rules of law, but also found in many religious and moral codes, and the enforcement of such standards are attempts to reduce victimisation and secure justice. However, what is dispensed as purportedly justice via these legal and regulatory codes can seem bizarre to others who do not share the same values (Greer and McLaughlin, 2012).

It is believed in criminal law that there are strict rules and procedures, which ostensibly must be observed in order to achieve a conviction. There is also the belief that if convicted, the consistent punishment of offenders accomplishes justice for both offenders and victims. However, in recent years, the frequent exposure of discriminatory practices, against both victims and suspects, has seriously undermined public confidence in the rule of law and the liberal rhetoric of equality for all before the law. Contrarily, these procedural requirements have

---

led to sweeping claims that they are overly bureaucratic and inflexible, and, in actuality, ostensibly deny natural justice (for an exemplar, see Stevens, 2002).

The probity of wishing to help worthy victims achieve justice is easily exploited for political and ideological gain by both liberals and conservatives, but their approaches and the values that inform these can be diametrically oppositional. Therein, and depending on the social status of the victims, more liberal approaches tend to emphasise factors impacting on victims that are beyond their personal control, while more conservative approaches can counter with a rhetoric of victim responsibilisation. The complexities of these discordant and often inconsistent ideologies are shaped by revisions in socio-economic, political and cultural circumstances that can radically reshape policies and practices for victims (Tombs and Whyte, 2003).

Despite the claims of a monolithic international legal order and all-encompassing globalisation, the varieties of justice available to victims remain politically and culturally diverse. Advocates of retributive justice assert that only by punishing offenders can victimisation be recompensed and justice fulfilled; therefore, they maintain, the failure to punish is morally reprehensible. In an attempt to move away from the obsession with punishment, which is not the simple or common-sense panacea that it is so often proclaimed to be, restorative justice proponents argue that justice can be achieved more effectively by restoring victims' losses and/or getting offenders to understand the harms that they have caused and to empathise with their victims (Randal, 2013). Being professedly much less punitive, despite the potential emotional turmoil for both victims and offenders, restorative justice is often caricatured as an insufficient mechanism for facilitating justice for victims simply because it insufficiently punishes.

Natural justice has similarities to the religious concept of karma, wherein good and bad deeds naturally and correspondingly produce good and bad repercussions. This can be highly problematic for victims and their pursuit of justice as their victimisation can be used to imply that a wide variety of purportedly 'inappropriate' actions caused their victimisation, thereby diminishing or denying offender culpability.

The pursuit of social justice for victims takes justice beyond merely the rules of law and seeks to address many forms of harm that deny them the core requirements of a decent life. Social justice is strongly influenced by socialist values. Herein opposing poverty and exclusion in order to secure a more just and fair society together with a peaceful existence, are at odds with the driving force of capitalism: labour exploitation. Thus, while the pursuit of social justice is observed by a dedicated United Nations Social Justice Day, in practice, this is discordant with levels of human exploitation and inequality permitted in contemporary neoliberal capitalist states. Accordingly, such victims are extensively denied justice from the crimes of the powerful and, in particular, the crimes of the state (Klein and Lavery, 2011). While it is clear that such crimes have received much greater scrutiny in recent years, there remains inadequate improvement in consistently achieving justice for the vast majority of such victims.

LIAM McCANN

See also: **Blame and Victims; Victim Hierarchy; Victims of Crime**

Readings

Greer, C. and McLaughlin, E. (2012) 'This is not justice', *The British Journal of Criminology*, 52(2): 274–93.

Klein, J. and Lavery, C. (2011) 'Legitimising war by victimisation: state-corporate crime and public opinion', *Crime, Law and Social Change*, 56(3): 301–17.

Randal, M. (2013) 'Restorative justice and gendered violence? From vaguely hostile skeptic to cautious convert: why feminists should critically engage with restorative approaches to law', *Dalhousie Law Journal*, 36(2): 461–99.

Stevens, J. (2002) 'The search for truth in the criminal justice system'. Available at: http://www.le.ac.uk/press/press/scalesofjustice2.html

Tombs, S. and Whyte, D. (eds) (2003) *Unmasking the crimes of the powerful: Scrutinizing states and corporations.* New York, NY: Peter Lang.

JUSTICE FOR ALL

In January 2015, the Victims' Commissioner for England and Wales reported on the efficacy of complaint handling under the Code of Practice for Victims. First introduced in 2004, this Code of Practice was implemented on the back of the Domestic Violence, Crime and Victims Act 2004, part of the then Labour government's initiative focused on the theme of 'justice for all'. The 2015 report states that 'There is a gap between the handling of complaints as described by criminal justice agencies, and how victims feel they have been treated' (Home Office, 2000, p 6). This statement infers that little has changed in the intervening decade. One question might be: why, and, as a consequence, what does 'justice for all' actually mean?

Many commentators have observed that the victim is the 'forgotten' party of the criminal justice system. Nonetheless, the first Victims' Charter of 1990, extended in 1996, significantly reoriented the work of the Probation Service to the victim rather than the offender, and these developments were given an added impetus with the embrace of the Human Rights Act in 1998. That Act was taken to mean giving entitlements to protection for victims as well as suspects. Alongside the greater willingness to listen to women's experiences of the criminal justice system, and the unfolding legacy of the Lawrence Inquiry, an overall review of policy towards victims was established. In the light of that review, the White Paper *Justice for all* (Home Office, 2000) was published. As Clark (2004, p 21) stated: '*Justice for All* is guided by a single clear priority – to rebalance the criminal justice system in favour of the victim and the community so as to reduce crime and to bring offenders to justice'. This preoccupation with rebalancing the justice system has been a key policy platform since then, although it reached a notable high point in the legislation referred to earlier. The Domestic Violence, Crime and Victims Act 2004 introduced surcharges on fines and fixed penalties for motoring offences that contribute to the funding of the Victims' Fund. It allowed the Criminal Injuries Compensation Authority to recover payments made to victims from their offenders, and widened the opportunities for victims to be given information and to provide information in cases where their offender receives a prison sentence. It also provided for a Commissioner for Victims and Witnesses, and set out a Code of Practice for Victims. The breadth of this legislation in relation to victims was without precedent in England and Wales.

So, it would seem that 'justice for all' implies rebalancing the criminal justice system. Miers (2007, p 337) has observed that this metaphor of 'rebalancing' is contentious. It not only puts victims/witnesses (complainants) and offenders (defendants) in an oppositional relationship with one another (which may be more imagined than real), but also begs the question as to the purpose of the criminal justice system itself. Some time ago, McBarnett (1988, p 300, emphasis added) observed that 'The offence is not just against the victimised person, the offence is against the state.... If the victim feels that nobody cares about their suffering, it is in part because *institutionally* nobody does'. Understanding this relationship between the state and the offender is central to understanding the problematic nature of the rebalancing metaphor: what or who is being rebalanced, and in what direction?

The preoccupation with rebalancing is underpinned by at least two concerns: to ensure the continued legitimacy of criminal justice (ie that people as victims/ witnesses continue to participate in it); and to respond to populist pressures in appearing to address the actual and/or perceived victims' needs for punishing the offender (politicians securing votes). Thus, the *Justice for all* White Paper and all that has followed in its wake has not only failed to address the concerns raised about the operation of the criminal justice system from the victims' perspective, but also failed to appreciate the central purpose of the criminal justice system itself. Indeed, the Victims' Commissioner's report referred to earlier consistently refers to complainants as victims, a nomenclature that, in and of itself, implies guilt and/or innocence. This presumption undermines the purpose of the criminal justice system as outlined by McBarnett (1988). Herein lies a fundamental problem with the notion of 'justice for all' as envisaged by politicians and interpreted by policymakers.

SANDRA WALKLATE

See also: **Code of Practice for Victims in England and Wales; Criminal Injuries Compensation Authority; Victims of Crime**

Readings
Clark, P. (2004) 'Redressing the balance: the Criminal Justice Bill 2002', in E. Capes (ed) *Reconciling rights*. London: LAG.
Home Office (2000) *Justice for all*, Cm5563. London: Home Office.
McBarnett, D. (1988) 'Victim in the witness box – confronting victimology's stereotype', *Contemporary Crises*, 7: 279–303.
Miers, D. (2007) 'Looking beyond Great Britain: the development of criminal injuries compensation', in S. Walklate (ed) *Handbook of victims and victimology*. Cullompton: Willan Publishing, pp 337–62.
Victims' Commissioner (2015) 'A review of complaints and resolution for victims of crime'. Available at: http://victimscommissioner.org.uk

K

KNOWLEDGE–POWER NEXUS

The concept of the knowledge–power nexus is derived from the work of French philosopher and historian Michel Foucault (1926–84), most notably, from his writings during the 1970s and 1980s. While Foucault focuses on the operation of the knowledge–power nexus in the regulation of offenders, the concept also has relevance for victims' experiences, in particular, with regard to: victims' exclusion from access to knowledge sources; the subjugation of victims' voices; and the judging of victims in comparison with ideas of respectability.

In his seminal account of the birth of the modern prison system (Foucault, 1977) (first published in French in 1975), Foucault charts the shift in 18th-century Europe from the hierarchical system of 'sovereign power' in which absolute obedience to the monarch was required, to the more dispersed systems of power that operate in modern 'disciplinary' society. Sovereign power had become an increasingly ineffective way of controlling growing urban populations, paving the way for disciplinary power, which operates through more subtle and measured forms of coercion (Foucault, 1977). Foucault uses Bentham's panopticon design as illustrative of the function of surveillance in the exercise of power; prisoners in the panopticon never know whether or not they are being observed and must thus employ self-discipline in order to avoid punishment.

Foucault portrays power as being 'exercised', rather than 'possessed'. In contrast to the Marxist concept of top-down power relations, Foucault (1977, pp 26–7) argues that power is not the 'privilege' of a ruling class, nor is it unilaterally imposed by the powerful upon the powerless. Rather, a network of 'micro-powers' go 'right down to the depths of society', involving 'innumerable points of confrontation' and instability, and creating an ever-present possibility of at least a temporary 'inversion of the power relations' (Foucault, 1977, p 27). Power is 'everywhere' and 'comes from everywhere' (Foucault, 1990 [1976], p 93). Within this nexus, individuals are 'the vehicles of power, not its points of application' (Foucault, 1980, p 98). For Foucault, where there is power, there is always resistance (Foucault, 1990 [1976]). In contesting the notion of power as merely repressive, Foucault (1980, p 119) asks: 'if it never did anything but say no, do you really believe that we should manage to obey it?' Rather, what 'gives power its hold' is that 'it produces things, it induces pleasure, it forms knowledge, it produces discourse' Foucault (1980, p 119).

The 'scientific' disciplines are identified by Foucault as playing a critical role in the operation of disciplinary power, with experts involved in the examination, codification and classification of bodies and minds. Within criminal justice processes, scientific knowledge is used to assess the offender and design techniques for their correction: 'It is no longer simply: "What law punishes this offence?" But: "What would be the most appropriate measures to take? How do we see the future development of the offender? What would be the best way of rehabilitating him?' (Foucault, 1977, p 19).

Through the assessment, diagnosis and 'normative judgements' made about the offender, knowledge produced by the scientific disciplines has become part of the system of punishment (Foucault, 1997, p 19). Rejecting the notion that 'true' scientific knowledge is free from power relations, Foucault (1977, p 27) states that 'power produces knowledge ... power and knowledge directly imply one another'. This is a two-way process whereby power relations cannot exist without a corresponding 'field of knowledge', just as knowledge must 'presuppose and constitute' power relations (Foucault, 1977, p 27). Through his concept of bio-power, Foucault describes the use of technologies to manage populations in the areas of 'life, death and health' (O'Farrell, 2005, p 106), involving the official collection of detailed information about the public health of populations, including on sexuality.

Foucault's concept of the knowledge–power nexus throws light on the experience of victims in criminal justice system processes. The operation of bio-power can be seen in the collection and analysis of detailed information about victims as a population by state and non-state agencies. Historically, victims have been marginalised in court processes, giving them little role other than to provide evidence of the crime, and leading to 'secondary victimisation', whereby victims experience being examined, assessed and judged by professional experts in comparison with the ideal of respectability. Victims of institutional abuse, in particular, have had their experiences nullified and voices silenced by those with greater power. The connections between power and knowledge may be seen in the struggles of victims individually and collectively to challenge dominant narratives and to have their voices heard and experiences recognised, for example, through historical inquiries or in court proceedings.

LINDA MOORE

See also: **Resistance to Crime, Harm and Victimisation**

Readings
Foucault, M. (1977) *Discipline and punish*. London: Allen Lane.
Foucault, M. (1980) *Power/knowledge: Selected interviews and other writings 1972–1977* (ed C. Gordon). New York, NY: Pantheon.
Foucault, M. (1990 [1976]) *History of sexuality*. London: Penguin Books.
O'Farrell, C. (2005) *Michel Foucault*. London: Sage.

L

LABOUR AND VICTIMISATION

For Marxists and thinkers influenced by the tradition, labour is central to understanding of exploitation in capitalism. Valorisation, the process during which surplus value is extracted from workers, is identified in *Capital* (Marx (1974/1867), as the dynamic at the heart of the political economy of capitalism. Why, then, is labour so significant, and, importantly, why is labour often the subject of victimisation? 'Victimisation' is a term describing punishment or discrimination against an individual or collective in a selective and unfair manner – at its root are notions of both disproportionality and unfairness. A key to this understanding lies in the nature of labour itself, together with its specific qualities.

As an artificial but explanatory lens, it is possible to separate a holistic or 'philosophical' conception of labour from one that is ostensibly utilitarian or 'economic' in its orientation. First, the corralling of workers into factories, offices and call centres is not an invariant 'fact of life', but a product of the development of capitalism and the historical generalisation of the commodity as an almost universal entity in economic exchange. As this development unfolds, labour – originally an activity where humans expressed their interaction with nature in a sensual manner – becomes de-sensualised and alienated, losing touch with its purpose, eventual outputs and, ultimately, its connectivity with the labourer (Ollman, 1976). Second, despite the growth and power of capital, labour does not give up without a fight. Labour, or, more correctly, labour power, unlike the fixed capital of production – plant, machinery and raw materials – is variable and malleable, allowing workers either to perform in excess of what is in their employment contracts or to resist and do less (Friedman, 1986; Smith, 2006; O' Doherty and Willmott, 2009). These specific qualities of labour produce incessant problems for its valorisation, which is based on the operation of an indeterminate dialectic. It is this that is at the core of workplace conflict, which can and does often lead to the victimisation of labour.

Having briefly outlined the analytical framework explaining why labour may be subject to victimisation, does this help with application to actual incidents and examples? The 1970s were a turbulent period for industrial relations in the UK. In the context of inflation, rising levels of unemployment and failing economic performance, management interventions directed at gaining further control over the exercise of indeterminate labour power became especially pronounced. In response, organised labour resisted in a series of strikes, 'lockouts' and 'go slows'. In 1972, there were more strikes in the UK than at any time since the General Strike of 1926. During that year, a national building industry strike was organised to protect workers against job insecurity and dangers to health and safety in an industry characterised by temporary employment on transient sites. Many worked on the so-called 'lump', a system facilitated by government-backed tax and national insurance concessions allowing some workers to be regarded as 'self-employed' and therefore potentially difficult to organise collectively. At the time, secondary, or 'flying', picketing – trade unionists joining in collective action to support their colleagues – was not illegal, but inevitably heavily disapproved of by employers and the government. Building industry employers were well organised nationally. One feature of this organisation was the maintenance of dossiers on 'troublesome' individuals who subsequently risked being denied future work.

A key 'moment' in the strike involved the arrest of the Shrewsbury 24, a group of secondary pickets; many of the group were subsequently imprisoned for infringement of a variety of apparently arcane laws, including an 1875 Act designed to protect private property. Over four decades later, the extent of alleged government interference in the arrest, charge and conviction of a group of workers who supported the strike action of their colleagues is still under scrutiny. An active campaign to overturn the convictions is in operation and continues to force debate in Parliament and in more dispersed political arenas. The longevity of the campaign, together with its continuing ability to seek out the raw nerves of injustice, conveys something about the relationship between labour and victimisation. In retrospect, 1972 may be seen as a high-water mark in the UK of the working through of the irreducible conflict between capital and labour, which is based on the particular qualities of labour itself. In the decade that followed, a raft of legislation circumscribing the abilities of trade unions to engage in collective action emerged. Secondary picketing was made illegal in 1974. The apparent discriminatory punishment of a group who took action to support the withdrawal of labour by others is one example of how labour may be victimised. It is rendered particularly significant by the symbolic and material context operative at the time, including the selective deployment of the legislative apparatus of the state.

DAVID BALSAMO

See also: **Justice and Victims**

Readings

Friedman, A. (1986) 'Developing the managerial strategies approach to the labour process', *Capital and Class*, 10(3): 97–124.

Marx, K. (1974/1867) *Capital Volume 1* (Translated from the fourth German edition by E. and C. Paul) Dent: London.

O' Doherty, D. and Willmott, H. (2009) 'The decline of labour process analysis and the future of the sociology of work', *Sociology*, 43(5): 931–51.

Ollman, B. (1976) *Alienation: Marx's conception of man in capitalist society*. London: Cambridge University Press.

Smith, C. (2006) 'The double indeterminacy of labour power: labour, effort and mobility', *Work, Employment and Society*, 20(2): 389–402.

LEGAL CRIMES – LAWFUL BUT AWFUL

Ideally, what the law proscribes coincides with what people in society regard as undesirable and unethical. The concept of white-collar crime refers to misconduct in business and the professions punishable by law, but it does not cover acts reflecting some serious disparities between legality and legitimacy. One such disparity falls in the category of *lawful but awful* activities: acts and practices that the law allows, and governments often encourage or even subsidise, which have adverse social, economic and environmental consequences, occasionally worse than those of serious and organised criminal activities.

An older example regarding toxic waste disposal is provided in the US. In the 1970s, when the definition of 'toxic waste' was delegated to the states, New Jersey had a comparatively advanced definition which meant that factories based in that jurisdiction had to dispose such waste in special ways that were much more expensive than those of ordinary waste. Pennsylvania, on the other hand, had much lower standards, which brought about a situation where New Jersey's waste was collected, transported to Pennsylvania and dumped there, polluting the environment without breaking either state's laws.

Such victimisation is produced by several industries and in different ways, sometimes due to their production processes and sometimes due to the product or services they deliver. For instance, the run-off of manure and artificial fertiliser from the mass factory farming of chickens and hogs in the Mississippi River basin has created an oxygen-depleted zone thousands of square miles off the coast of New Orleans. The (ab)use of intellectual property laws in order to commercialise breast cancer test products and prevent the use of the technology for research geared towards the prevention of breast cancer, or the continuing manufacture and export of domestically banned products, illustrate health and quality-of-life victimisation. Additional physical costs and environmentally or public-health-damaging production processes can be found in the car manufacturing, private security, pharmaceutical, petrochemical, extractive, energy, defence or biotechnology industries.

Heavy financial costs to national and global economies are generated by financial institutions for example: first, excessive risk-taking and non-accountability when investments prove imprudent caused a global financial crisis; second, so-called 'de-risking' involved the draining of finance from developing countries and needy communities; and, third, the 'bail-out' of Greece, which was essentially the return of capital to German, French and US banks who knowingly engaged in at first profitable and risky lending, led to austerity, loss of sovereignty and humanitarian disaster in a whole country. Sizeable financial costs are produced through the manipulation of tax, transfer pricing and public procurement law by entertainment, technology, defence and many other industries that undermine the tax base and create huge opportunity costs. The facilitative role played by law and accounting firms could also be added to this list.

Other victimisation is hard to quantify, such as the cultural, moral, anthropological and historical costs of the 'laundering' of stolen art and looted antiquities through mainstream galleries, auction houses and museums. Difficult to quantify are also the growth efforts of private prison companies that would benefit from unduly rising rates of incarceration or the increasing length of sentences that may undermine livelihoods, families and communities. Similarly difficult to calculate are the criminogenic effects of gambling industries, the redlining and 'de-risking' of financial institutions, the (non-)regulation of obscure derivatives products, and the overfishing of the waters of Somalia that undercut the local economy and contributed to the emergence of maritime piracy. Also, democracy and justice are victims when powerful corporations non-transparently or sometimes even openly influence foreign and domestic policies, as illustrated by a memo urging the elimination of Zapatistas (poor farmers) in Mexico so that the government could 'demonstrate their effective control' as '[f]inancial markets might not respond positively to increased democracy because it leads to increased uncertainty' (Passas and Goodwin, 2004, p 12).

On the other hand, there are industries profiting from inherently harmful products, such as the tobacco or weapons and small arms industries. Finally, lobbying industry activities enable such practices to remain legal even though they undermine the public interest.

The more such industries and practices flourish, the more societies lose overall. Very similar acts are outlawed when committed on smaller scales or by less powerful actors. If a more consistent substantive definition of crime was to be adopted, it would be misconduct entailing avoidable and unnecessary harm to society, which is serious enough to warrant state intervention and similar to other kinds of acts criminalised in the countries concerned or by international law. Under this framework, the aforementioned practices, which externalise costs to the weakest and least privileged groups, amount to 'crimes without law violations' or 'legal crimes' – the 'lawful but awful' (Passas, 2005, p 771).

Public policy and priorities are thus misconstrued due to power asymmetries, globalisation in a context of fragmented and inconsistent laws, ill-considered regulation, media and public opinion manipulation on 'trickle down' and 'free market' benefits for the national economy, security and emergency arguments, and short-term concerns obscuring serious future problems. Answers can thus be found in awareness-raising regarding negative externalities, appeal to the public sense of justice and fairness, and balancing corporate and societal influence on law and its enforcement.

NIKOS PASSAS

See also: **State–Corporate Crime and Harm; White-Collar Crime, Harm and Victimisation**

Readings
Passas, N. (2005) 'Lawful but awful: "legal corporate crimes"', *Journal of Socio Economics*, 34(6): 771–86.
Passas, N. and Goodwin, N. (eds) (2004) *It's legal, but it ain't right: Harmful social consequences of legal industries.* Ann Arbor, MI: University of Michigan Press.

MALE VICTIMS OF VIOLENCE

Males are over-represented as both offenders and victims of violent crime. Male victimisation rates for homicide (murder and manslaughter), physical assault (aggravated and non-aggravated) and robbery are typically double or more those of females (Bureau of Justice Statistics, no date; Australian Bureau of Statistics, 2015; Office for National Statistics, 2015). Only in instances of sexual assault and related sexual violence are male rates of victimisation lower than those of females, although boys and girls experience equivalent rates of victimisation from this category of violent crime.

Despite this over-representation, male victims of violence and their victimisation experiences went largely unacknowledged in the academic literature (Walklate, 2007). The exclusion of men as victims of crime was, in part, an effect of revised examinations of victimisation and the induction of the concept of gendered victimisation, which rendered men's involvement in crime as principally that of the perpetrator. Males, and, in particular, the heterosexual, white male, were relegated to 'the victimological other: that which cannot be spoken' (Walklate, 2007, p 151). Theoretical constructs of masculinity accommodated to explain the predominance of males as perpetrators of violence (against women) provided the medium where discussions of masculinity, crime and victimisation was eventually given greater prominence in the academic literature. The validity of male victimisation was accordingly accepted.

Subsequent studies of male violent victimisation describe, for some men at least, substantial physical and psychological injury, including post-traumatic stress disorder, depression and anxiety. Victimised males report poorer health and well-being, difficulties in maintaining or initiating social and intimate relationships, and increased levels of alcohol and substance misuse post-victimisation compared to men who have not been victimised.

Males also generally recover more quickly from their victimisation and are less likely to suffer prolonged harm. The difference in the nature of male and female victimisation (unknown versus known; public versus private) is a conventional explanation for observed variation in victimisation response and recovery. Also of pertinence are the effects of the normalisation of violence and the 'constraints' of hegemonic masculinity (Walklate, 2007) on males and how they express the effects of violent victimisation. The normalisation and consequent social acceptability of male-on-male violence provides its protagonists with an excuse not only to take part in violence, but also to deny the seriousness or impact of harm. When harm occurs, males often express a reluctance to identify and relate to the victimisation (Stanko and Hobdell, 1993).

At the core of this response is the way males 'manage their membership in two culturally conflicting categories – males and victims' – and, by so doing, 'defend ... one identity from the threat of another' (Burcar and Åkerström, 2009, pp 32, 51). Males interviewed in victimisation studies often minimise or deny the seriousness of the event or the seriousness of the injury and rationalise both the way the violence was initiated (eg not responsible but tried to confront or alleviate where possible) and their response to the violence (eg circumstances did not permit resistance). In a study of male victims of rape, men described their victimisation as a result of being overpowered, overridden, intimidated or entrapped (Allen, 2002).

A denial of victimisation also translates into patterns of help-seeking behaviour among male victims of violence. Some men do seek support but when they do, it is often from formal rather than informal support. Males are less inclined to seek informal support because of concerns of the effect on family and friends, and the risk of social contempt, or because their social networks are, or are perceived to be, less developed. Men are equally likely not to seek any support at all for reasons of denial, preferring not to involve or upset family, or a lack of knowledge about the existence of support services. In addition, there are structural and systematic barriers. Males (and the violence they experience) have generally not been seen as a priority for formal support and the availability and appropriateness of services for males has consequently had less attention.

SAMANTHA BRICKNELL

See also: **Night-Time Economies, Victims and Victimisation**

Readings

Allen, S. (2002) 'Male victims of rape: responses to a perceived threat to masculinity', in C. Hoyle and R. Young (eds) *New visions of crime victims*. Oxford: Hart, pp 23–48.

Australian Bureau of Statistics (2015) *Recorded crimes – victims, Australia 2014*, Catalogue no 4510.0. Canberra: ABS.

Burcar, V. and Åkerström, M. (2009) 'Negotiating a victim identity: young men as victims of violence', *Journal of Scandinavian Studies in Criminology and Crime Prevention*, 10(1): 37–54.

Bureau of Justice Statistics (no date) 'NCVS victimization analysis tool (NVAT)'. Available at: http://www.bjs.gov/index.cfm?ty=nvat

Office for National Statistics (2015) *Crime statistics – focus on violent crime and sexual offences, 2013/14*. London: ONS.

Stanko, E. and Hobdell, K. (1993) 'Assault on men: masculinity and male victimisation', *British Journal of Criminology*, 33(3): 400–15.

Walklate, S. (2007) 'Men, victims and crime', in P. Davies, P. Francis and C. Greer (eds) *Victims, crime and society*. London: Sage, pp 142–64.

MEDIA REPRESENTATIONS OF VICTIMS

The media plays a primary role in the portrayal of crime and victims, and in the social construction or the denial of victimhood. However, one of the key problems with discussions of the media is a tendency to caricature it as being monolithic and overly deterministic. In reality, there is great diversity in media forms as, for example, the prefixes 'mass', 'news', 'print', 'digital' and 'social' suggest; multimedia is therefore a more accurate analytical focus. Questioning the degree to which aspects of media are politically biased, sexist, racist, xenophobic, Islamaphobic and/or homophobic in their portrayals of victims is, in itself, a political and ideological assessment. However, in reality, even the so-called liberal and/or reactionary media can sometimes represent victims in ways that appear at odds with their more typical viewpoints. To understand the complexity of diverse political and ideological beliefs and values that shape media requires more detailed analysis. Nonetheless, it would be difficult to dispute that media representations of victims are framed within the dominant neoliberal ideological values that pervade most of contemporary media discourses.

Similarly, the media is too often mistakenly spoken of as if independent of key 'experts' who are often, sometimes incongruously, called upon to explain crimes and victimisation and thus also play a key role in the social understanding of such.

This is important because it is well known that news media reporting of crime, and victimisation in particular, has a determining effect upon people's perception of the levels of crime and their probability of victimisation (Jewkes, 2015). The often disproportionate portrayal of victimisation leads to people overestimating their own probability of meeting the same fate. Such, often prurient, over-reporting of some crimes, in particular, sex and violent crimes, can have a seriously detrimental impact upon people's lives and lead some to self-imposed curfews that can exclude them from society (Weitzer and Kubrin, 2004).

This is particularly pertinent to the huge growth of television portrayals of what are claimed to be 'true crime' re-enactments, which implicitly invite the viewer to comprehend the experience of victimisation. There is much contestation as to the legitimacy of showing such, often graphic, depictions of victimisation and whether they fuel disproportionate fears and anxieties. The problem herein is the difficult field of quantifying and qualifying the impact of media portrayals of crime and victimisation on people's fears and precariously trying to assign 'appropriateness' to those fears. The complexity of factors that impact on victimisation rates makes the ability to calculate an individual's probability of victimisation extremely difficult, besides sheer misfortune (Sparks, 1992). Conversely, claims are made that some media portrayals of victimisation, particularly in the area of sexual violence, induces offending (Boyle, 2005), and this has led to increased legislative restrictions on extreme pornography. Such changes have impinged upon consensual sadomasochism participants' freedoms as they strongly deny that any victimisation is involved.

The 24-hour news media's preference for reporting stereotypical victims and sensational crimes can have a distorting impact on the public's and practitioners' understanding of crime and victimisation. However, not all media reporting is as biased or conspiratorial in respect of victimisation as some reductionist analysis contends. Media fragmentation has led to a dilution of dominant discourses and even to the emergence of empowered 'citizen journalists' who have utilised phone and media technology to challenge the credibility of, for example, police accounts of events resulting in victimisation (Greer and McLaughlin, 2010). The complexity of these variations in representations of victims is also augmented by an individual's own interpretations of the images that they are presented with. For example, many have observed what has been described as 'benefits porn' and beheld disapprovingly purported 'scroungers', yet others who are more liberal and empathetic interpreted such portrayals as the heroic struggles of the marginalised victims of neoliberalism to subsist.

Prejudicial ideas can also inform abhorrent media representations that blame victims for behaviours that allegedly precipitated their victimisation. Contrarily, some real-life portrayals of practices dispensed to victims have outraged public opinion and led to promises of change, most notably, in the exposure of police practices increasingly revealed via social media. Consequently, anyone wishing to study the media's portrayal of victims is entering a highly contested and complex area that is experiencing both rapid and radical changes.

LIAM McCANN

See also: **Notoriety and Victims; Visual Victimology**

Readings

Boyle, K. (2005) *Media and violence.* London: Sage.

Greer, C. and McLaughlin, E. (2010) 'We predict a riot? Public order policing, new media environments and the rise of the citizen journalist', *British Journal of Criminology*, 50(6): 1041–59.

Jewkes, Y. (2015) *Media and crime* (3rd edn). London: Sage.

Sparks, R. (1992) *Television and the drama of crime: Moral tales and the place of crime in public life.* Milton Keynes: Open University Press.

Weitzer, R. and Kubrin, C. (2004) 'Breaking news: how local TV news and real-world conditions affect fear of crime', *Justice Quarterly*, 21: 497–520.

MEDICALISATION, HARM AND VICTIMISATION

Medicalisation has been a subject of much interest for social scientists for some time, largely gaining prominence in the latter half of the 20th century. Medicalisation, namely, what it is, and the effects of it, has sparked considerable critical debate and discussion on matters of power relations, conformity/deviance and social control. Early definitions of medicalisation described it as a process where socially non-conforming behaviours became known and controlled through explanations of sickness (Parsons, 1951). These have subsequently been developed with several seminal writings sculpting this landscape of enquiry. What these analyses have in common is their concern for the effects of the exercising of medical power in societies – what is the character and nature of medical power, and what are the consequences and effects of it?

Foucault (1973 [1963]) illuminates on medical power and the process of medicalisation in significant depth. He posits that differential power relations between the clinician and the individual develop through a staged process. First, contact with the medical profession and the 'gaze' of the doctor on an individual renders them an object that is subject to medical knowledge. Second, the body becomes an object of analysis; a site where disease and illness finds its place. Third, Foucault (1973) describes a process whereby the 'gaze' of the doctor shifts from the individual to the disease or illness; a prioritising of symptoms over the individual. Fourth, 'grids of specification' and understanding are formulated. This is the process of examining symptoms or illnesses in a way where elements are separated and investigated independently. The outcome of these stages is that the 'gaze' creates new languages and understandings, specifically new alliances or relationships between words and discoveries.

Zola (1972) contends that significant shifts in the roles and responsibilities of social institutions have occurred. With a focus on medical domination, Zola (1972) explains how trust and confidence gained popularity over time, and had gained prominence alongside (and, in some cases, in place of) the more traditional institutions of religion and law. Fundamentally, this prominence gave way to power, and with power came social control. The medical 'gaze' then became ever-more invasive into networks of society and community, creating a 'reluctant reliance on the expert' (Zola, 1972, p 487). This is aided by the esoteric knowledge exercised by medical professionals and the complex technological and bureaucratic society that people live their lives within. Illich's (1976) documenting of medical power also outlines concerns over medical imperialism and the systems of governance exercised through biomedical classifications of deviant behaviours. Illich's (1976) explanations derive from dissatisfaction with a pursuit of happiness that is technologically manufactured. Technologies of medicine, and their interventions, have gone too far and, in Illich's (1976) view, can cause harm, coining the term 'iatrogenesis'.

Illich's (1976) iatrogenesis comprises three specific types: clinical, social and cultural. The first (clinical iatrogenesis) comes to represent the harm caused by injury sustained during inappropriate or ineffective medical interventions or procedures. Social iatrogenesis refers to the monopoly of medical expertise over everyday life. Medicine and its processes of medicalisation hold the capacity to expand categories of behaviours that warrant medical classification and intervention. With an intention to address newly classified symptoms comes the demand for treatments, not least pharmaceuticals. Drug treatments for conditions that are created by the medical expert are not always seen as legitimate or warranted. For example, in 2014/15, there was controversy in the UK over official guidance to doctors and the financial incentives available to prescribe statins (a cholesterol-reducing pharmaceutical intervention) to patients of low risk of heart disease. Illich's (1976) final type of iatrogenesis is cultural. Here, Illich describes a situation where medical dominance has eroded and destroyed traditional ways of comprehending and dealing with death, sickness and pain. Illich (1976) describes the way in which, culturally, societies make sense and judgements over their and others' sickness, pain and death within the parameters of medical opinion and discourse. Doing so removes individual agency and autonomy and keeps routes patent for collaborating institutions such as the pharmaceutical market.

Other authors such as Conrad (2007) have made substantial contributions to the subject of medicalisation – what it entails, and what it brings with it. Again, reinforcing the deliberate attempts of medicine to understand and classify human behaviours in medical frameworks, Conrad (2007) draws critical attention to the conversion of non-conformity to sickness or illness. Understanding the sophistication of medical institutions is a necessary undertaking; indeed, it is also how medical discourse is maintained and the methodologies utilised so that it permeates aspects of social life on a global scale. However, as Conrad (2007) and other authors such as Rose (2007) acknowledge, there is no single medical entity, but, rather, a complexity of political, economic, cultural and social forces, making such enquiry intricate.

Social deviance is very much a legitimised domain of the medical profession, who work in a bid to understand complex social behaviours in biomedical terms. The power relations between doctor and patient are an area of contestation and potential harm. Indeed, if illness is confirmed, the patient is obliged to cooperate with medical instruction. Being a victim of medical intervention may be conceived of as somewhat perverse with regards to the Hippocratic Oath taken by doctors 'to do no harm'. That said, medical models obscure social processes and forces on individual behaviour and render the individual's deviance as a fault in their individual biology (Moncrieff, 1997). This may be particularly evident in examples of the medical management of mental illness, whereby the production of diagnosis (such as schizophrenia) and treatments (such as psycho-surgery, electro-convulsive therapy) has had a catastrophic impact on the therapeutic experience and contributed directly to the continued stigmatisation of recipients of classifications of psychiatric illness and disorders.

Debate exists over the extent of the imperialistic tendencies of the medical profession in processes of medicalisation; rather, some authors determine that health-care consumers play an active role in bringing about or resisting medicalisation (Ballard and Elston, 2005). That said, the analyses and theorisations over medical power remain a salient matter for social scientists and the medical profession to wrangle with. The works of Foucault, Zola, Illich and Conrad, to name but a few, cannot be disregarded, and serve a conceptual and practical usefulness in determining how, and in what ways, medical institutions can be complicit in the production of less-than-desirable, harmful and victimising experiences of individuals.

PAUL TAYLOR

See also: **Iatrogenic Harm, 'Crime' and Victimisation; Social Harm; Zemiology**

Readings

Ballard, K. and Elston, M.A. (2005) 'Medicalisation: a multi-dimensional concept', *Social Theory & Health*, 3(3): 228–41.

Conrad, P. (2007) *The medicalization of society: On the transformation of human conditions into treatable disorders.* Baltimore, MD: The John Hopkins University Press.

Foucault, M. (1973 [1963]) *The birth of the clinic* (trans A.M. Sheridan). London: Tavistock.

Illich, I. (1976) *Medical nemesis.* New York, NY: Pantheon.

Moncrieff, J. (1997) 'Psychiatric imperialism: the medicalisation of modern living', *Soundings: A Journal of Politics and Culture*, 6. Reprinted and available from: http://www.critpsynet.freeuk.com/sound.htm

Parsons, T. (1951) 'Illness and the role of the physician: a sociological perspective', *American Journal of Orthopsychiatry*, 21(3): 452–60.

Rose, N. (2007) 'Beyond medicalisation', *The Lancet*, 369(9562): 700–2.

Zola, I.K. (1972) 'Medicine as an institution of social control', *The Sociological Review*, 20(4): 487–504.

MISCARRIAGE OF JUSTICE, WRONGFUL CONVICTION AND VICTIMS

'Miscarriage of justice' and 'wrongful conviction' are terms that are synonymously used in the literature and in public discourse to refer to innocent victims of wrongful convictions. Yet, they refer to very different legal and moral standards that impact on the crucial issue of how victims are conceived and quantified (see Naughton, 2007).

As this relates to the criminal justice system in England and Wales, the essential distinction between a miscarriage of justice and a wrongful conviction is that a miscarriage of justice relates to a criminal conviction that is overturned on appeal and does not indicate that the successful appellant is innocent. For instance, police not abiding by the strict rules of the Police and Criminal Evidence Act 1984, governing how evidence is to be treated, which has led to convictions being overturned for murder and other serious offences, would be a miscarriage of justice even though the successful appellant were guilty. Another common cause of miscarriages of justice is when prosecutors fail to disclose evidence to the defence under the terms of the Code for Crown Prosecutors, again notwithstanding the reality that successful appellants in such cases can be guilty (see Naughton, 2013a).

Alternatively, a wrongful conviction relates entirely to the wrongful conviction and/or imprisonment of an innocent individual who did not commit the alleged crime that they were convicted of and who may or may not overturn their conviction depending on whether they have the required legal grounds. An example of a wrongful conviction that is also a miscarriage of justice is the case of Sean Hodgson who had his conviction for the rape and murder of Teresa De Simone overturned when developments in DNA testing were utilised to totally exonerate him.

Thus, miscarriages of justice are best understood as miscarriages of the criminal justice process, which may or may not include innocent victims of wrongful convictions who are able to overturn their convictions on appeal by showing breaches of procedure or that they are not guilty through new evidence that was not available at the time of the original trial. In this context, the data on successful appeals against criminal conviction are a reflection of what the legal system sees as a miscarriage of justice. It reflects the criminal justice system's notion of a fair process rather than a lay notion of fairness in terms of the outcome of criminal trials and appeals and the conviction of the guilty and the acquittal or successful appeal of the innocent. Moreover, this official legal view of miscarriages of justice will change, as will the official statistics, as the rules and procedures of the criminal justice system change, for instance, reforms to the guidelines on how the police are required to treat suspects when the Judges Rules of 1912 were replaced with the Police and Criminal Evidence Act 1984 (see Naughton, 2013b).

It is also important to note that in public discourse, a miscarriage of justice can also refer to a guilty offender who escapes justice. This creates a fundamental tension with a legal system that overturns the convictions of guilty offenders on points of law while innocent victims languish in prison unable to overturn their convictions, which also has relevance to debates about 'deserving' and 'undeserving' victims of miscarriages of justice.

Indeed, the victimology on miscarriages of justice and wrongful conviction is not straightforward (see Tan, 2011; Naughton, 2013c). It is only on rare occasions that it can be known for sure whether successful appellants, legal miscarriages of justice, are, in fact, innocent or guilty. For the most part, victims of miscarriages of justice fall into a grey area in which it is not or cannot be known whether they are actually innocent or guilty as the criminal appeal system overturns convictions on the basis that they are 'unsafe' in law as opposed to morally wrongful. At the same time, alleged victims of wrongful convictions who are unable to overturn their convictions will never be acknowledged as victims of miscarriages of justice by the legal system, with the subsequent consequence that they will not be eligible to apply for compensation or aftercare services post-successful appeal.

MICHAEL NAUGHTON

See also: **Appeals Against Wrongful Conviction**

Readings

Naughton, M. (2007) 'What is a miscarriage of justice?', in M. Naughton (ed) *Rethinking miscarriages of justice*. Basingstoke: Palgrave Macmillan, pp 14–36.

Naughton, M. (2013a) 'Perspectives and definitions', in M. Naughton (ed) *The innocent and the criminal justice system*. Basingstoke: Palgrave Macmillan, pp 15–33.

Naughton, M. (2013b) 'The key causes of abortions of justice', in M. Naughton (ed) *The innocent and the criminal justice system*. Basingstoke: Palgrave Macmillan, pp 34–69.

Naughton, M. (2013c) 'Victimology', in M. Naughton (ed) *The innocent and the criminal justice system*. Basingstoke: Palgrave Macmillan, pp 191–208.

Tan, G. (2011) 'Structuration theory and wrongful imprisonment: from "victimhood" to "survivorship"?', *Critical Criminology: An International Journal*, 19(3): 175–96.

MUSIC, CONFLICT AND TORTURE

'Music as torture' is a term that covers a range of harms associated with the systematic use of music as a weapon. There are two main aspects to consider: 'acoustic bombardment', mostly used on the battlefield/zones of conflict; and music as a technique of psychological torture undertaken for the purpose of breaking the victim's will.

The use of music in battle has two main purposes, one of which is to communicate with fellow soldiers, and the other is as a psychological weapon against the enemy. Music has been used within the 'theatre of war' throughout history (Pieslak, 2007). For example, the long-established use of drums and horns and the employment of music in the armed services reflects a notion that music can inspire courage and patriotism and can also form the boundaries between 'us and them'.

During the Nazi period, official orchestras were a feature of many concentration and death camps (Johnson and Cloonin, 2009), and prisoners with musical talent were usually treated better than other camp prisoners. Although the orchestras would put on shows for SS officers, music was also used for more nefarious purposes, for example, music was used, via loudspeakers, to drown out sounds of gunfire that might have led to panic or rebellion within the camps. Music was also utilised as a 'welcome' to greet new arrivals at the train station in Treblinka as it had the purpose of deceiving the new arrivals about the true nature of the camp.

Recent interest in music as torture arose with reports from Guantanamo Bay about the use of a range of so-called 'torture-lite' techniques that were designed to inflict psychological torment but not leave physical signs of harm (Cusick,

2006). One example was waterboarding, designed to make the victim feel as if they are drowning. In addition to the use of sensory deprivation, such as hoods, darkness and disorientation, techniques of sensory overload, such as bright light and loud repetitive sounds, were also used. Music was utilised to induce sleep deprivation and to prolong the shock of being captured for the detainees.

There is an implicit assumption that music provides pleasure and spiritual comfort. However, music, or any noise, can be a source of pain and victimisation, and beyond a certain limit, it becomes a weapon of death. The consequences of excessive sound can result in slower thinking, neurosis, increased respiration and heart rate, raised blood pressure, and difficulties in speaking (Attali, 1985).

To some extent, any repetitious noise could be used for harm but in cases such the Iraq war and in Guantanamo Bay, the choice of music used is culturally alien and discordant to the enemy, such as heavy metal and rap. In addition, the use of music from TV programmes such as Sesame Street and Barney, symbolic of childhood innocence, in order to 'break' detainees seems particularly brutal. However, these choices are illustrative of the appropriation of music by the state and its agents as a technique of power and a source of harm.

ELEANOR PETERS

See also: **Criminology and War; State-Corporate Crime and Harm**

Readings

Attali, J. (1985) *Noise: The political economy of music.* Minneapolis, MN: University of Minnesota.

Cusick, S.G. (2006) 'Music as torture/music as weapon', *Transcultural Music Review*, 10: 1–9.

Johnson, B. and Cloonin, M. (2009) 'Music accompanying violence', in B. Johnson and M. Cloonin (eds) *Dark side of the tune: Popular music and violence.* Farnham: Ashgate, pp 65–94.

Pieslak, J.R. (2007) 'Sound targets: music and the war in Iraq', *Journal of Musicological Research*, 26(2/3): 123–49.

N

NEOLIBERALISM AND THE POLITICISATION OF THE VICTIM

Miers (1978) first observed the politicisation of the victim in the processes that led up to the inception of what was then referred to as the Criminal Injuries Compensation Board (now known as the Criminal Injuries Compensation Authority). Endemic in those processes were claims to speak for the victim of crime independent of any evidence to support such claims. However, in the intervening years, the 'powerful motif' of the victim (Bottoms, 1983, p 172) has continued apace as victims groups have proliferated and occupied the spaces made available by an increasingly diffuse policymaking process. This process is not only more diffuse, but also, simultaneously, less partisan and more political, with the consequence that whose voice is listened to, how, why, when and what about are all questions that pertain to this politicisation in its contemporary form. The changing policy climate that is exemplified by politicisation is linked to the changing role of public services and service delivery. This more recent mode of service delivery, dressed up as 'new managerialism', has been one of the main ways that neoliberal economics have seeped into and driven public services (see, eg, McLaughlin et al, 2001). The presence of new managerialism, often referred to as the audit culture, has also penetrated victim services in the different ways in which claims to speak for the victim of crime have been articulated.

Since 1979, which coincided with the marked development of victim services in England and Wales, Clarke et al (2000) have suggested that there have been a number of iterations of what might be claimed to be in the public interest, of which claims to speak about victims of crime are a constituent part. The first

---

views the public as taxpayers, with their interests being equated with economy, efficiency and effectiveness, and whom it is presumed have an antagonistic relationship with non-taxpayers. This view was popular during the 1980s, when government policy began to put tighter economic reins on the public sector with a view to promoting the voluntary sector. It is no surprise that this decade also saw the phenomenal growth of Victim Support as a voluntary organisation claiming to speak for victims. The second is a view of the public as consumers, as active choice makers within public services. This view could be identified in the various charters of the late 1980s and early 1990s put in place for crime victims, contemporarily illustrated by the Code of Practice for Victims first introduced in 2004. The last view of the public interest identified by Clark et al (2000) is one of a community of diverse interests, a community now 'responsibilised' (Clark, 2005) in a whole range of relationships it has with the state. Contemporarily, this view has permitted an increased diversification in the range of groups claiming to speak for victims, often focused around one particular interest (like Mothers Against Drunk Driving) rather than the more generic concerns of Victim Support.

There are specific difficulties with all of these visions of the public interest but they share a common view of the citizen as having rights to call upon the state, but rights that are contingent on citizens' willingness and ability to fulfil their obligations to the state. This is a significant shift from the relationship of the 1950s in which the citizen had rights and the state had obligations. Of course, what has been assumed in these processes, especially in the claims made on behalf of the crime victim, is that the victim of crime equates with 'us all'. Thus, Young (1996) has argued that victimhood has become elided with citizenship. Yet, as has been observed earlier, the proliferation of victims' groups, all with differential access to the policy process, along with the differential fragmentation of articulations of the public interest, militate against any meaningful understanding of what is to be understood as 'all of us'. Nonetheless, these processes clearly point to the way in which successive governments, in their desire to manage the problem of crime in changing economic circumstances and in the light of an increasing awareness of the nature and extent of criminal victimisation, have looked to the victim of crime as a solution to that problem. It is a solution, however, that Fraser (2009) has argued has subjected 'us all' to the 'cunning of history'.

Fraser's (2009) analysis is focused on feminism. However, the points that she makes are pertinent for understanding the relationship between the politicisation of the victim and neoliberalism. Put simply, in its essence, neoliberalism can handle claims of difference and identity but cannot accommodate claims rooted in notions of class or collective action. As she observes, second-wave feminism coincided with the emergence of neoliberalism and thrived under the conditions of privatisation, deregulation and imperatives for personal responsibility, and it is these conditions that, she suggests, facilitated the 'resignification' of feminist ideals. So, as neoliberalism took a hold, the feminist challenge to the economy, in which women suffered from (mis)distribution, (mis)recognition and (mis)representation, became resignified as claims for justice centred on identity and difference. Thus, the feminist desire to democratise state institutions and promote gender justice through citizen participation has become resignified as citizen empowerment in 'the big society', in which the state is considered to be increasingly redundant. Thus, second-wave feminism has become an unhappy bedfellow of neoliberalism, similar to the way in which both those of the Far Right and feminists would like to ban pornography – an alliance produced by very different motivations.

In the context of criminal justice policy, Fraser's observations add significantly to Garland's (2001) analysis of a 'culture of control'. The adaptation to failure of the criminal justice system to solve the problem of crime, alongside the emergence of performance indicators under the guise of new managerialism, informs the specific institutional setting in which many of the policy initiatives introduced in the UK to address the victim of crime need to be understood: a particular manifestation of neoliberalism. So, in that wider socio-economic context of neoliberal capitalism, it is easy to see how there has been an apparent successful proliferation of organisations speaking for the victim in all their different guises, yet, simultaneously, little fundamental change in their collective experiences of the criminal justice process and its service delivery.

SANDRA WALKLATE

See also: **Code of Practice for Victims in England and Wales; Criminal Injuries Compensation Authority; Victims of Crime**

Readings
Bottoms, A.E. (1983) 'Neglected features of the contemporary penal system', in D. Garland and P. Young (eds) *The power to punish*. London: Heineman, pp 166–202.

Clarke, J. (2005) 'New Labour's citizens: activated, empowered, responsibilized, abandoned?', *Critical Social Policy*, 25(4): 447–63.

Clarke, J., Gewirtz, S., Hughes, G. and Humphrey, J. (2000) 'Guarding the public interest? Auditing public services', in J. Clark, S. Gewirtz and E. McLaughlin (eds) *New managerialism: New welfare?* London: Sage, pp 250–66.

Fraser, N. (2009) 'Feminism, capitalism and the cunning of history', *New Left Review*, 56, pp 98-117.

Garland, D. (2001) *The culture of control*. Oxford: Polity.

McLaughlin, E., Muncie, J. and Hughes, G. (2001) 'The permanent revolution: New Labour, new public management and the modernisation of criminal justice', *Criminal Justice*, 1(1): 301–18.

Miers, D. (1978) *Responses to victimisation*. Abingdon: Professional Books.
Young, A. (1996) *Imagining crime*. London: Sage.

NIGHT-TIME ECONOMIES, VICTIMS AND VICTIMISATION

As its name suggests, the night-time economy reflects a range of industries that mainly, but not exclusively, operate at night and weekends. These include bars, restaurants, live entertainment, taxi services, prostitution and drug sales, although more recent definitions of the night-time economy are limited to legitimate industries (Wickham, 2012). Given that, in many countries, these industries tend to cluster in urban centres, the term 'night-time economy' reflects loosely defined geographical rather than economic entities that include the space between venues as well as the venues themselves. In many Western countries, night-time economies are synonymous with alcohol consumption (World Health Organization, 2005).

As official definitions of night-time economies rarely exist, these settings have no official boundaries. Consequently, estimating how much crime and victimisation, specifically violence, sexual assault and antisocial behaviour, takes place in night-time economies is difficult. For example, during 2012–14, approximately 21% of violence against adults in England and Wales took place in or around a bar or nightclub. However, a further 20% of all violence against adults took place in the street, some of which is likely to be a direct result of engagement with the night-time economy (Office for National Statistics, 2015). Statistics on crime and victimisation in the form of sexual assaults and antisocial behaviour in these environments are less freely available.

Violent night-time economies are a primarily Northern European, North American and Australasian phenomenon. The relationship between violence and night-time economies appears to be largely influenced by the availability of alcohol in these areas, coupled with the heavy episodic drinking patterns that are prevalent in these cultures. Internationally replicated evidence indicates a cumulative effect of the number of alcohol outlets in an area (outlet density) on rates of violence, and a positive relationship between hours of alcohol sale and violence. Therefore, for many, the night-time economy 'problem' is an alcohol 'problem'. However, the causal role of alcohol in the generation of violence is highly contested as many cultures with liberal alcohol licensing laws and high alcohol availability and affordability have few problems with alcohol-related violence. While psychological evidence shows that alcohol can increase the potential for aggression by impairing executive functioning and communication skills, individual trait aggression, alcohol–violence expectancy effects, competition for scarce resources, poor place management and hypersexualised, hypermasculine environmental cues also contribute to the explanation of night-time economies as violent places (Graham and Homel, 2008; Parker and McCaffree, 2014).

Compared to violence in other settings, violence in night-time economies tends to be disproportionately between male strangers. As night-time economies are associated with violence and excessive alcohol consumption, the population that these areas attract is disproportionately male and young. This population frequents these environments despite, or perhaps because of, its reputation for risk. Victims of violence in night-time economy settings are less likely to regard it as a crime and less likely to report the victimisation to the police than similarly harmful violence in other settings, reflecting a normalisation of heightened risk of harm and victimisation in this environment (Brennan, 2015). Interventions to reduce levels of crime in night-time economies have typically employed a routine activities approach and focused on reducing alcohol intoxication in the general public through social marketing and training bar staff, identifying and eliminating environmental risk factors, and police crackdowns on problematic licensed premises. Very few approaches have demonstrated medium- or long-term effectiveness (Brennan et al, 2011).

For many local governments, thriving night-time economies generate revenue, provide a forum for leisure and cultural activities, and are a signal to visitors of a vibrant urban environment. However, the side effect of increased social disorder creates pressure on police and health services and the fear of victimisation in these areas marginalises groups such as the elderly. Consequently, local governments must find a balance between tax revenue/inclusivity and crime, victimisation and social harm in these environments.

IAIN BRENNAN

See also: **Alcohol and Harm; Anti-Social Behaviour, Harm and Victimisation**

Readings

Brennan, I.R. (2015) 'Victims responses to violence: The effect of alcohol context on crime labelling', *Journal of Interpersonal Violence*, DOI: 10.1177/0886260514564068, 31(6): 1116-11140. Available at: http://jiv.sagepub.com/content/early/2014/12/31/0886260514564068.abstract

Brennan, I.R., Moore, S.C., Byrne, E. and Murphy, S. (2011) 'Intervention for disorder and severe intoxication in and around licensed premises, 1989–2009', *Addiction*, 106: 706–13.

Graham, K. and Homel, R. (2008) *Raising the bar: Preventing aggression in and around bars, pubs and clubs*. Cullompton: Willan Publishing.

Office for National Statistics (2015) *Nature of crime Table 3.10*. London: Office for National Statistics. Available at: www.ons.gov.uk/ons/rel/crime-stats/crime-statistics/focus-on-violent-crime-and-sexual-offences--2013-14/chd--figure-5-8.xls

Parker, R.N. and McCaffree, K.J. (2014) *Alcohol and violence: The nature of the relationship and the promise of prevention*. Plymouth: Lexington Books.

Wickham, M. (2012) *Alcohol consumption in the night-time economy: Working paper 55*. London: Greater London Authority.

World Health Organization (2005) *Alcohol and interpersonal violence: Policy briefing*. Geneva: World Health Organization.

NOTORIETY AND VICTIMS

A high-profile victim case, exceptional in terms of the global profile it generated and its perceived newsworthiness, was the abduction of three-year-old Madeleine McCann from a holiday resort in Praia da Luz, Portugal, in May 2007. The international coverage that this story received was particularly intense and reached unprecedented levels in the summer of that year and continues to spike media interest many years later.

Few crimes generate high-profile, emotionally charged news coverage and public outcry as much as the abduction of a child (Critcher, 2011). Along with the very old, children are viewed as the most vulnerable members of society, and the least able to resist victimisation, harm and abuse. A child who has been abducted is readily accorded the status of 'ideal victim' (Christie, 1986). Yet, only a minority of such cases are deemed worthy of sustained news media coverage. Disproportionate attention is given to children but, within that, often to those who are young, white, pretty and female. The social construction of such 'legitimate' victims in this way indicates the power of the media and their tendency to sympathise with some (innocent) victims while blaming others (Jewkes, 2015). Assumptions based on this stereotypical image of the 'ideal victim' may help to generate criteria by which those in the media assess the 'newsworthiness' of specific crime stories.

Time and space available for news in most mediums is finite; crime news is selected, shaped and presented according to certain 'news values' – professional benchmarks that help to explain the broad profile of media representations of crime, control and victimisation. Most consumers of crime news are seeking to engage with stories on an emotional level. Many high-profile victim cases invoke feelings (often fear, uncertainty, anger) for the public, who tend to empathetically follow these stories, and journalists and editors are well versed in giving the public what it wants (Jewkes, 2015).

As the experience of crime and control has become more mediatised, so, too, has it become more image-oriented, capitalising on the highly visual nature of contemporary culture. Stories are more readily personalised and individualised when accompanied by visual images. Increasingly, crime stories are 'selected and produced' on the basis of their visual (portrayal in images), as well as their lexical-verbal (portrayal in words), potential (Greer, 2007). Central to the superordinate high-profile status of the McCann case were the poignant and iconic photographs and images taken of Madeleine enjoying the family holiday in the hours and days before her abduction.

However, as hinted at earlier, a 'hierarchy of victimisation' is also reflected and reinforced within crime news reporting of high-profile victim cases. This refers to a 'pecking order' of sorts, signifying the differential status of particular types and categories of crime victim in media and official discourses, including ideal victims (eg some child abduction or murder victims) at the top of the hierarchy, and undeserving/illegitimate victims (eg young people injured who had been drinking) near the bottom (Greer, 2007).

The increased interest around crime victims in the media is one of the most significant qualitative changes in media representations of crime and control over the second half of the 20th century. Here, the case of Madeleine McCann exemplifies the complex interconnections between crime news reporting, victimisation and public reaction, and the processes by which particular high-profile crimes are selected, produced and consumed. Yet, the victim voices that find resonance in the media represent only a small fraction of those who experience criminal victimisation and harm. So, many victims of crime or harm remain marginalised or ignored in official and mediated representations.

It is crucial, therefore, to also consider those victims who feel the pains of victimisation most acutely but whose voices are stifled rather than amplified in news media discourses. More attention could be directed at understanding the role of the media in constructing and representing victims, offenders and the processes of criminal victimisation. Researching the media representation (or lack of representation) of victims of the powerful (corporate crimes, deaths in custody, war crimes and genocide) or those who are stereotyped as less 'legitimate' victims, for example, should be a central concern for such academic enquiry.

NICOLA O'LEARY

See also: **Blame and Victims; Victim Hierarchy**

Readings

Christie, N. (1986) 'The ideal victim', in E. Fattah (ed) *From crime policy to victim policy: Reorientating the justice system*. Basingstoke: Macmillan Press, pp 17–30.

Critcher, C. (2011) 'For a political economy of moral panics', *Crime, Media, Culture*, 7(3): 259–75.

Greer, C. (2007) 'News media, victims and crime', in P. Davies, P. Francis and C. Greer (eds) *Victims, crime and society*. London: Sage.

Jewkes, Y. (2015) *Media and crime* (3rd edn). London: Sage.

NUCLEAR EXPERIMENTS AND VICTIMISATION

Between 1953 and 1963, numerous atomic tests were undertaken on mainland Australia as a result of a partnership between the British and Australian governments. Official discourse (ie opinion expressed by many British and Australian politicians and scientists) assured that: atomic tests would be of no detriment to Australian populations; the land to be used was 'useless'; the removal of indigenous populations from their land was unproblematic; and illnesses experienced were the result of other health issues. Conversely, private memories (those of indigenous populations) provide a very different narrative, suggesting experiences of multiple victimisation in terms of: immediate health issues post-tests; long-term and secondary illnesses and conditions passed down generationally; displacement; and long-lasting land contamination (McCelland, 1985). It is perhaps the lesser-considered 'land victimisation' and 'land harm' that this piece focuses on.

Post-Second World War, Britain was keen to have an atomic weapon since the only defence against the Soviet atomic threat was deemed the possession of a deterrent. Australia was also concerned that it may become a target without help from powerful allies. It is thought that in order to secure this, the then Australian Prime Minister Robert Menzies offered to host the tests as England had the bomb and the know-how and Australia had the wide open spaces. Hundreds of tests were conducted on land throughout this era, land 'officially' considered uninhabitable; however, in some cases, the land was, in fact, inhabited by Aboriginal populations, or *was* until their removal, ostensibly for their own safety.

Acknowledging Aboriginal ties with land goes some way to understanding the 'land victimisation' and 'land harm' experienced. Fundamental to the well-being of Aborigines, the land holds great spiritual and cultural significance; sacred sites include rocks, waterholes, hills and trees.

Private memories detail forced removal and the splitting up of families in order to relocate populations to Yalata Station, a large Aboriginal reserve established to the North of Maralinga, one of the main targets for nuclear testing. Removed from the Ooldea mission, officially described as abandoned (much evidence suggests that its closure in 1952 coincided with preparations for tests), indigenous peoples described how conditions at Yalata drove many to crime, rebellion, violence and alcohol. The indigenous peoples experienced sadness for Ooldea, the red desert land they felt related to, a connection that they did not have with the grey limestone of Yalata (Mattingley, 2009).

Although relocated from Ooldea, the presence of occasional 'blacks' was acknowledged on a known track to the North of Maralinga (Arnold, 1987), and official discourse via the Royal Commission report (McCelland, 1985) discussed the necessity of blocking people's movement, specifically former residents of Ooldea, who were discouraged from returning. Discouragement involved rationing, restricted train travel and the threat of *mamu tjuta* (evil spirits) and *putjina* (poison) from bombs (Mattingley, 2009).

The existence of the Yalata reserve seemed to lead official opinion to the conclusion that Aboriginals had no *need* to enter test areas; indeed, the effects of short-term fallout were considered a potential danger only to intruders or Aboriginal Nomads (Arnold, 1987). This officially acknowledged nomadic lifestyle is problematic: first, land that had been traversed for generations was now 'prohibited', meaning a restriction on movement; and, second, 'danger' and 'prohibited' signs were erected in *English* (McCelland, 1985; Arnold, 1987; Mattingley, 2009). This official discourse means that, in addition to their movement being known about, indigenous populations who may have entered the land not only were at risk health-wise, but could also be constructed as intruders and therefore 'deserving' of any ill effects experienced.

Incredibly strong Aboriginal ties with land, water and kin make it questionable whether their removal from future prohibited areas was ever likely to be successful; indeed, despite continued official assertions of indigenous safety, after the last major test in 1959, indigenous peoples were found living far inside a prohibited zone (Mattingley, 2009).

In order for tests to be successfully undertaken on the Australian mainland, it can be argued that Aboriginal ties with the land necessarily had to remain officially *unacknowledged* outwardly, thereby allowing official atomic-era discourse to pave the way for its use, all the while maintaining the invisibility of victims. Land returned to traditional owners post-tests remains contaminated to this day (Doran,

2014), further illustrating the long-term 'land victimisation' and 'land harm' of indigenous peoples.

BETH McJURY

See also: **Environmental Harm and Victimisation; State–Corporate Crime and Harm**

Readings

Arnold, L. (1987) *A very special relationship: British atomic weapon trials in Australia.* London: Crown Copyright.

Cohen, S. (2001) *States of denial.* Cambridge: Polity.

Doran, M. (2014) 'Maralinga traditional owners get greater atomic test site access and have tourism hopes', ABC News. Available at: http://www.abc.net.au/news/2014-06-05/traditional-owners-gain-greater-maralinga-access/5502848

Mattingley, C. (2009) *Maralinga: The Anangu story.* Australia: Allen and Unwin.

McCelland, J.R. (1985) *Royal Commission into British nuclear tests in Australia.* Canberra: Australian Government Publishing Service.

O

OFFENDERS AS VICTIMS OF SOCIAL POLICY AND CRIMINAL JUSTICE PROCESSES IN ENGLAND

The English summer riots emerged after peaceful protests about the death of Mark Duggan, a 29-year-old black resident of Tottenham (London), who was shot by the police on 4 August 2011. Rioting erupted on 6 August, spreading to many other cities in England over the next six days. Using these events as an example, this entry puts forward how those involved can be conceived of as victims of social policy and criminal justice processes, that is, as victims of the deprived contexts and communities in which many of them reside, as well as victims of a consequent 'uplift' in their processing through the criminal justice system.

The immediate public and political response to the dissent of 2011 framed those involved as mindless apolitical thugs and 'feral youth', without any consideration of the underlying social and economic context in which these acts emerged. However, to mask the rioting as 'mindless criminality' is to ignore wider social-structural inequalities, denying the very real contextual, socio-economic and structural factors that framed the disturbances of the summer of 2011.

Those from disadvantaged backgrounds are disproportionately represented in the criminal justice system through a combination of greater criminogenic risk and preferential attention and processing by the police. Moreover, evidence highlights an association between deprivation and those involved in the 2011 riots (Lightowlers, 2015; Lightowlers and Shute, 2012). This, alongside the fact that many who participated in the riots described their actions as a response to heightening injustice and inequality of opportunity (Lewis et al, 2011), continues to be downplayed when developing responses to crime and crime prevention policy. However, to enable more enlightened responses and, perhaps more importantly, to prevent the reoccurrence of such events in the future, such issues need to be meaningfully addressed as the actions of rioters are necessarily shaped by their social and economic context. Indeed, more critical scholars would argue that they are victims of brutal forms of social policy that inflict upon them the deprivation they experience and the lack of power to challenge or change their circumstances.

Sentencing also formed an immediate and highly politicised part of the public debate about the riots, with criminal justice agencies working under great pressure to restore order. Lightowlers and Quirk (2015) identify that, from arrest to sentence, a tougher stance was adopted for sentencing riot-related offending, and an air of prosecutorial zeal and judicial abandon was commonplace. Much of the drive came from the Crown Prosecution Service. Suspects were charged with burglary rather than theft, which carries a tougher sentence. However, it was not just the courts that overreacted; an 'uplift' was applied at every stage, from arrest, to charge, to remand, to which court dealt with the case.

Furthermore, a blanket decision that all disorder-related offending should fall outside the existing guidelines, as was seen in the wake of the riots, was a substantial policy decision made hastily, without consultation, and was not consistent with consideration and decision-making on an individual basis. This is deemed to have led to excessive and arbitrary punishments.

Without wanting to deny that the actions of those involved did have very real repercussions for the 'deserving' victims who suffered as a result of the riotous and criminal behaviour, the blurred lines between offenders and victims are apparent in the case of those who *engaged* in offending behaviour during the riots. Clearly, these were termed 'offenders' in much of the government and media rhetoric, defying notions of the 'ideal victim' (Christie, 1986). The demonising rhetoric used to describe the rioters was effective in 'othering' them in order to justify excessive and exemplary punitive treatment. However, they can also be conceived of as victims of both 'context' (namely, deprivation and social policy) and 'consequence' (the uplift in their processing through the criminal justice system), although they remain low in the 'hierarchy of victims' politically speaking and present particular challenges in terms of social policy.

Nonetheless, the impact of being drawn into the criminal justice system should not be underestimated, especially for those people who have not previously been involved with criminal justice. It can have a serious impact on family and community relations, as well as resulting in diminished educational and employment opportunities, especially for individuals in deprived communities who may have less social and economic capital to withstand the effects of incarceration. The rioters and their communities can therefore be seen as 'doubly disadvantaged' as their deprivation exacerbates their lived experience of contact with the criminal justice system and the punishment they receive.

CARLY LIGHTOWLERS

See also: **Blame and Victims; Victim Hierarchy**

Readings

Christie, N. (1986) 'The ideal victim', in E. Fattah (ed) *From crime policy to victim policy: Reorientating the justice system.* Basingstoke: Macmillan Press, pp 17–30.

Lewis, P., Newburn, T., Taylor, M., Mcgillivray, C., Greenhill, A., Frayman, H. and Proctor, R. (2011) 'Reading the riots: investigating England's summer of disorder'. Available at: http://eprints.lse.ac.uk/46297/1/Reading%20the%20 riots(published).pdf

Lightowlers, C. (2015) 'Let's get real about the "riots" – exploring the relationship between deprivation and the English summer disturbances of 2011', *Critical Social Policy*, 35: 89–109.

Lightowlers, C. and Quirk, H. (2015) 'The 2011 English 'riots': prosecutorial zeal and judicial abandon', *British Journal of Criminology*, 55(1): 65–85.

Lightowlers, C. and Shute, J. (2012) 'Rioting and area deprivation in Greater Manchester', *Radical Statistics*, 106: 22–9.

OFFENDERS, HARM AND RISK ASSESSMENT

'Risk of harm' is a term used within the criminal justice system to denote the future likelihood of an offender causing harm to others or to themselves. It is most often used as a measurement of probability that a further offence or harmful act will occur, and as an assessment of the relative impact or harm of the offence. The focus on risk as a cornerstone of criminal justice theory has arisen as part of the 'new penology', replacing a concern with guilt and morality with a preoccupation over public protection and safety (Feeley and Simon, 1994). Within this context, 'harm' is defined as behaviour that is 'life-threatening and/or traumatic, and from which recovery, whether physical or psychological, can be expected to be difficult or impossible' (National Offender Management Service, 2009, p 5).

The assessed level of harm may impact on how the offender is managed. For example, in England and Wales, those assessed as having a 'high' or 'very high' risk of harm will be managed by the National Probation Service (NPS). In some localities, those with a 'medium' or 'low risk' of harm will be supervised by their local, privately run Community Rehabilitation Company.

An offender's risk of harm is assessed at the point of sentencing, and as an ongoing process throughout their sentence. As an initial assessment, a tool called 'Risk of Serious Recidivism' (RSR) is completed at court by a member of the NPS. The RSR assesses how likely offenders are to commit a seriously harmful re-offence within the next 12 months. If the RSR score indicates that there may be an ongoing risk of harm from the offender, this will lead to a full risk of harm assessment.

Assessing risk of harm is a continuous and dynamic process. Although many established predictors of risk are static, such as type of offence, gender and age at first conviction, many are dynamic and will change according the offender's circumstances. A full assessment will include examining a range of risk factors that may influence the offender's future behaviour. Risk factors cover a range of circumstances, behaviours and attitudes that could increase the likelihood or seriousness of future harm. Such risk factors include alcohol and drug use, employment status, and peer associations.

There is a range of tools to fully assess risk of harm, one being the 'Offender Assessment System' or 'OASys'. OASys asks specific questions in relation to the offender's risk of harming themselves, the general public, the vulnerable (eg children) and previous victims. The tool provides a summary that categorises the offender's risk of harm as ranging from 'low', defined as having no current or significant indicators of harm, to 'very high', defined as posing an imminent risk with serious impact.

The offender's particular risks and behaviours will feed into, inform and influence a risk management plan. This is an essential part of managing an offender, and ensures that appropriate measures are put in place to minimise potential future harm. This can be viewed both in terms of the reduction of the frequency of behaviours that could pose a risk, as well as a reduction in the impact of those behaviours.

A risk management plan should be proportionate to the risk of harm posed by the offender. The plan should offer protection to potential victims, be realistic and achievable, and be based on clear and defensible decision-making (Kemshall et al, 2008). It will usually have three elements: monitoring and surveillance; restrictive elements that may limit the opportunity to offend; and interventions to alter risky behaviour.

The focus on risk has not been without its criticisms from a variety of quarters, including academia, campaigners concerned with civil liberties and those tasked with implementing sanctions or controls. To date in England and Wales, managing an offender according to their risk of harm and their propensity to commit future crime is a key element of the Ministry of Justice's commitment to protecting the public. However, theories focused on the 'risk society' and concerns over the pervasiveness of risk-based discourses, policies and practices warn that as risk becomes a general preoccupation, the expectation that risk can be fully removed, rather than managed, leads to false expectations within and beyond the justice system (Hudson, 2003). In addition, the use of standardised tools to assess risk of harm can disregard the individuality of each offender within the system, and excludes any examination of protective factors that could form a solid basis for rehabilitation.

RACHAEL STEELE

See also: **Probation and Victims; Risk, Risk Management and Victimisation**

Readings

Feeley, M. and Simon, J. (1994) 'Actuarial justice: the emerging new criminal law', in D. Nelken (ed) *The futures of criminology*. London: Sage, pp 173–201.

Hudson, B. (2003) *Justice in the risk society*. London: Sage.

Kemshall, H., Mackenzie, G. and Wilkinson, B. (2008) 'Risk of harm guidance and training resources', De Montford University in association with the National Offender Manager Service.

National Offender Management Service (2009) *Public protection manual*. London: NOMS.

OFFICIAL CRIME STATISTICS AND VICTIM SURVEYS

Crime statistics have served as indicators of the amount of criminal victimisation against a population since the 19th century. The counting of crime forms part of the suite of 'moral statistics' that early social scientists such as Adolphe Quetelet, André-Michel Guerry and Emile Durkheim used to explore the trends and characteristics of deviance in societies. Since these works, measures of crime and the characteristics of those crimes have served as a moral barometer, as well as indicators of police and political performance, but their reliability as accurate measures of crime has regularly been called into question. Internationally, the primary source of data on victimisation is the recording of these incidents by the police when they are reported by victims or witnesses (although the police witness a small amount of crime themselves).

The reliability of police-recorded crime as an overall measure of notifiable crime varies between crime types. It is regarded as a reliable measure of murder and vehicle theft but is very poor at capturing and reflecting sexual assault and domestic abuse. The likelihood of a crime being reported to the police varies by crime type: for example, approximately half of all violence but only 3% per cent of vehicle theft goes unreported (Office for National Statistics, 2013, 2014). The primary reason for the weaknesses in police-reported crime data lies in the fact that the organisation responsible for collecting information about victimisation also has a statutory duty to respond to these incidents. For a variety of reasons, victims may not wish to pursue the perpetrator through the criminal justice system, reducing the likelihood that they will report the crime. In many jurisdictions, crime statistics are used to indicate the performance of a police force; therefore, political pressure creates an incentive to minimise the severity of or to not record reported crimes. As a result of this conflicting, dual purpose, confidence in police crime statistics has been undermined internationally by a series of high-profile scandals involving the manipulation or downgrading of police-recorded crime. In England and Wales, this practice led directly to police-recorded crime losing its 'official statistics' status in 2014.

Beginning in the 1960s, surveys that ask samples of the population about their recent experience of victimisation have emerged worldwide. Data collection is usually conducted face-to-face but surveys can also be completed via telephone or self-completed and returned by post. These surveys are able to capture experience of crime that is not reported to the police (often referred to as the 'dark figure' of crime), along with detailed demographic, historical and attitudinal information that was also not ascertained by police records. While all members of a population are eligible to be included in police records, victimisation surveys only include small proportions of the population, which can be adapted to reflect the goals of the survey. For example, national victimisation surveys like the US National Crime and Victimization Survey and the Crime Survey for England and Wales target a representative sample of adults from the population. The European Union Violence Against Women Survey only samples adult women, while the England and Wales Commercial Victimisation Survey samples businesses rather than individuals. Using census data, survey data can be extrapolated to provide population-wide estimates of victimisation. Often, countries will present measures of police-recorded crime alongside survey estimates of victimisation.

Victimisation surveys are not a perfect estimate of national victimisation: they rarely sample young people, the homeless or those living in institutions, who are all disproportionately at increased risk of victimisation. The method of survey data collection (Mirrlees-Black, 1999) and the question style (Hall and Smith, 2011) affect the reporting of domestic abuse and sexual violence; survey respondents are often limited to a fixed number of reported victimisations, which will inevitably result in underestimation. Moreover, surveys are more receptive to offending between individuals than groups, and crimes that happen in the real world as opposed to the online world.

Crime statistics, in the form of police-recorded crime or victimisation survey reports, are susceptible to a range of biases and weaknesses that diminish their reliability and validity: for example, their myopic focus on conventional crime and victimisation, and their predominant omission of the crimes, victimisation and harms of the powerful, including social harm. However, taken as imperfect indicators of the prevalence and characteristics of criminal victimisation, they remain an important tool in the understanding of criminal victimisation and police performance.

IAIN BRENNAN

See also: Criminal Justice and Victims; Social Harm; State-Corporate Crime and Harm

Readings

Hall, P. and Smith, K. (eds) (2011) *Analysis of the 2010/11 British Crime Survey intimate personal violence split-sample experiment.* London: Home Office.

Her Majesty's Inspectorate of Constabulary (2014) *Crime-recording: Making the victim count.* London: Her Majesty's Inspectorate of Constabulary.

Maguire, M. (2012) 'Criminal statistics and the construction of crime', in M. Maguire, R. Morgan and R. Reiner (eds) *The Oxford handbook of criminology* (5th edn). Oxford: Oxford University Press, pp 206–44.

Mirlees-Black, C. (1999) *Domestic violence: Findings from a new British Crime Survey self-completion questionnaire.* London: Home Office.

Office for National Statistics (2013) *Focus on: Violent crime and sexual offences, 2011/12.* London: Office for National Statistics.

Office for National Statistics (2014) *Crime statistics, focus on property crime, 2013/14 bulletin tables 01.* London: Office for National Statistics. Available at: www.ons.gov.uk/ons/rel/crime-stats/crime-statistics/focus-on-property-crime--2013-14/rft-1.xls

P

POLICY AND VICTIMS IN THE UK

Since its inception, the criminal justice system (CJS) has mainly been focused on dealing with offending and offenders, with much criticism being levied at the fact that victims constituted little more than an afterthought. With the establishment of voluntary organisations such as Victim Support representing victims in the otherwise imbalanced CJS, a raft of policies relating to victims' needs, wants and expectations finally emerged late in the 20th century.

In 1984, the publication of two key documents – *A new deal for victims* (Parliamentary All-Party Penal Affairs Group, 1984) and *Compensation and support for victims of crime* (House of Commons, 1984-85, in Miers, 1985) – indicated the first of a series of changes whereby the government sought to inform, support and assist victims of crime, especially those who may be required to attend court. Further investigation by victims' advocates into the needs of victims and witnesses attending court led to the establishment of the Home Office-funded Crown Court Witness Service, a policy outlined by the government in 1990 in their first Victims' Charter. The subsequent revised Victims' Charter of 1996 has been replaced by several Codes of Practice for Victims (2005; 2013; 2015), usually referred to as the 'Victims' Code'. Each edition outlined the procedural and service rights that victims could expect from the CJS. However, the development of policies aimed at making the criminal justice process easier to negotiate has consistently fallen short of codifying victims' rights comparable to the substantive rights afforded to an accused person. Even the recent Victims' Right to Review, which provides the opportunity to review Crown Prosecution Service decisions to discontinue cases, is still more reflective of a procedural rather than substantive right.

A growing political concern with, and for, particular victims of crime as being *symbolic* in socio-political contexts has become more evident in government policies. The contemporary co-opting of certain groups of victims by ministers seeking to further enhance their party's punitive crime policies has been illustrated through the establishment of specific spokespeople. In addition to policy, the establishment of several victims' figureheads indicated the increasing visibility being afforded to victims of crime. This began with Sara Payne being appointed Victims' Champion in 2009. Payne's five-year-old daughter Sarah had been murdered by paedophile Roy Whiting in 2000, prompting her to successfully campaign for public access to information on sex offenders in the community, which later became the Sex Offender Disclosure Scheme ('Sarah's Law', similar to 'Megan's Law' in the US). The high-profile campaign resulted in Payne becoming seen as an unofficial spokesperson for victims and their families. In 2010, Louise Casey was appointed Victims' Commissioner, a role occupied by Baroness Helen Newlove since 2012. The remit of these various figureheads has thus far been to consult with victims in order to review and report on the operationalising of various victim policies.

The aforemention roles have been complemented by a succession of Victims' Ministers, each of which has had the responsibility for victims added on to an existing portfolio. As victims' interests have not yet comprised of a singular ministerial remit, and there has been little evidence to suggest a coordinated approach between figureheads and ministers, victim policy remains fragmented and lower down the law and order hierarchy. However, in the lead-up to the 2015 general election, the two main political parties – the Conservatives and Labour – both indicated their intentions to develop a 'victims' law', which involved the statutory enforcement of the existing Code alongside several new provisions. The renewed focus on victims was predicated on a desire to enhance the protection of victims in the CJS while also providing new and improved victim services. This was in addition to the first hearing of a proposed Victims' Bill of Rights, instigated by Plaid Cymru, to enshrine existing measures set out in various Codes and Charters.

Victim policy currently occupies a high political status, which is unprecedented in the UK. It is notable how ministerial rhetoric capitalising on popular social issues has traditionally proven to be a successful tactic for governments in fighting, and winning, elections on the basis of law and order. It remains to be seen whether this strategy, which is now being applied to victims, is as beneficial for the public as politicians.

MARIAN DUGGAN and VICKY HEAP

See also: **Code of Practice for Victims in England and Wales; Neoliberalism and the Politicisation of the Victim**

Readings

Hall, M. (2010) *Victims and policy making: A comparative perspective*. Abingdon: Willan Publishing.

Miers, D. (1985) 'Compensation and support for victims of crime', *Brit. J. Criminology*, 32: pp 382–389.

Parliamentary All-Party Penal Affairs Group (1984) *A new deal for victims*, London: HMSO.

Spalek, B. (2006) *Crime victims: Theory, policy, practice*, Basingstoke: Palgrave Macmillan.

POSTIVITIST VICTIMOLOGY

Positivist victimology is recognisable through its: examination of patterns of victimisation; emphasis on conventionally defined crime types, such as interpersonal 'public' forms of crime; search for the cause of victim involvement in their own victimisation; and promotion of risk-based, situational victimisation prevention (Miers, 1989; Walklate, 2003, 2007). It has roots in the mid-20th century, draws closely upon positivist social science and has been influential in framing contemporary debate about, and research on, victims of crime and victimisation.

The origins of positive victimology lie in Von Hentig's belief that an understanding of 'victim' attributes, motives and experiences can aid explanations of crime and its control. In *The criminal and the victim* (Von Hentig, 1948), published in 1948, he constructed a victim typology, comprising of various victim types, conceptualising the role that victims may play in their own victimisation through the idea of 'victim-proneness'. Utilising a similarly speculative and somewhat flawed methodology, Mendelsohn (1956), following in the footsteps of Von Hentig, suggested a sixfold typology underpinned by the notion of 'victim culpability'. However, it was the publication of research carried out in Philadelphia in the US by Wolfgang (1957) on homicide, and his PhD student Amir (1971) on forcible rape, that positivist victimology gained real disciplinary footing, albeit in controversial ways. Both writers analysed criminal records data and, through the concept of 'victim precipitation', explored the contribution that victims make to their own victimisation (Davies et al, 2003).

It is this body of work that has, arguably more than any other tradition in victimology, influenced the development of contemporary thinking about victimisation. Today, the central tenets of positivist victimology include: an emphasis on ordinary, normal and public forms of victimisation as legally defined; a concern with the fear and risk of crime and disorder; and a theoretical focus on the routine everyday activities and lifestyles of victims. Its empirical basis derives from the analysis of 'official' data collected by police and local criminal justice organisations, and through crime surveys carried out in specific geographical locations. Its policy solutions are often concerned with managing the risk and probability of criminal victimisation occurring and reoccurring through various forms of prevention and problem-oriented policing.

Positivism is the golden thread that connects Von Hentig with much contemporary thinking about victims of crime and victimisation. It continues to influence the nature and type of research undertaken, including decisions about what is studied, how and the research questions that are asked. It provides conceptual and theoretical frameworks within which research is framed, and it continues to inform various policy ideas. The repackaging of early positivist victimological concepts of victim-proneness, culpability and precipitation as victim lifestyle, routine activity and vulnerability (see Cohen and Felson, 1979; Hindelang et al, 1978) highlights the influence that positivism has had on much victimological thought (Walklate, 2003). Similarly, the predominance of actuarial approaches to specific, repeat and multiple victimisation can be suggested as further evidence of the continuing influence of positivism.

Positivist victimology has been decried for 'victim blaming' through its focus on the participation of victims in their own victimisation, alongside their active contribution to specific incidents. It has been pilloried for its limited assessment of 'invisible' victims and social harms, of actions that go on behind victims' backs (Walklate, 2003), and for its lack of analysis of state, government and corporate victimisation. Criticisms have also been levelled at its gendered assumptions, lack of wider structural and social analysis, overuse of quantitative methodologies, and reliance on conventional strategies of crime control.

Despite such criticisms, the impact of positivist victimology has been considerable, not least in providing information about the nature, extent and impact of crime and victimisation. Analysis of crime survey data has provided important insights into the rates, patterns and trends of crime, as well as the distribution of crime and its impact on individuals and communities. Crime surveys have also provided data on victims' experiences, perceptions and fears, and have allowed for multivariate analysis on crime, victimisation, place and variables such as class, race, age, gender, sexuality and so forth (Davies et al, 2003). The victim survey has ensured that the traditions of positivistic science, and the conceptual and methodological techniques associated with it, are synchronistic with much victimological research and thinking today.

PETER FRANCIS

See also: **Blame and Victims; Ethics and Methods in Victim Research**

Readings
Amir, M. (1971) *Patterns of forcible rape*. Chicago, IL: University of Chicago Press.

Cohen, L. and Felson, M. (1979) 'Social change and crime rate trends: a routine activity approach', *American Sociological Review*, 4(44): 588–608.

Davies, P. and Francis, P. (eds) (2010) *Doing criminological research*. London: Sage.

Davies, P., Francis, P. and Jupp, V. (eds) (2003) *Victimisation: Theory, research and policy*. Basingstoke: Palgrave Macmillan.

Davies, P., Francis, P. and Greer, C. (eds) (2007) *Victims, crime and society*. London: Sage.

Hindelang, M.J., Gottfredson, M.R. and Garofalo, J. (1978) *Victims of personal crime: An empirical foundation for a theory of personal victimisation*. Cambridge, MA: Ballinger.

Mendlesohn, B. (1956) 'A new branch of bio-psychological science: La Victimology', *Revue International de Criminologie et de Police Technique*, 10: 782–89.

Miers, D. (1989) 'Positivist victimology: a critique', *International Review of Victimology*, 1(1): 3–22.

Von Hentig, H. (1948) *The criminal and his victim*. New Haven, CT: Yale University Press.

Walklate, S. (2003) 'Can there be a feminist victimology?', in P. Davies, P. Francis and V. Jupp (eds) *Victimisation: Theory, research and policy*. Basingstoke: Palgrave Macmillan.

Walklate, S. (2007) *Imagining the victim*. Buckinghamshire: Open University Press.

Wolfgang, M. (1957) *Patterns of criminal homicide*. Philadelphia, PA: University of Philadelphia Press.

PREVENTING VICTIMISATION

Efforts to prevent crime and victimisation have addressed a variety of measures, such as changing the mentality of the perpetrator ('social prevention'), making the target more difficult to access ('situational prevention') and increasing the nature and remit of the criminal law. Prevention efforts such as 'target hardening' drew upon criminological theories which suggested that some crimes were opportunistic and could be deterred with evident barriers such as visible security and surveillance measures (such as CCTV cameras, removing valuables from sight in vehicles or installing gates around properties). However, this form of crime prevention, based on situational factors, may have deflected the crime from happening to *that* victim but did not necessarily omit the likelihood of it happening to another victim with fewer or no security measures in place.

Target hardening largely addressed crimes of acquisition; these initiatives proved less useful for crimes of violence, particularly in relation to interpersonal victimisation. In such cases, victims may be subject to repeat incidents, most notably, in cases of domestic violence, 'hate crime' (targeted victimisation predicated on identity prejudice) and anti-social behaviour. Preventing future victimisation in these cases may be the responsibility of several different organisations. Domestic violence victims, for example, may rely on statutory agents (ie the police) to enhance their safety, ensure that restraining orders are adhered to or locate refuge services if alternative accommodation is required. In many cases, this will involve a multi-agency approach, particularly if the victim has children or is at high risk of repeat or increased harm. Recently, policies such as the Domestic Violence Disclosure Scheme have shifted some of this preventive responsibility onto the victim themselves by giving them the opportunity to find out about a partner's abusive past and make an informed decision about whether or not to continue with a relationship.

For victims of 'hate crime' and anti-social behaviour, safety and prevention literature encourages measures that may be undertaken by the individual themselves, whereby changing their patterns of behaviour, dress, movement or social interaction illustrates a desire to reduce the likelihood of being targeted for abuse. Not only does this have a potentially detrimental impact on the social and psychological well-being of the individual, but it also means that the social and cultural prejudices informing such targeted victimisation remain unchallenged. Harmful cultures informing sexual victimisation have similarly avoided scrutiny as a result of criminal justice awareness and prevention campaigns traditionally advising potential victims (usually younger women) of the steps *they* should take to reduce the likelihood of experiencing sexual violence. Criticisms have highlighted the gendered stereotyping of victim blaming inherent in such prevention literature that neglects to target or focus on preventing perpetrators.

More recent approaches to preventing victimisation have emerged that focus on three stages: primary, secondary and tertiary interventions. Primary prevention strategies focus on combating the creation of victims on individual and societal levels. They aim to reduce the likelihood of crime by changing cultures, attitudes and perceptions around a given issue, usually in relation to interpersonal forms of victimisation. For example, a key part of the 'End Violence Against Women' national coalition involves challenging harmful or debilitating representations of women, promoting discussions around consent and positive sexual relationships, and combating harmful forms of sexism in society. In North America, primary measures have emerged in schools and colleges that are focused on promoting 'bystander intervention'. These schemes aim to equip people with the confidence, techniques and abilities to challenge harmful or negative situations they may encounter, deflecting instances of domestic, sexual or hate-based victimisation.

In addition to early measures, secondary and tertiary prevention strategies are focused on reducing repeat offending and/or victimisation with identified victims and perpetrators. These interventions address existing factors informing and sustaining abusive behaviours through individual or couple counselling, group therapy, or community support involving volunteers with a vested interest in seeing a reduction in criminal victimisation. These work to enhance an offender's ability to desist from further criminality by offering pastoral support while recognising a need for accountability for the harm caused. Such measures offer an alternative to the traditional criminal justice responses of increased penalties or longer sentences, which may serve to enhance punishments but have little impact on reducing criminal victimisation.

MARIAN DUGGAN

See also: **Victims of Crime**

Readings

Cerise, S. (2011) *A different world is possible: Ending violence against women.* London: End Violence Against Women. Available at: http://www. endviolenceagainstwomen.org.uk/resources/19/a-different-world-is-possible-ending-violence-against-women-2011

Corteen, K. (2002) 'Lesbian safety talk: problematizing definitions and experiences of violence, sexuality and space', *Sexualities*, 5(3): 259–80.

PRIMARY, SECONDARY AND TERTIARY VICTIMS AND VICTIMISATION

The terms 'victim' and 'victimisation' are pivotal to the study of the impact of crime (Karmen, 2016). Those concerned with victims and victimisation within and beyond academia predominantly imagine perpetrators, victims and intentional acts to harm and victimise to be obvious and clearly demarcated. However, victimologists 'recognise that not all victims, including victims of crime, are publically, officially and politically perceived, received and responded to as such'

(Corteen et al, 2014, p 26). Subsequently, *who* is a 'victim' and *what* is 'victimisation' cannot be taken for granted.

In order to understand the nature and level of harm and suffering as a result of victimisation, what has been described as a 'victim hierarchy' has emerged, with distinction made between three different types of victims and victimisation, namely, 'primary', 'secondary' and 'tertiary' (Spalek, 2006; Davies, 2011). These three concepts take precedence in victimological literature and in literature on victims inside and beyond academia, although they are often interpreted and applied differently (Corteen et al, 2014).

The term 'primary' victim predominantly encapsulates 'those that experience harm directly' (Davies, 2011, p 194) and who are individually 'targeted or personalized' as a victim (Burgess et al, 2011, p 67). As such, primary victims experience the *act* of victimisation and its consequences, impacts and effects first-hand.

Following this, 'secondary' victims comprise those victims that do not experience the harmful act or act of victimisation directly. They experience victimisation as a result of the direct victimisation caused to another (or others), for example, those who know the victim, witnesses of the victimisation or family and friends of the primary victim. 'Tertiary' victims can suffer vicarious victimisation, a kind of second-hand harm, or a harmful ripple effect after witnessing, being involved in or hearing about a particularly disturbing and distressing event. Professionals and workers in a variety of fields can be identified as tertiary victims due to the stress and fatigue that arises as part of their occupation (Spalek, 2006).

The concepts 'primary', 'secondary' and 'tertiary' create or lend themselves to a 'hierarchy in the level of suffering experienced' (Spalek, 2006, p 13). However, 'it cannot be assumed that secondary and tertiary victims necessarily suffer less trauma than primary victims', as Spalek (2006, p 13) highlights, 'secondary and tertiary victims can also face significant, physical, psychological and emotional pain'.

That said, there has been the application of such victim hierarchies across several studies (including sexual violence and domestic abuse). In this instance, examples of primary, secondary and tertiary victims and victimisation are discussed by Corteen et al (2014) in their analysis of the UK's coroner's inquest into service-user self-inflicted deaths. Such deaths are viewed as a 'victimising event' in the context of health and social care professions (Corteen et al, 2014, p 25). Culpability aside, the compulsory participation in the public coronial process, together with the media's reporting of it, can be particularly harmful and victimising for professionals. Yet, unlike other individuals affected by a service-user death, the victim status and experiences of victimisation of professionals is less obvious.

Within academia, the media and social and health services, service users who take their own lives are automatically bequeathed the status of primary victims having encountered primary victimisation.

Corteen et al (2014, p 29) acknowledge this and they do not 'wish to diminish or minimize service users' suffering as a result of the primary victimisation they endured'. They do, however, recognise and highlight how the self-inflicted death of a service user can result in *additional* primary victims and occupational-related primary victimisation. This is due to a potential iatrogenic victimising effect on health and social care professionals as a result of the coroner's inquest in the aftermath of a service user's self-inflicted death. The process, the verdict (especially if it is a narrative verdict), the public nature of the event and media reporting can lead professionals to become a primary victim of a 'witch-hunt'. In such cases, health and social care practitioners may feel vulnerable and powerless as they are held personally and professionally responsible for such a tragedy, being publically blamed, vilified and attacked (for more detail, see Taylor et al, 2013; Corteen et al, 2014). The subsequent production of primary victims and primary victimisation can be evidenced 'when public sector workers harm and even kill themselves in response to public negativity including naming and shaming' (Corteen et al, 2014, p 23). In addition, health and social care professionals suffer and experience primary *victimisation* as 'the loss of a service user in their care or under their supervision has a primary harmful impact', especially if they witnessed the event or the immediate aftermath (Corteen et al, 2014, p 30).

Furthermore, for Corteen et al (2014), health and social care professionals in this situation may be more readily conceived as experiencing secondary *victimisation*. The common usage of the 'two distinct meanings' of secondary victimisation (Davies, 2011, p 194) is explained as follows. Secondary victimisation may be experienced by those 'indirectly harmed' – the secondary victims, as identified earlier – family, friends, witnesses and those who know the victim. Secondary victimisation can also be experienced by those with 'exacerbated' emotions and experiences of victimisation (Davies, 2011, pp 194–5). The latter form of secondary victimisation describes the process of being 're-victimised' (Davies, 2011, p 195). This can be as a result of the victimising effects of negative social or institutional responses to the initial experience of victimisation. Secondary victimisation may be experienced by health and social care professionals due to their treatment within and beyond the coroner's inquest (Taylor et al, 2013; Corteen et al, 2014). Thus, as secondary victims due to the loss of a service user in their care or under their supervision, the coronial process aimed at bringing some resolution can actually be harmful and damaging personally and professionally. Health and social care professionals may also experience secondary victimisation in a vicarious way as they witness 'the victimising effects experienced by family, friends, other service users and colleagues' (Corteen et al, 2014, pp 36–7).

Tertiary *victimisation* 'includes a wider circle of "victims" who may have been affected by a particularly shocking event' (Davies, 2011, p 196). For Corteen et al (2014), health and social care professionals belong to an occupational community, and, in so doing, they experience tertiary victimisation. This is due to the visceral public response together with sensationalist and simplistic news reporting in which professionals involved and the profession itself are publically blamed or inferred as culpable in some way.

To conclude, primary, secondary and tertiary victims are constructed from an initial victimising event. While secondary and tertiary victims may differ from primary victims in that the direct act of harm and victimisation was not directed at them, they may experience primary victimisation as well as secondary and tertiary victimisation. The initial primary victim and victimising event may also inadvertently produce *additional*, different but related primary victims and victimisation that, in a professional context, may be occupation-related.

KAREN CORTEEN

See also: **Blame and Victims; Victim Hierarchy; Victimology**

Readings

Burgess, A.W., Regehr, C. and Roberts, A.R. (2011) *Victimology: Theories and application*. London: Jones and Bartlett.
Corteen, K., Taylor, P. and Morley, S. (2014) 'The coroner's inquest and visceral reactions: considering the impact of self-inflicted deaths on the health and social care professional', in P. Taylor and P. Wagg (eds) *Work and society: Places, spaces and identities*. Chester: University of Chester Press, pp 37–45.
Davies, P. (2011) *Gender and victimisation*. London: Sage.
Karmen, A. (2016) *Crime victims: An introduction to victimology* (9th edn). Boston, MA: Cengage Learning.
Spalek, B. (2006) *Crime victims: Theory, policy and practice*. Basingstoke: Palgrave Macmillan.
Taylor, P., Corteen, K. and Morley, S. (2013) 'Service user suicides and the coroner's inquests', *Criminal Justice Matters*, 92: 32–3.

PROBATION AND VICTIMS

Although probation is offender-focused in England and Wales, there is a historic interest in victims among probation officers and within the service through probation order conditions and compensation, and, later, an interest in the development of Victim Support. More recent involvement with victims post-sentence has imposed new responsibilities while raising the question of conflicting interests. However, with recent fundamental changes to probation in England and Wales, it is likely that the involvement of probation will be limited to these post-sentence responsibilities.

First, while probation has traditionally focused on the supervision of offenders, its ethos of reconciliation and community cohesion means that it has favoured sentences that allow offenders to provide reparation to their victims. The possibility of compensation as a discretionary requirement of a probation order was established early in probation's development, and provided the platform from which senior probation managers, like John Harding in the 1980s, advocated the benefits of restitution by offenders to their victims. Many smaller-scale local initiatives, including the Victim/Burglar Group in Plymouth, were precursors to the involvement of probation in mediation and, later, restorative justice initiatives. This is especially so with young offenders, where probation officers, as members of Youth Offending Teams, have become increasingly involved in assessing the needs of crime victims and addressing them in the context of the most appropriate ways of dealing with offenders. Similarly, many of the 'accredited programmes' offered by the Probation Service provide an extension of the offence-directed aspects of intensive probation and may also incorporate a victim focus. However, the provision of such programmes may be called into question following recent governance changes (see later).

Second, probation's interest in reparation was, in part, responsible for the key role played by officers in the creation and expansion of the organisation Victim Support. It was one of the key promoters of the first Victim Support schemes in Bristol, England, in 1973, and as Victim Support expanded its base nationally, probation officers featured prominently on local management committees and in providing resources such as office space. At the same time, Victim Support's commitment to partnership working meant that its first constitution required each scheme to include on its management committee at least one representative from either probation or social services, and this was, in practice, usually a probation officer.

Third, the involvement of probation with supporting victims was acknowledged when, following the 1990 Victim's Charter, the Probation Service was made responsible for establishing contact with the victims of long-term prisoners so that victims were informed of release plans and any concerns they might have could be passed on to the prison and/or Parole Board. Subsequent policies formalised and expanded the duties of probation in this respect. A statutory victim contact scheme was introduced in 2004 for victims of offenders convicted of certain sexual and violent offences and sentenced to imprisonment for 12 months or more. Different local probation services handled this responsibility in different ways: one franchised the service out; others gave responsibility to the probation officer supervising the offender; and others deployed specialist victim liaison officers (VLOs), who were usually Probation Service officers (salaried at a grade below a probation officer). In theory, providing one officer to deal with both the offender and their victim might be seen as a continuation of the reconciliation-based approach, but questions of divided loyalties mean that VLOs are the most common option used. This, in turn, has led to criticism of poor communication between VLOs and offender managers in reports by both the victim's commissioner and Her Majesty's Inspectorate of Probation. Following these reports, the contact scheme has also been revised in the 2013 Victims' Code of Practice and Parole Board guidance.

Since February 2015, the governance of probation in England and Wales has changed radically, with a public sector centralised body – the National Probation Service (NPS) – responsible for high 'risk of harm' offenders and local privatised agencies – Community Rehabilitation Companies – dealing with low 'risk of harm' offenders. This move towards an NPS responsible for policing criminals rather than one working with offenders and victims in their communities is the culmination of a process started under the then New Labour government. The recent Coalition government also enthusiastically committed itself to this approach. As such, it suggests an erosion of the more positive features of probation work, including working with victims, except in the case of victims of offenders serving long-term sentences, which remains a responsibility of the NPS.

ROB I. MAWBY

See also: **Code of Practice for Victims in England and Wales; Victims' Charters; Victims of Crime**

Readings
Walklate, S. (ed) (2007) *The handbook of victims and victimology*. Cullompton: Willan Publishing.

PROFESSIONAL WRESTLING, 'SPORTS ENTERTAINMENT', HARM AND VICTIMISATION

A promoter once said to me, 'If you die, kid, die in the ring. It's good for business'. ('Piper', cited in Swartz, 2004, p 3)

Cohen, 'a professional wrestling expert', states: 'while many people think of wrestling as a big joke, there is one thing about wrestling that isn't funny. The death rate among wrestlers is alarmingly high' (2015, para 1). Professional wrestling is a profitable business and a corporate enterprise and it is also a highly harmful industry. As workers within this profit-oriented venture, professional wrestlers are subject to, and endure, 'multiple harms and layers of victimisation' (Corteen and Corteen, 2012, p 48). To summarise, 'the least common way that wrestlers seem to be dying is due to old age' and, unfortunately, 'because it is wrestlers, no one cares' (Cohen, 2015, paras 7–8). This includes the industry itself as it 'appears to have acted in an almost shameless manner to what is a shameless state of affairs' (Corteen and Corteen, 2012, p 52).

Some attention has been given to the harm caused to the spectators of professional wrestling, especially children (see, eg, Bernthal, 2008); yet, limited serious academic attention has been paid to the harms and victimisation experienced by professional wrestlers or professional wrestler sports entertainers.

Focusing on the wrestling and sports entertainment business in the US, Corteen and Corteen (2012) attempt to address this omission within academia. They discuss the victimisation of professional wrestlers and they argue that such workers comprise the 'victimological other' (Walklate, 2007); the victimological other 'falls outside the normative imagery of theory and practice' (Walklate, 2007, p 53). Professional wrestlers constitute the victimological other as 'their status as victims is not in keeping with commonsense thinking and mainstream academic victimology or victim activism' (Corteen and Corteen, 2012, p 49). This is compounded by their status as performing sports entertainers within a sports entertainment industry.

Due to changes in the nature of the wrestling business from the early 1980s, in the public imagination, 'professional wrestlers became more firmly established as exhibitionist actors as opposed to athletes' (Corteen and Corteen, 2012, p 48). In sum, 'wrestlers went from fighting men in tights to bona fide televised personalities' (Lagorio, 2005, p 1). The majority of professional fans understand that there is more to the profession than this; they 'look to see the fake and to see through the fake to see the real ... examining each punch for its impact and non-impact' (Mazer, 1998, p 6). However, by 1985, the marketisation and commodification of the wrestling profession had taken a hold and despite resistance inside and outside of the industry, by 1986, the profession was refashioned into the genre of family entertainment and the term 'sports entertainment' was invented.

Professional wrestler sports entertainers do enact violence; however, such violent performances result in real injuries and actual violence (Mazer, 1998; Blaustein, 1999) and victimisation (Corteen and Corteen, 2012): behind the 'staged combat, real violence, harm, and repeat victimization permeates the ring and the industry'

(Corteen and Corteen, 2012, p 49). The performative violence that professional wrestlers engage in as part of their craft and the corporate sports entertainment industry that they are located in comes at a high cost. These include occupational self-inflicted and occupational-inflicted harm and victimisation.

Within the political economy of sports entertainment, professional wrestlers are under immense pressure to deliver more extreme and dangerous performances. The pursuit of profit, entertainment and celebrity status results in 'the expectation of professional wrestlers to push the boundaries of health and safety and to take more extreme risks' (Corteen and Corteen, 2012, p 51). This can be seen with wrestling taking place on concrete floors, the use of weapons, including chairs, and matches conducted within and on top of cages. In so doing, 'accidents do happen and injuries occur' (Cohen, 2015, para 3), and 'conflict erupts with violence spilling over from display to actuality' (Mazer, 1998, p 22).

Inside the professional wrestling industry, there exists a predominantly ignored and uncontrolled alcohol and substance abuse among wrestlers (Swartz, 2004; Cohen, 2014, 2015). This is a result of: relentless work schedules with no off-season; constant travel from one event to another; living in (non-glamorous) hotels and being away from home for extended periods of time; and working when in pain and injured. This working environment results in 'the deadly slope that many wrestlers have found themselves facing' both while working and in retirement (Cohen, 2015, para 3), namely, the use and abuse of steroids, prescription drugs (such as sleeping pills and painkillers), illicit drugs (such as cocaine and other recreational drugs) and human-growth hormones.

The cumulative effect can be seen in 'the very high rate of premature mortality from cardiovascular disease, cancer, and substance abuse' of 'professional wrestlers who are part of the entertainment industry' (Herman et al, 2014, p 6). The strain on the heart is further endangered due to wrestler's having to 'carry either an enormous amount of muscle or a tremendous amount of fat' in order to fulfil the 'larger than life' appearance necessitated 'to be successful in the business', thus making 'the heart work harder than it must' (Cohen, 2015, para 5). Other fatalities include accidental and intentional self-inflicted deaths and death 'as a result of injuries suffered in the ring' (Cohen, 2015, para 6). Further harms comprise: alcohol and substance dependency; degenerative and debilitating long-term and short-term injuries; and individual, marital and familial breakdowns.

The disproportionate number of wrestlers who have died since 1985 before reaching the age of 65 is a key concern (for details of such deaths, see Cohen, 2015; Corteen and Corteen, 2012). Possibly the most disturbing of this awful 'scary epidemic' of wrestlers dying young is the death of Chris Benoit (Cohen, 2014, para 2). He died at age 40, killing himself, his wife Nancy and their young son in their family home. This professional wrestler (plus two of his family members) is one example 'amongst an ever-increasing list that includes over 100 famous wrestlers who have arguably died a pre-mature death' (Corteen and Corteen, 2012, p 51). The list compiled by Cohen (2015) does not include wrestlers who have not appeared on national television, who may work in similar or worse working environments, and thus this scary epidemic may be even more frightening. There are also 'the secondary and tertiary victims – those who are left behind: families and the wrestling community, including fans' (Corteen and Corteen, 2012, p 51).

The ambiguous classification of professional wrestling as sports entertainment, 'at best, facilitates the mystification and neglect of the harm and victimization caused to professional wrestlers as part of their craft, or at worst causes the victimisation of professional wrestlers' (Corteen and Corteen, 2012, p 47). There are other occupational-related factors that cannot be discussed in depth here, such as the independent contractor status of wrestlers and 'contracts' that encompass 'death clauses' that free the wrestling business from liability when a wrestler dies or is injured in the ring (Michak, 2010 (see also Sonneveld's [2012] discussion on the connection between the lack of wrestlers' employment rights and protections as workers, and the harms they endure).

It is paramount to acknowledge the harm, victimisation, injustices and lack of accountability that is endemic to this industry and to contextualise it within the political economy. The extent to which such harm and victimisation can be attributed to the commodification of the business and to the corporation that monopolises it is debatable. However, the occupational nature and disproportionate extent of harm and victimisation within this industry cannot be ignored. With reference to his list of over 100 premature deaths of famous professional wrestlers, Cohen (2014, para 6) states: '[v]ery few of deaths on the list could be blamed 100% on the wrestling business and very few have a 0% blame'. Further investigation is warranted. Despite efforts to improve the industry, professional wrestler sports entertainers continue to die and be harmed at extraordinary rates and the industry remains predominantly unregulated, deregulated and unaccountable. The author agrees with Herman et al's (2014, p 6) call for the need for 'an intensive prevention strategy with aggressive treatment of each of the risk factors' to secure the health and well-being of the workers in this corporate enterprise – sooner rather than later.

KAREN CORTEEN

See also: **Sport, Crime and Harm; Victimological Other**

Readings

Bernthal, M.J. (2008) 'How viewing professional wrestling may affect children', *The Sports Journal*, ISSN: 1543-9518, February 22. Available at: http://thesportjournal.org/article/how-viewing-professional-wrestling-may-affect-children/

Blaustein, B.W. (producer and director) (1999) *Beyond the mat*, documentary, Universal Family and Home Entertainment.

Cohen, E. (2014) 'The death secret exposed', 15 December. Available at: http://bit.ly/RWoqTj

Cohen, E. (2015) 'Wrestling's dirty secret', 3 March. Available at: http://bit.ly/NvpTnk

Corteen, K. and Corteen, A. (2012) 'Dying to entertain? The victimization of professional wrestlers in the USA', *International Perspectives in Victimology*, 7(1): 47–53.

Herman, C.W., Conlon, A.S.C., Rubenfire, M., Burghardt, A.R. and McGregor, S.J. (2014) 'The very high mortality rate among active professional wrestlers is primarily due to cardiovascular disease', *PLoS One*, 9(11): 1–7.

Lagorio, C. (2005) 'Wrestling with the margins', *The Village VOICE*, 4 January. Available at: http://bit.ly/9pCYAQ

Mazer, S. (1998) *Professional wrestling: Sport and spectacle.* Jackson, MS: University Press of Mississippi.

Michak, D. (2010) '"DEATH CLAUSES": talent contracts release WWE from liability in wrestlers' deaths', *Journal Inquirer.com*, 3 September. Available at: http://www.journalinquirer.com/page_one/death-clauses-talent-contracts-release-wwe-from-liability-in-wrestlers/article_07fb72d4-acf1-5cc1-9a04-d61402718de0.html

Sonneveld, S. (2012) *Why WWE Pro Wrestler should form a Professional Wrestling Union*, Available at: http://bleacherreport.com/articles/1110575-wwe-news-wrestlings-risks-warrant-a-labor-unions-rewards

Swartz, J. (2004) 'High death rate lingers behind the fun facade of pro wrestling', *USA TODAY*, 3 March. Available at: http://usat.ly/4rcACC

Walklate, S. (2007) *Imagining the victim of crime.* Berkshire: Open University Press.

PROPERTY CRIME, VICTIMISATION AND HARM

In October 2014, the Sentencing Council (SC) for England and Wales published its extensive *Robbery guideline consultation* (Sentencing Council, 2014). The SC's predecessor body (the Sentencing Guidelines Council [SGC]) had previously published a definitive guideline for the sentencing of robbery offences in July 2006. Interestingly, the 2006 guidelines did not include guidance for every possible 'type' of robbery. In particular, robberies in dwellings (or robberies in the home) were not included within a discrete category. It is therefore now pleasing to see that the current draft consultation does include a specific grouping relating to 'robberies in a dwelling'.

Although there exists only a single offence of robbery (s 8, Theft Act 1968), the 2014 consultation recognises three broad 'types' of robbery for sentencing purposes. They are 'street robberies', 'commercial robberies' and 'robberies in dwellings'. While 'robberies in dwellings' comprise the smallest of those three categories, it is nonetheless a significant minority. In 2013, for example, of the approximate 4,400 adults sentenced for robbery, 13% were for dwelling robberies. Furthermore, even though the smallest numerical category, the impact of robbery in a dwelling can often be a significant factor, as the *Robbery guideline consultation* (Sentencing Council, 2014, p 7) notes: 'In 2013 approximately 560 adult offenders were sentenced for robbery in a dwelling. The impact of this type of offence occurring in the home, where one should feel safe, can be profound and long lasting'.

It is arguable (with support from authorities [see later]) that where two otherwise identical robberies occur (one in the street and one in the victim's home), the latter is more serious because of the sole fact that it occurred where the victim should feel secure. Thus, there is often a corresponding impact upon the victim in terms of distress and anxiety. Victims frequently experience emotional distress (eg in relation to the loss of items with strong sentimental value), feelings of isolation and insecurity, and fears about repeat attacks and victimisation (Lammy, 2015). However, harm (in its broadest sense) can extend beyond the immediate victim in such offences. Neighbours can become fearful for their own safety, and families of the immediate victims can be caused distress and anxiety. These are all instances of the wider negative impact of 'victim proximity'. Fears of victims and those in the surrounding local community can be more real than imagined and this is especially so for vulnerable individuals and groups and those living in already deprived areas (see Lammy's [2015] comprehensive report in this respect).

As noted earlier, Part 1 of the 2006 SGC *Robbery: Definitive guideline* (Sentencing Guidelines Council, 2006) covered three specific types of robbery: street robberies ('muggings'), robberies of small businesses and less sophisticated commercial robberies. All other robberies, covered in Part 2, were subject to guidance from the Court of Appeal. Part 2 did extend to 'violent personal robberies in the home', but specifically only those with a 'high level of violence'. Consequently, there was no overt guideline covering robberies in dwellings that involved less serious violence, including instances of threats of violence.

The absence of such specific guidance in the 2006 guidelines has already been the subject of comment by the Court of Appeal. In *A-G's Reference (Nos. 38-40 of 2007) (Crummack and others)* [2007] EWCA Crim 1692, the Court of Appeal increased an unduly lenient sentence, noting specifically the age and vulnerability of the victims, threats with weapons, and physical assaults on them with the appellants' fists.

In *A-G's Reference (No. 124 of 2008) (Doran)* [2008] EWCA Crim 2820, the Court of Appeal (per Hughes L.J.) stated specifically that: 'It seems to us that sentence for this kind of *unpleasant robbery, targeting elderly householders without weapons or significant violence*, ought to be in the very general range of five to six years after a trial' (emphasis added).

More recently, in *Alexander and White* [2014] EWCA Crim 1768 (although the sentences were reduced slightly on appeal), the Court of Appeal identified the elderly victim's learning disability and hearing impairment, and the acute anxiety and depression that he suffered as a result of the robbery, as all being relevant factors in sentencing.

Thus, the 2014 draft SC guidelines on robbery provide a timely contribution to the issue of the appropriate sentence for robberies in dwellings where moderate violence, or the threat of violence, is used. It is important to note the precise approach to be taken by the court.

First, the sentencer determines the 'offence category'. This is done by assessing the culpability of the offender (set against an exhaustive list of factors in the guidelines) and the harm to the victim (also set against an exhaustive list of factors). It is important to note for the purpose of dwelling burglaries that 'harm' in the guidelines extends to both physical and/or psychological harm. Based on the authorities, it is suggested that the latter is often a significant consideration.

The 'culpability factors' will determine whether the case in question falls within: A – High culpability; B – Medium culpability; or C – Lesser culpability. Similarly, the 'harm factors' range across Categories 1, 2 and 3 (from most serious to less serious).

The guidelines then determine an appropriate 'Category Range' and 'Starting Point' dependent upon the culpability and harm calculation. So, for example, high culpability (A) plus high harm (1) would result in the highest Category Range (9–13 years' custody), with a Starting Point of nine years' custody. Similarly, medium culpability (B) with medium harm (2) results in a Category Range of 4–8 years' custody, and a Starting Point of five years' custody. Finally, at the lower end, lesser culpability (C) with low harm (3) produces a Category Range of 1–3 years, with a Starting Point of 18 months' custody.

Lastly, the sentencer must consider if there are any factors constituting aggravation or mitigation. These are contained in a table of additional factors relating to both the context of the offence and the offender. Importantly, it is a non-exhaustive list, which will give some further limited discretion to future sentencers.

Finally, property crimes in Britain continue to 'take their toll' and yet such crimes 'enjoy *de facto* decriminalisaton' (Lammy, 2015, p 9). However, it is hoped and expected that, once fully applied, the current SC draft guidelines on robbery will fill the small but important gap that exists in the 2006 guidelines relating to some 'domestic robberies'. In particular, there is an opportunity here to enable the wider harms to victims of such offences to become important considerations in the general sentencing process.

DAVID W. SELFE

See also: **Crime, Victimisation and Vulnerability**

Readings

Ashworth, A. (2002) 'Robbery re-assessed', *Criminal Law Review*, November 851–72.

Lammy, D. (2015) *Taking its toll: The regressive impact of property crime in Britain*. London: Policy Exchange. Available at: http://www.policyexchange.org.uk/images/publications/taking%20its%20toll.pdf

Sentencing Council (2014) *Robbery guideline consultation (October)*. London: Sentencing Council.

Sentencing Guidelines Council (2006) *Robbery: Definitive guideline*. London: Sentencing Guidelines Council.

QUALITATIVE AND QUANTITATIVE INQUIRY INTO VICTIMS

See: Ethics and Methods in Victim Research; Official Crime Statistics and Victim Surveys

R

RACIST HATE CRIME

Identification of what constitutes hate crime victimisation is essential for enacting related legislation. Protected groups can be added to hate crime legislation, but determining the elements and actions of a hate crime and associated victimisation can be challenging. In the US, under federal law, race, religion, gender, sexual orientation, ethnicity/national origin and disability are considered protected groups. State laws vary in relation to whom or what may fit the definition of a protected group, and the crime is viewed as an offence against an entire group. Overall, target characteristics must account for the harm. For example, with regard to racist hate crime, the crime of assault must include a specific intent to hurt the victim because of skin colour. In Britain, ethnic minority groups are affected by racism and racist hate crime (Craig, 2013). Racist hate crime, in keeping with other hate crimes, thus occurs because of target characteristics as defined in legislation.

The extent of racist hate crime necessitates a careful examination of actions, harm and motives. A critical question is what constitutes enough harm for the act to be considered a criminal act motivated by hate and bias. Determining the physical and or mental status of the offender is crucial in decisions to charge a defendant with a hate crime enhancement. Other difficult questions revolve around sentencing and achieving justice at trial because ethnic minority groups are disproportionately criminalised in Britain (Craig, 2013).

Racist hate crimes often receive an extensive amount of media attention, where reports may be unreliable because of the emotional aspects of the crime. In Britain, racist views of Muslims after the London bombings in 2005 increased and racist hate crime was influenced by Islamophobia (Frost, 2008). Public sentiment may frame what the media portrays, even if the information is questionable. In court proceedings, the burden is on the prosecution to prove beyond a reasonable doubt that a crime was committed and that the offence inflicted harm on the victim because of their actual or perceived identity. However, bias and stereotypes may impact in court proceedings. Stereotypes influence the categorisation of who is a legitimate or typical victim (Plumm et al, 2014).

Many activists in the US are demanding that police officers be considered a protected category in hate crime legislation. Media reports tend to focus on the victims of police use of force, especially when a minority ethnic citizen is assaulted or killed. These actions may be viewed as a hate crime if they were based on racial bias. Police officers may also become targets for threats and violence based on their occupation status. Opponents argue that classifying police officers as a protected hate crime group is unreasonable. Adding occupation to hate crime legislation is a slippery slope that may apply to dozens of jobs and people outside of law enforcement. The issue is yet to be decided.

Hate crime legislation creates a sentencing enhancement to already-existing criminal statutes. The sentences for individuals convicted of hate crimes are harsher because the goal of the sentence is to serve as a specific and general deterrent. If a potential offender is aware of the harsher punishment, then he or she may be deterred from committing criminal acts based on prejudicial views about certain groups. When a crime is committed based on hate and bias, racial or otherwise, there is a tendency to prefer retributive practices in sentencing. However, if harm has been done to the victim and the community is affected, perhaps punishment should transition towards a restorative justice model. Through restorative justice practices, the harm as a result of racist hate crime and other forms of hate crime can be repaired within the community, and between the victim and perpetrator. Under these circumstances, the offender is given the opportunity to be reintegrated back into the community. However, deeply ingrained racial and other prejudices and hatred towards certain groups are difficult, and, in some cases, impossible, to change despite serious consequences. Extended imprisonment may represent the best approach in dealing with hate crimes in order to satisfy the community's need for closure (Spieldenner and Glenn, 2014). The community and the victim may want the offender to receive a longer prison sentence because hatred of a social group motivated the crime, which serves as an aggravating circumstance.

NANCY CONTRERAS

See also: **Hate Crime and Victimisation**

Readings

Craig, G. (2013) 'Invisibilizing "race" in public policy', *Critical Social Policy*, 33(4): 712–720.

Frost, D. (2008) 'Islamophobia: examining causal links between the media and "race hate" from "below"', *International Journal of Sociology & Social Policy*, 28(11/12): 564–78.

Plumm, K., Terrance, C. and Autin, A. (2014) 'Not all hate crimes are created equal: an examination of the roles of ambiguity and expectations in perceptions of hate crimes', *Current Psychology*, 33(3): 321–64.

Spieldenner, A.R. and Glenn, C.L. (2014) 'Scripting hate crimes: victim, space and perpetrator defining hate', *Continuum: Journal of Media & Cultural Studies*, 28(1): 123–35.

RADICAL VICTIMOLOGY

All strands of victimological thought are differently concerned with questions of power relations, suffering and the nature of individual choice (see McGarry and Walklate, 2015). However, radical victimology does not just centre power and power relations in framing explanations of victimhood; it gives primacy to them. The origins of radical victimology can be found in the work of Mendelsohn, one of the founding fathers of victimology, who argued for a victimology concerned with all aspects of victimisation, not only those that were associated with law-breaking behaviour. However, a more focused development of these ideas is frequently attributed to the work of Richard Quinney. In an essay published in 1972, Quinney asked 'Who is the victim?', and was at pains to point out that 'our conceptions of victims and victimisation are optional, discretionary and are by no means given' (Quinney, 1972, p 314). In making this observation, his intention was to bring to the foreground victims of state crime, victims of corporate victimisation, victims of oppression and so on. In other words, he wanted to focus attention on all those victims not so readily visible or heard within criminal justice responses. Arguably, the subject matter of radical victimology is informed by human rights rather than criminal law. Thus, the main proponents of radical victimology have been Elias (1986) and Kauzlarich et al (2001). However, in developing this radical agenda further, Rothe and Kauzlarich (2014) have outlined a 'victimology of state crime', and it is worth reflecting on their agenda for a more finely tuned appreciation of what might constitute a radical victimology.

Rothe and Kauzlarich (2014) eschew both the criminal law and human rights as their starting point and prefer to make the case for thinking about the nature of the harm perpetrated as the entry point for (radical) victimology. The contributions in their edited collection illustrate how this might be operationalised. These include analyses of: harm done to 'street' children and to children in institutional 'care'; the violence(s) perpetrated in the 'Mukaradeeb Massacre'; the normalisation of civilian bombing; victimisation during and after war; the harms generated by Somali piracy; and the role of immigration policy in victimising both displaced persons and people without papers. For Rothe and Kauzlarich (2014), the victim label could have been reasonably and justifiably applied to the harms generated as a result of these experiences. They are all connected to systematic state violence(s) on those deemed vulnerable. By implication, those who hold power are the arbiters of social harm. Thus, this version of victimology brings to the agenda a much wider appreciation of who can or cannot be a victim, including those who might be the least likely to acquire such a label. It is also an agenda that focuses attention on whose voices are heard and whose are not in the process of arbitrating the harm done. For example, those less likely to be listened to, for example, the homeless or the street prostitute, whose harmful experiences might be deemed a matter of their own choice, are nevertheless victims of the state's violence(s) in this version of victimology. Herein lies a conceptual problem.

In giving primacy to power and power relations, this version of victimology does rather erase the question of individual choice and, as a result, denudes individual agency. This can raise difficult empirical questions when it is evident that individual and/or collective choices were made, resulting in harm that could have been foreseen (see, eg, Rafter and Walklate, 2012). Nonetheless, as Box (1983, p 17) pointed out some time ago, 'the majority of those suffering from corporate crime remain unaware of their victimisation – either not knowing it has happened to them or viewing their "misfortune" as an accident or "no-one's fault"'. This is referred to by Geis (1973) as 'victim-responsiveness'. Such issues notwithstanding, the case for widening conceptions of victimhood as proposed by radical victimology is a sound one and is especially evidenced as victimological concerns have increasingly reached into the arena of mass victimisation and atrocity crimes (see, eg, Letschert et al, 2011). In these contexts, the question of individual choice is clearly a less pertinent one as such harms are self-evidently perpetrated by the powerful on the less powerful.

SANDRA WALKLATE

See also: **Social Harm; State-Corporate Crime and Harm; White-Collar Crime, Harm and Victimisation**

Readings
Box, S. (1983) *Power, crime and mystification.* London: Tavistock.
Elias, R. (1986) *The politics of victimisation.* Oxford: Oxford University Press.

Geis, G. (1973) 'Victimisation patterns in white collar crime', in I. Drapkin and E. Viano (eds) *Victimology: A new focus, 5*. Lexington, MA: D.C. Heath and Co, pp 86–106.

Kauzlarich, D., Matthews, R.A. and Miller, W.J. (2001) 'Toward a victimology of state crime', *Critical Criminology*, 10: 173–94.

Letschert, R., Haveman, R., De Brouwer, A.-M. and Pemberton, A. (2011) *Victimological approaches to international crimes*. Cambridge: Intersentia.

McGarry, R. and Walklate, S. (2015) *Victims: Trauma, testimony, justice*. London: Routledge.

Quinney, R. (1972) 'Who is the victim?', *Criminology*, 10: 314-23.

Rafter, N. and Walklate, S. (2012) 'Genocide and the dynamics of victimisation: some observations on Armenia', *European Journal of Criminology*, 9(5): 514–26.

Rothe, D. and Kauzlarich, D. (eds) (2014) *Towards a victimology of state crime*. London: Routledge.

RELIGION AND HATE CRIME

See: **Hate Crime and Victimisation; Religion and Victimisation**

RELIGION AND VICTIMISATION

Religion can be an important aspect to individuals' coping strategies in relation to victimisation. Victims can draw upon religious frameworks of understanding in order to help try to explain why it is that they have suffered. Suffering may be understood as part of the experience of being human, as involving important learning for the development of one's soul, as involving temporary suffering until the person is reunited with their God and/or as being due to something that they may have done in a previous life (karma). Religion can also be used as a way of gaining a sense of justice, in that some religious frameworks provide a victim with the understanding that their offender will be punished in the future. Religion can also be drawn upon in relation to feelings towards the perpetrator, in that some religions stress forgiveness.

Religion can also present a victim with challenges in relation to their beliefs. If a victim believes in a just and loving God, they may question why it is that they have been victimised. Victimisation can lead to a loss of faith in some victims. Some victims may change their beliefs, choosing to find a religion that perhaps makes more sense to them in the aftermath of their victimisation. For example, a woman who has experienced domestic violence may turn against any patriarchal religion that she has been brought up to believe, preferring a religion that has greater equality between men and women.

Religion can also provide individuals with coping skills. Prayer and meditation may be used as a response to crime. This may be to invoke feelings of relaxation and calm within the victim, and may also involve seeking protection from future risks of being a victim through divine intervention. Religion can also provide individuals with a wider social support system, which they can draw upon to help them cope. For instance, some African-American women may gain social, as well as spiritual, support by participating in a religious congregation as a way of coping with racism and sexism. It is also important to consider spirituality in relation to coping with victimisation. Spirituality might be thought of as a sense of humans belonging to a central energy or principle. Some victims of crime may experience an increased sense of spirituality after being victimised. Traumatic events can lead individuals to reassess their lives. Literature on post-traumatic growth suggests that individuals can grow into having new and positive beliefs, interests and emotional and physiological reactions (Tedeschi and Calhoun, 1996). Some victims may also cope better with their victimisation as a result of drawing upon their spirituality, perhaps because, for some people, spirituality involves a belief that there is a divine plan for the world, or that everything that happens in a person's life has spiritual meaning.

Members of faith communities may be victimised by religious hate crime. This involves crimes that are motivated by a hatred of a particular religion. Hate crime on the basis of religion can occur within all societies. In stable societies, there can be events that happen locally, nationally and internationally that increase the number of religious hate crimes, and therefore that increase the number of victims. Post-9/11, there have been a number of terrorist-related incidents that have fed into tensions within and between communities. In particular, Muslim and Jewish communities have been victimised by religious hate crime. Following the terrorist attacks in 2015 against the premises of the French satirical magazine *Charlie Hebdo*, both Jewish and Muslim communities experienced a greater amount of victimisation from religious hate crime. Religious hate crime carried out on a particular person or a particular place of worship can impact upon a much larger number of people, in that those individuals who identify with the faith that is under attack may feel vulnerable and fearful of future attacks themselves.

Within societies characterised by conflict, religion may be part of wider political and ethnic tensions between groups that are in conflict with each other. Political and religious leaders can draw upon religion in order to justify acts of violence in the name of protecting one's faith. As part of avoiding future victimisation, some people may hide their religious identities and they may avoid going to locations that heighten the risk of them being victimised. For some people, being victimised may lead to them developing religious beliefs that are more extreme than the beliefs that they have been brought up with.

BASIA SPALEK

See also: **Hate Crime and Victimisation; Terrorism and Victimisation**

Readings
Kennedy, J., Davis, R. and Taylor, B. (1998) 'Changes in spirituality and well-being among victims of sexual assault', *Journal of the Scientific Study of Religion,* 37(2): 322–8.
Spalek, B. (2008) *Communities, identities and crime.* Bristol: The Policy Press.
Tedeschi, R. and Calhoun, L. (1996) 'The post-traumatic growth inventory: measuring the positive legacy of trauma', *Journal of Traumatic Stress,* 9(3): 455–71.

RESILIENCE

See: **Survivorology; Victim Recovery**

RESISTANCE TO CRIME, HARM AND VICTIMISATION

Resistance can take many forms; it can be active or passive, collective or individual. In all cases, though, irrespective of the form, resistance is difficult and painful, with any victories being tainted by the effects of struggle. The following offers two contrasting examples of resistance to victimisation in the UK. Both, however, have resulted in detrimental and devastating costs to those involved and those around them. There is a huge difference between those politicised, who make a conscious decision to challenge state norms, and those people who are unexpectedly confronted with injustice through state action or inaction. The Hillsborough 'disaster' and the death of Christopher Alder are examples of the latter and also serve as good examples of the longevity of campaigns against the state.

In 1989, 96 Liverpool football supporters were killed at a football stadium in Sheffield, England, hundreds were injured and thousands were traumatised by the experience of the day. In the aftermath of the disaster, fans were blamed in spite of a public inquiry clearly stating that the cause of the 'disaster' was the breakdown of police control. No prosecutions followed and verdicts of accidental death were recorded against all the dead (see Coleman et al, 1990). These stark facts led to an organised challenge to the established version of events, and that challenge continues to the present day.

The majority of bereaved families and survivors were not political people; they had little or no experience of challenging officialdom at any level. However, what they had was a fundamental sense of injustice. The families felt the injustice of no one person or organisation being held accountable for the deaths of their loved ones, and, indeed, the bereaved families were meant to accept that the deaths were an accident. The survivors suffered the acute injustice of lies, corruption and being labelled as complicit in the cause of the deaths through their behaviour. The city of Liverpool, England, collectively mourned but, moreover, rejected and resisted the negative labelling of so many of its inhabitants.

The Hillsborough Justice Campaign (HJC) was a vehicle that enabled the aforementioned three groups (the bereaved families, the survivors and the inhabitants of Liverpool) to come together, to resist and to fight back. It serves as a great example of a grassroots, collective campaign. It came into existence some nine years after the 'disaster', born out of the frustration of a number of bereaved families with the existing family support group that, by its very nature, excluded survivors. The HJC had few practical resources and no money whatsoever. However, what it did have was a collective sense of injustice and a unified aim of fighting for the true verdicts of the 'disaster' to be established. The strength of this unity would, in time, generate support from millions across the world and raise funds to assist in campaigning. Those who had hands-on involvement volunteered their time and skills freely and generously. Many still do.

Throughout the many years of resistance, the HJC was subject to numerous questionable practices on the part of members of the 'establishment', and a number of campaigners' allegations of being under surveillance are currently the subject of ongoing investigations. Campaigners were also subject to court action in respect of their website, which was used as a vehicle for the truth. However, the longer the HJC continued, the more confident it became. The longevity of the campaign meant that it went through various phases and changing priorities at times. However, the central tenet of the HJC remained the fight for truth and justice and the practical aim of having the original inquest verdicts quashed. There were many dark years when very little seemed to be happening. During those times, people drew strength from those who had a long history of challenging the state, for example, the Bloody Sunday Campaign.

The sustained pressure of the campaign and its increasingly visible presence (eg banners being seen at high-profile football matches that were and are broadcast on television across the world) led to the government establishing a panel to review all available documentation relating to the 'disaster' and its aftermath in 2010. The resultant panel report in September 2012 supported what campaigners had known and had been saying for 23 years (Hillsborough Independent Panel, 2012). The government admitted not only a cover-up, but also a conspiracy, leading to the British Prime Minister David Cameron publicly apologising for both. By December, 2012, the original inquest verdicts were quashed and fresh inquests ordered.

Finally, as this Companion goes to publication, a 27-year battle for truth and justice resulted in a landmark legal vindication. The longest legal proceedings ever heard by a jury in England, conducted in a temporary courtroom over a two-year period, came to a close. On 26 April 2016 the Hillsborough inquest concluded that the 96 Liverpool football supporters were unlawfully killed as a result of negligence and mistakes made on the part of the police and other authorities. One immediate outcome was the suspension of the Chief Constable of South Yorkshire Police and fresh investigations. Further repercussions are unfolding. Whilst it is shameful that this campaign has taken so long, so needlessly, nevertheless it is hoped that others faced with an individual or collective battle with the establishment gain confidence and strength from the costly victory of all those involved in resisting the injustices of Hillsborough.

The preceding brief summary of events overstretches 27 years and has omitted the real cost to many of those involved in such resistance. The list is long but includes relationship breakdowns, job losses, the premature death of bereaved family members and numerous suicides of survivors. For those who are still surviving, Hillsborough continues to inform much, if not all, of their life.

Christopher Alder was unlawfully killed by the police. Evidence is that following a five-minute journey in a police van, he emerged unconscious with his trousers to his knees. Closed-circuit television footage shows him being dragged into a custody suite and left on the floor, where he can be heard gasping for his breath. He died shortly after in spite of police looking on. In 2000, an inquest returned a verdict of unlawful killing, the jury stating that Christopher might have survived if police had helped him.

Janet Alder is the sister of Christopher and without her, not only would society not know of Christopher Alder, but neither would the true facts of his death be officially recorded. Janet fought for a full inquest into how Christopher died; fighting for all the evidence that enabled the verdict of unlawful killing. Moreover, when no police officer faced any criminal or disciplinary penalty, despite the verdict, Janet took her fight to the European Court of Human Rights in Strasbourg. In spite of the UK government continuing to fight her, they eventually admitted to violations of Article 2 (right to life), Article 3 (no torture, inhuman or degrading treatment) and Article 14 (no discrimination). More than 11 years on from Christopher's death, Janet was told that she had buried the wrong person and Christopher's body was still in the morgue.

Janet's fight took 13 years before the human rights ruling and it continues to the present day. It was a fight that took its toll on her health and damaged her relationship with her two children. She has stated that normal life was put on hold: 'Your priorities change, issues that are probably quite normal to other people don't seem as important as somebody losing their life. They [her children] lost their mother' (cited in Bell, 2012, para 14).

In this sense, Janet's experience mirrors that of many Hillsborough families and survivors. Likewise, her words resonate when she states how she could have progressed with her life: 'I would have moved on a long time ago if the state had said, "look, there's been something wrong here and we're not having this" ... once somebody tells the truth, you can't help but accept it and move on' (cited in Bell, 2012, para 18). Janet also discovered that not only herself, but also her barrister, was subject to surveillance, and in May 2015, the Independent Police Complaints Commission decided to refer its report to the Crown Prosecution Service. The fight for justice for Christopher Alder was, for a long time, a one-woman fight. This was in stark contrast to the huge support that the HJC experienced. The fact that Janet went on to gain the support of an organisation of the calibre of Liberty is a testimony to the strength of this remarkable woman.

As an individual challenging the state, it can be argued that you are more likely to fail and are certainly easier to label negatively. However, conversely, it can be argued that resistance on a larger scale might have greater implications and therefore be less likely to succeed. Either way, it is not for the faint-hearted. The two examples offered in this brief piece indicate that whether you are an individual or part of a larger campaign, your resistance will be met with a response that renders you vulnerable on a number of levels. The examples demonstrate that the establishment will always reorganise to protect its own interests and that, moreover, any victory will be offset by the damaging costs endured.

SHEILA COLEMAN

See also: **Social Harm; State–Corporate Crime and Harm; Survivorology**

Readings

Bell, D. (2012) 'Deaths in police custody. Case study: Christopher Alder', *The Bureau of Investigative Journalism*, 7 February. Available at: https://www.thebureauinvestigates.com/2012/02/07/case-study-christopher-alder/

Coleman, S., Jemphrey, A., Scraton, P. and Skidmore, P. (1990) 'Hillsborough and after: the Liverpool experience, first report: April 1990'. Available at: http://hillsborough.independent.gov.uk/repository/SYP000046650001.html

Hillsborough Independent Panel (2012) *Hillsborough: The report of the Hillsborough Independent Panel*, September. London: The Stationery Office. Available at: http://hillsborough.independent.gov.uk/repository/report/HIP_report.pdf

RESTORATIVE JUSTICE AND VICTIMISATION

Restorative justice brings victims, offenders and the community together to talk about and respond to crime and other types of harmful behaviour. It has its roots in Christian beliefs and indigenous tribal justice from North America, Australia and South Africa, and aims to achieve healing, reconciliation and forgiveness as opposed to the more common criminal justice focus on proof, guilt and punishment (Zehr, 1990). Although often understood as an *alternative* to criminal justice, in many instances, it is *additional* to the formal justice system. However, restorative justice is also increasingly used outside the criminal justice system in settings such as schools to deal with bullying and discipline, workplaces to deal with grievances, and communities to deal with neighbourhood disputes. It has also been successfully used in divided and transitional societies in the form of truth commissions designed to help address historical wrongs and build a sense of shared nationhood. Northern Ireland, South Africa and Rwanda would be examples where restorative justice has been used for these purposes (Johnstone, 2011).

There are many models of restorative justice, including victim–offender mediation, family group conferencing, sentencing circles and youth offender panels, but they all contain a core set of principles that define them as types of restorative justice. The most important of these principles is the creation of a safe space in which people can talk to each other about the harm caused, why it was caused, how it has affected them and how it can be resolved. This is intended to generate mutual understanding through a managed conversation, with a trained mediator or facilitator taking responsibility for organising a meeting and preparing those who will attend. Other important restorative principles are that the process should be voluntary and inclusive – involving not just the victim and offender, but family members and relevant community members, such as school teachers or shop owners (Johnstone, 2011).

Restorative justice starts from the position that crime and other types of harm damage relationships and it is these that need to be restored (Zehr, 1990). Unlike a courtroom trial, restorative justice avoids questions of guilt and often replaces criminal justice language with its own terminology; for example, restorative 'encounters' often take place when the 'wrongdoer' accepts responsibility for what they have done. Lawyers are not involved and the purpose of each restorative encounter is for those involved to reach some common understanding that results in a contract about how the harm will be 'repaired'. This might be a formal apology, financial reparation, community service or additional support mechanisms to ensure the harmful behaviour does not continue. These restorative contracts must be decided and agreed upon by all parties and should provide the basis of repairing the harm and rebuilding relationships between victim, offender and the community (Zehr, 1990). At its best, this process can be genuinely transformational and there are some very powerful examples of victims and offenders crying, hugging and becoming friends in the aftermath of a successful restorative encounter.

One of the most important aspects of restorative justice is the central involvement of the victim in the decision-making process. In a courtroom trial, it is the state that acts as the victim. Crimes are committed against the state – not against an individual – and it is the state that prosecutes and punishes. This has led to criticism that the trial system ignores the victim, relegating them to witnesses rather than active participants in the criminal justice process. Restorative justice can comprise different meanings amid different groups and in different contexts. Although this can be problematic, there is some agreement that when implemented properly, restorative justice provides an entirely different approach. This approach removes the state, the judiciary and legal professionals entirely and puts authority for crime and conflict back into the hands of those directly involved. This had led to some concerns that restorative justice may place an unnecessary burden on victims and possibly lead them to be further harmed by having to relive traumatic events or face aggression or disinterest at the hands of the offender (Green, 2007). Further fears that the victim might also be unduly disadvantaged by an offender-focused process that criminals might take advantage of and that fails to deter them from reoffending appear not to have been realised. In sum, restorative justice should not be assumed to be an alternative panacea with regard to justice for victims, the rehabilitation of the offender and the negation of recidivism. However, some evidence suggests that, in general, restorative justice does have a positive impact on reconviction rates and leads to improvement in the victim's satisfaction, security and sense of closure when compared to courtroom justice (Sherman and Strang, 2007; Shapland et al, 2011).

SIMON GREEN

See also: Criminal Justice and Victims; Justice and Victims

Readings

Green, S. (2007) 'Restorative justice and the victims' movement', in G. Johnstone and D. Van Ness (eds) *A handbook of restorative justice*. Cullompton: Willan Publishing, pp 171–93.

Johnstone, G. (2011) *Restorative justice: Ideas, values, debates* (2nd edn). London: Sage.

Shapland, J., Robinson, G. and Sorsby, A. (2011) *Restorative justice in practice*. London: Routledge.

Sherman, L. and Strang, H. (2007) *Restorative justice: The evidence*. London: Smith Institute.

Zehr, H. (1990) *Changing lenses: A new focus for crime justice*. Scottsdale, PA: Herald Press.

RISK, RISK MANAGEMENT AND VICTIMISATION

The importance of risk, risk management and victimisation in relation to crime is a relatively recent phenomenon; however, Goodey (2005) argues that it has moved from a simplistic determination of the likelihood of a crime occurring, to being adopted as a term that covers a wide range of social insecurities. Garland (2001) identifies a recent ideological shift from crime being seen as individual pathology or moral aberration, to crime being seen as a risk to be managed in the context of the failure of the rehabilitative ideal, and a new regressive and less inclusive civic narrative. Feeley and Simon's (1992) 'new penology' identified the necessity to calculate the risk of crime actuarially and manage it appropriately, which has affected the discourses and policies on offenders, who are defined in terms of the risk they present, and victims, who are personally responsible for minimising personal risk. Cohen and Felson's (1979, p 588) routine activity theory takes a risk-based approach, identifying the differing risks for victimisation that individuals and/or places present. It refers to the presence of 'likely offenders', 'suitable targets' and the 'absence of capable guardians against crime', rather than focusing on the characteristics of offenders. Within this context, Kemshall (2003) argues that the approach to 'crime control' in modern neoliberal states has undermined the Hobbesian notion of the social contract between the individual and the state. Instead, individuals have become personally responsible for avoiding risky behaviour and taking adequate security measures against crime. This personal responsibility becomes a measure of good citizenship instead of assuming collective protection by the state.

However, perceptions on the responsibility of risk avoidance do affect judgements on the deservedness of victims and how they are formally and substantively treated in the criminal justice system. Early victimology looked at victim culpability, with Mendelsohn's research on 'victim-proneness' and Wolfgang's 'victim precipitation' (see Goodey, 2005). Goodey (2005) argues that while these ideas have been discredited, the criminal justice system continues to blame victims, most notably, in cases of rape, where adverse judgements can be made about 'risky behaviour' based on lifestyle, clothing and alcohol consumption. This is known to affect decisions as to whether to prosecute, conviction rates and sentencing. Victims of corporate crimes are also judged differently to those who fall foul of more traditional crimes. The harms caused by problematic corporate behaviour are often defined as accidental, or 'a disaster', and Croall (2007) argues that the principle of *caveat emptor* (let the buyer beware) results in consumers being blamed for not making 'informed choices' and also blaming themselves for being 'taken in'. Workers may also be blamed for increasing their personal risk by apparently ignoring health and safety regulations. Apart from this, Dignan (cited in Croall, 2007) argues that victims of white-collar or corporate crime are generally excluded from 'victim-oriented policies', such as support in court or state compensation schemes.

Levels of risk that victims actually face appear to play little part in judging their worthiness, this being associated more with the 'harms' they suffer, their vulnerabilities and whether they conform with the 'ideal victim' type (Christie, 1986). In comparison to the elderly, young unemployed men, particularly from minority ethnic groups, are routinely labelled as 'offenders' rather than being recognised as a member of a vulnerable, frequently victimised group (Green, 2007). Vulnerability and the risk of victimisation also have a political currency and market value. Williams (1999, cited in Green, 2007) argues that the greater the level of harm likely to be suffered, the greater the need to take preventive actions to minimise risks. Bauman (2006, cited in Green, 2007, p 111) argues that 'the market thrives under conditions of insecurity, it capitalises on human fears and feelings of haplessness', which fuel the demand for security goods, private policing, gated communities and other technologies to minimise the risk of victimisation, the take up of which becomes normalised as a responsibility of citizenship.

JILL JAMESON and KATE STRUDWICK

See also: **Blame and Victims; Deviant Victims**

Readings
Christie, N. (1986) 'The ideal victim', in E. Fattah (ed) *From crime policy to victim policy: Reorientating the justice system.* Basingstoke: Macmillan Press, pp 17–30.
Cohen, L. and Felson, M. (1979) 'Social change and crime rate trends: a routine activity approach', *Sociological Review*, 44: 588–608.
Croall, H. (2007) 'Victims of white collar and corporate crime', in P. Davis, P. Francis and C. Greer (eds) *Victims, crime and society.* London: Sage, pp 50–77.
Feeley, M.M. and Simon, J. (1992) 'The new penology: notes on the emerging strategy of corrections and its implications', *Criminology*, 30(4): 449–74.
Garland, D. (2001) *The culture of control: Crime and social order in contemporary society.* New York, NY: Oxford University Press.
Goodey, J. (2005) *Victims and victimology: Research, policy and practice.* Harlow: Pearson Education Ltd.
Green, S. (2007) 'Crime, victimisation and vulnerability', in S. Walklate (ed) *Handbook of victims and victimology.* Cullompton: Willan, pp 91–118.

Kemshall, H. (2003) *Understanding risk in criminal justice*. Maidenhead: Open University Press.

ROLE OF VICTIMS IN COMMON LAW JURISDICTIONS

The common law legal system has largely been inherited by countries originally colonised by the British, including the US, Canada, New Zealand, India, Nigeria and Australia. The origins of the system can be traced from the time of the Norman Conquest of England in 1066, where King's Courts travelled across England presiding over local disputes and applying general rules developed in the context of previous disputes with similar circumstances. These general rules formed the basis of the common law legal system. The key feature of the system is the adversarial trial, where the presiding judicial officer plays a relatively passive role and it is rather the parties to the case that decide how to present their respective cases, relying mainly on witnesses (including victims) giving live oral evidence and then being subject to cross-examination (Langbein, 2003).

The role of victims of crime in the criminal justice system (CJS) has evolved over history and continues to develop. While there are some differences between jurisdictions within common law nations, two overall trends are clearly discernible. The first was a result of the parties to the adversarial trial changing from the victim and the defendant, to the present day, where the parties are the state and the defendant. This trend evolved over some time and resulted in the sidelining of the victim (Victorian Law Reform Commission, 2015). The second trend, starting from the 1970s with the advent of the modern 'victims' movement', sees an attempt to provide greater consideration for victims, including perhaps restoring some role for victims in their dealings with the CJS.

From pre-Norman times to the start of the 1400s, the CJS could be seen as a private dispute system similar to the way common law civil claims operate today, whereby prosecutions were conducted almost solely by the individual crime victim against wrongdoers (defendants). Victims were responsible for the investigation of crime, the instigation of criminal charges and the prosecution of those charges through the courts. Victims paid for warrants, did their own investigative work (or paid somebody to do it for them) and hired their own lawyer to draw up the indictment and prosecute the offender. The victim was the key decision-maker in the CJS and the direct beneficiary of it because restitution to the victim was the main form of punishment, with a system of fixed payments for various wrongs established. In parallel with this, however, there was increased involvement by the king and his officials in the settlement of criminal justice disputes. From the early 1200s, some serious offences (such as homicide, robbery, arson and treason) came to be seen as breaches of the king's peace and were prosecuted by agents of the king. This was the beginnings of the distinct branch of criminal law (as opposed to civil law), which focused on public interest and the maintenance of society, with offences being seen as against the state rather than individual victims (Kirchengast, 2006).

Although right up until the early 1700s the state had become increasingly involved in the CJS, in the majority of cases, victims were still parties to cases and thus retained the central role and responsibility for prosecutions. Significant changes in British society since the 1700s, such as mass industrialisation and urbanisation, resulting in the need for a centralised police force, led to the state gradually taking over from the victim as the party to proceedings. From the mid-1850s onwards, this led to the sidelining of the victim, who virtually lost all decision-making power. The state assumed the functions of criminal investigation and the identification, prosecution and punishment of offenders. The emphasis on restitution to the victim as the usual penalty changed to the emphasis being on deterrence and punishment, with prison sentences becoming the main form of punishment.

The victim's role in the CJS was thus reduced to two matters: first, deciding to report the crime against them (thereby, in most cases, triggering the CJS); and, second, being required to give evidence at court if the prosecution desired them to do so. Victims lost the ability to decide whether or not they wished to testify, and no longer being a party to proceedings also meant that they could not be legally represented at court. While victims still retained a residual power to launch a private prosecution, this power was used infrequently and is a very limited one anyway.

Since the 1970s in Britain and elsewhere, there has been considerable advocacy on behalf of victims. Disparate victim advocacy organisations and individuals argued that the sidelining of victims had led to the victim becoming the 'forgotten person' of the CJS, who thus often suffers from the phenomenon of 'secondary victimisation'. These advocates have been at the forefront of changes to various aspects of the CJS, the main purpose of which is to ensure that the system treats victims better and, perhaps more controversially from a civil liberties perspective (Henderson, 1985), reinstate some role for victims in the system. These changes have come in the form of victims' rights documents, which many governments have agreed to since the 1970s. While these may vary considerably between common law jurisdictions, they often set out in a wide-ranging manner how criminal justice agencies and individuals should treat victims, and the specific consideration that must be provided to victims at various stages of the CJS. Although rarely enforceable from a strict legal perspective, these documents do attempt to make the victim more of the focus within criminal justice decision-making and thereby endeavour to redress to some extent the sidelining of the victim. They may consist of one or more documents in combination (which might take the form of administrative directions or codes of conduct for criminal justice officials and agencies), legislation or even constitutional provisions, as found in many states in the US.

The principles contained in such documents commonly address multiple issues. First, there is normally a general exhortation for criminal justice personnel and agencies to treat victims fairly and with respect for their rights and dignity. There are also various measures to protect the safety, security and privacy of victims as they navigate the CJS. Such measures include separate court waiting areas for victims and defendants where feasible and making it less traumatic for victims when testifying at court, for example, by limiting cross-examination of previous sexual history, utilising screens and closed-circuit television during testimony to reduce contact with the defendant, the non-disclosure of victims' identifying information, and providing for a civil order that makes it a criminal offence for the defendant to be within a certain distance from the victim. These measures are often emphasised for particularly vulnerable victims, such as children and sexual assault victims. Another category of measures tries to ensure that victims are provided with the information relevant to their role in the criminal case proceedings, including the progress of the case, their role as witnesses and an understanding of aspects of criminal procedure. There is also often a requirement that information be provided to enable victims to access non-criminal justice remedies that have also come about due to modern victim advocacy – various victim support services and government-funded victim compensation. Other important measures are those that attempt to provide reparation or compensation to victims, such as greater emphasis on and use of restitution orders as part of the offender's sentence. The modern movement towards the implementation of more restorative justice principles and processes may also facilitate reparation for victims, and arguably provide them with a greater sense of psychological satisfaction and participation in the outcome of cases. Victims' rights principles often also attempt to provide victims with a voice during various important stages of the CJS, such as bail, plea bargaining, sentencing and parole, by allowing victims to provide information and their perspectives to relevant decision-makers. Perhaps the most outstanding example of this is that most common law jurisdictions now have legislation allowing victims to provide the sentencing court with a victim impact/personal statement – this is probably the most tangible form of the return of a victim role in the CJS.

The effectiveness of these principles clearly varies between common law jurisdictions and is often dependent on: how seriously criminal justice officials and agencies take the principles; the resources that are devoted to their implementation; to what extent the principles are written in mandatory terms; whether there is any adverse consequences for officials and agencies in not abiding by the required principles; and a myriad of other factors that may be particular to the jurisdiction in question. In summary, these are clearly piecemeal reforms that without fundamental changes to the adversarial system, can only go some of the way in redressing the sidelining of victims.

SAM GARKAWE

See also: **Victims of Crime; Victims' Rights**

Readings

Henderson, L. (1985) 'The wrongs of victims' rights', *Stanford Law Review*, 37: 937–1021.

Kirchengast, T. (2006) *The victim in criminal law and justice*. Basingstoke: Palgrave MacMillan.

Langbein, J. (2003) *The origins of the adversarial criminal trial*. Oxford: Oxford University Press.

Sebba, L. (1996) *Third parties: Victims and the criminal justice system*. Ohio, OH: Ohio State University Press.

Victorian Law Reform Commission (2015) *The role of victims of crime in the criminal trial process, information paper no. 1: History, concepts and theory*. Melbourne: Victorian Law Reform Commission.

ROLE OF VICTIMS IN INTERNATIONAL LAW

The traditional conception of crime victims is that they are victims of common crimes such as assault and theft that are committed by private individuals, and not generally by the state or its agents. For this reason, they have not been thought of as having a role in international law (IL), IL being conventionally confined to the legal system between nations. However, these perceptions are changing and states are no longer considered to be the only legitimate subjects of IL – increasingly, individuals are seen to have rights and obligations under IL. Various international norms and standards have been developed in modern times that set out the manner in which states should treat crime victims. The most prominent international instrument in this regard is the 1985 United Nations (UN) Declaration of Basic Principles of Justice for Victims of Crime and Abuse of Power.

In terms of the relationship between crime victims and IL, three branches of IL stand out as where a crime victim may now be seen to have some role. The first and probably least helpful to victims is international humanitarian law, which is invoked only where there is an armed conflict or declared war taking place at the time of, or in the aftermath of, the crime. Civilian non-combatants subject to crimes that may be seen as the responsibility of one of the warring parties to the conflict, and combatants and prisoners of war being subject to crimes where there is no lawful excuse for such crimes under national law or IL, have no direct remedy under international humanitarian law. While this body of law declares that specified persons, such as civilian non-combatants and prisoners of war, are 'protected persons' and grants them certain rights, it does not directly provide such persons with an independent right to seek a remedy when their rights are violated (Schabas, 2011, p 343). The laws merely allow for the victim's state to take up their situation with the state or entity responsible for their victimisation, and these parties will hopefully agree to provide the victim with a remedy.

The second area of IL where victims may have a role is international human rights law. Most crime victims suffer either a violation of their bodily integrity rights (stemming from crimes such as homicide, assault against the person [including torture], robbery or sexual assault) or their property rights (stemming from crimes such as theft, burglary, robbery or fraud). Victims of such crimes thus suffer a violation of well-accepted international human rights norms. In cases where it is the state itself or one of its agents that has committed the crime against the victim, international human rights law is clear in obligating the relevant state to provide a remedy to the victim. Where the crime is committed by a private individual, it is not the state itself that is the direct cause of the violation. However, under international human rights law, the state has a duty to reasonably prevent such crimes taking place, and where such a crime does take place, it also has a duty to provide a remedy to the crime victim within their legal system. Where a state can be shown to have failed on either of these duties, there may then be a limited remedy for individuals who are the victims of such violations under international human rights law. There are now many major international human rights treaties that provide individuals with a right to complain (referred to as an 'individual complaints mechanism') to a body established by a relevant treaty to ensure state compliance with the treaty (such as the UN Human Rights Committee, established pursuant to the International Covenant on Civil and Political Rights). The substance of the complaint is that their rights under the treaty have been violated and they have been unable to obtain a remedy. This body can then issue a non-binding finding that may request the violating state to provide the individual with a remedy. In circumstances where the human rights violation amounts to a crime, this gives the crime victim only a limited right to a remedy for two reasons: first, such a right is dependent on the state first agreeing to the individual complaints mechanism; and, second, the state must be willing to carry out the ruling of the relevant body as, in reality, it is difficult to force a violating state to abide by the ruling.

The third and most promising area of IL where crime victims increasingly are seen as having a role is international criminal law. It is here where victims of crimes that amount to international crimes have increasingly been given a role in modern international courts or tribunals established to prosecute persons accused of such crimes. In the past, such tribunals and courts have followed the common law criminal justice model, where victims have traditionally had few rights. However, recently, international and part-international tribunals and courts have moved away from the pure adversarial criminal justice model and incorporated aspects of other models that provide some rights for victims. The most outstanding example of this is the International Criminal Court (ICC), which has operated since 1 July 2002 to prosecute the international crimes of genocide, crimes against humanity and war crimes (Funk, 2010; Leyh, 2010; Schabas, 2011). A person must first apply to the ICC to be recognised as a 'victim' of one of the crimes that are being prosecuted before the court according to the criteria and rules laid down in the court's Statute and Rules of Evidence and Procedure (Rome Statute of the International Criminal Court, 1998; Rules of Procedure and Evidence of the International Criminal Court, 2002). Once accepted as a 'victim', and provided that their 'personal interests are affected', then they are allowed to present the court with their 'views and concerns' at 'stages of the proceedings determined to be appropriate by the Court'. In order to do this, they may apply to the court to have their own legal representation appointed on their behalf during court proceedings. It is important to understand that recognised victims are only *participants* and not *parties* to the proceedings, and they thus do not have the full rights that the parties (the prosecutor and defendant) have. Nevertheless, the rights to victim participation are a very significant recognition under international criminal law that crime victims may have an input into the proceedings in their own right that is not dependent on the prosecutor. Not surprisingly, there have been considerable difficulties in implementing such a scheme of victim representation, but this is understandable given the sheer numbers of victims that could potentially be victims of the types of crimes the ICC deals with. The other very significant right of crime victims under the ICC is their right to seek reparation for the harm they have suffered, and the ICC establishes a trust fund for this purpose (Rome Statute of the International Criminal Court, 1998: s 79; Rules of Procedure and Evidence of the International Criminal Court, 2002). Similar participation rights for victims have also been established in other international or semi-international tribunals or courts, such as the Extraordinary Chambers in the Courts of Cambodia (Leyh, 2010).

SAM GARKAWE

See also: **Role of Victims in Common Law Jurisdictions; United Nations Declaration of the Basic Principles of Justice for Victims of Crime and Abuse of Power; Victims of Crime**

Readings

Funk, M. (2010) *Victims' rights and advocacy at the International Criminal Court*. Oxford: Oxford University Press.

Leyh, B.M. (2010) *Procedural justice? Victim participation in international criminal proceedings*. Utrecht: Intersentia.

Rules of Procedure and Evidence of the International Criminal Court (2002) 3–10 September, No ICC-ASP/1/3.

Rome Statute of the International Criminal Court (1998) 17 July, UN Doc. A/CONF. 183/9, 2187 UN TS 90.

Schabas, W. (2011) *An introduction to the International Criminal Court* (4th edn). Cambridge: Cambridge University Press.

S

SEXUAL OFFENDING, VICTIMS AND THE COURTS

The victims of all crimes were for many years the 'forgotten player' in the criminal justice system, whether they were the victims of sexual crime or any other crime. In the UK, that position has changed over the last 30 years and increasing provisions have been made to assist the victim of crime; additional measures have been made for the victims of sexual crimes.

In the criminal courts, procedural support has been included in the court procedures themselves. Some complainants acting as witnesses in a sexual offences trial may feel particularly vulnerable; others may feel intimidated in the presence of the person alleged to have committed the crime. The whole experience of a criminal court itself can also be intimidating. The surroundings are unfamiliar and the formalities of the court itself can be threatening.

Fierce cross-examination by barristers is not a pleasant experience. In one child sexual exploitation hearing, a barrister mocked some children, saying that they were 'enjoying all the attention from police and social services'; another told them that he supposed 'it's better to be a victim than a slag' (Norfolk, 2015, p 4). 'Special measures' have been introduced into courts to make the experience easier for both adult and child witnesses.

Section 32 of the Criminal Justice Act 1988 introduced live video-links for children under 14 to give their evidence to court. The government held back from introducing any pre-recorded tapes of statements or cross-examinations being used as evidence in court. Chelmsford Crown Court achieved the distinction of being the first UK court to hear evidence on a live video-link from a 13-year-old victim in a rape case; the judge reportedly tried to put the girl at ease with the words 'What's it like being on the telly, not too bad?' (*The Independent*, 1989). The Criminal Justice Act 1991 introduced the use of pre-recorded video interviews of children in court by amending the Criminal Justice Act 1988 with a new section 32A; the child was still expected to be available for cross-examination and the Act did not contain provisions for pre-recorded cross-examinations.

The Youth Justice and Criminal Evidence Act 1999 introduced eight more 'special measures' for what it termed the 'eligible witness' (ss 16–17) – in effect, this meant the child witness and the vulnerable or intimidated adult witness. They were:

- screening to prevent the witness seeing the defendant;
- live CCTV links to speak to the witness in another room;
- the witness giving evidence in private;
- the removal of wigs and gowns by court personnel;
- pre-recorded witness statements ('evidence in chief');
- pre-recorded cross-examination of the witness;
- use of an 'intermediary' by a witness; and
- use of an aid to communication by a witness. (Youth Justice and Criminal Evidence Act 1999, ss 22–30)

The use of an 'intermediary' was to assist a witness with, say, learning disabilities or other communication problems to present their evidence as clearly as possible to the court. Although the use of pre-recorded cross-examinations of witnesses was now on the statute book, the government still held back from implementing the relevant section 28 of the Act.

Three years later, the government returned to the subject and the Coroners and Justice Act 2009 amended the Youth Justice and Criminal Evidence Act 1999 with more 'special measures':

- raising the upper age limit of child witnesses automatically eligible for special measures from those under 17 to include those under 18;
- providing child witnesses with more choice and flexibility about how they give their evidence;
- making specific provision for the presence of a supporter to the witness in the live-link room;
- relaxing the restrictions on a witness giving additional evidence in chief after the witness's video-recorded statement has been admitted as evidence in chief; and
- making special provision for the admissibility of video-recorded evidence in chief of adult complainants in sexual offence cases in the Crown Court. (Coroners and Justice Act 2009, ss 98–103)

The search to make life easier for vulnerable and intimidated witnesses in criminal courts has continued. In 2012, the question of pre-recorded cross-examination was returned to:

> We are working to resolve the complex issues associated with implementation of pre-trial video-recorded cross examination (section 28 of the Youth Justice and Criminal Evidence Act 1999) with a view to establishing whether the provision can be made to work in practice. (Ministry of Justice, 2012, para 94)

Pilot measures for recorded pre-trial cross-examinations of children and other vulnerable witnesses eventually started in England in Leeds, Liverpool and Kingston on Thames in April 2014 (Ministry of Justice, 2014), 15 years after this had first been recommended.

TERRY THOMAS

See also: **Policy and Victims in the UK**

Readings
Ministry of Justice (2012) 'Getting it right for victims and witnesses: the government's response', Cm 8397, July, London.
Ministry of Justice (2014) 'First victims spared harrowing court room under pre-recorded evidence pilot', press release, 28 April.
Norfolk, A. (2015) 'They are slags, not victims, lawyer tells grooming trial', *The Times*, 7 March.
The Independent (1989) 'Girl gives evidence by video link', 10 January.

SEXUAL VIOLENCE

There is no universal definition of sexual violence; however, the World Health Organisation (2002, p 149) defines it as:

> any sexual act, attempt to obtain a sexual act, unwanted sexual comments or advances, or acts to traffic, or otherwise directed, against a person's sexuality using coercion, by any person regardless of their relationship to the victim, in any setting, including but not limited to home and work.

'Sexual violence' is thus an umbrella term used to describe a range of behaviours, the majority of which have been criminalised in the UK. Rape and sexual assault are two of the more serious offences contained in the primary legislation governing sexual offences in the UK. The Sexual Offences Act 2003, however, includes unwanted sexual touching, voyeurism and indecent exposure (commonly referred to as 'flashing') as sexual offences. Sexual violence against certain groups in society has been categorised separately, for example, sexual violence against children is often termed 'child sexual abuse', whereas offences against older people is termed 'elder abuse'. In the context of an intimate relationship, which research suggests is where the majority of sexual violence occurs, it overlaps with definitions and approaches to domestic violence.

Both men and women can be victims and perpetrators of sexual violence; however, globally, the majority of reported sexual violence involves a female victim and a male perpetrator (World Health Organisation, 2003). As such, sexual violence is considered a gendered phenomenon and is typically categorised as a form of violence against women. It is difficult to get accurate statistics on the prevalence of sexual violence. Sexual victimisation is often under-reported and unreported due to the shame and stigma that these offences carry and the culture of disbelief that exists in the criminal justice system. For example, in the UK, the Office for National Statistics estimates that only 15% of victims report the offence to the police. Furthermore, national and international victimisation surveys, which generally obtain much higher statistics and are considered a more reliable form of data collection, are methodologically limited as they only include samples of people aged 16–59 and do not include people living in institutions such as prisons, hospitals or care homes. This is problematic as it excludes significant proportions of the population and often those who are considered the most vulnerable. However, the most recent national statistics from the Home Office in 2015 estimate that, in England and Wales, 2.2% of women and 0.7% of men experienced some form of sexual assault in the previous 12 months, equating to over 400,000 women and over 90,000 men. In 2012/13, there were more than 22,000 recorded sexual offences against a child aged under 18 (Jütte et al, 2014).

The negative consequences and impacts of sexual violence have been well documented and include depression, drug and alcohol misuse, fears and phobias, high levels of anxiety, and suicidal feelings. Negative health impacts include increased risk of high cholesterol, heart disease, stroke and problems with the immune system, while a range of mental health issues have been associated with rape and sexual assault, including overall poor mental health, self-harm, suicidal thoughts, panic attacks and post-traumatic stress disorder (Chen et al, 2010; Machado et al, 2011).

The focus of researchers and campaigners has primarily been directed at sexual violence perpetrated against young people in the context of date rape or domestic violence. Sexual violence in war zones has received much less attention, with developments in this area still very recent. In the context of conflict zones, sexual violence is viewed as a weapon of war, a deliberate strategy used by military personnel and those fighting in wars. It has multiple uses, including ethnic cleansing, which refers to the systematic wiping out of cultures or ethnicities, for example, via the impregnating of women or the purposeful transmission of contagious viruses and infections, such as human immunodeficiency virus (HIV). Furthermore, as blame and shame are often attached to women who are raped in these communities, it serves as a strategy to break down and erode communities. Moreover, as men dominate the front line in war zones, this is a way of directly affecting women in the countries and areas where the war is concentrated.

Feminist theories have dominated sexual violence research and discourses and have made unique contributions to the field. They position sexual violence as a consequence of the inequalities that exist between women and men, rooted in a patriarchal society that views women as subordinate to men and attaches value to their sexuality. Sexual violence is seen as a weapon used by men to assert their masculinity and control and to oppress women. Feminist theories have arguably had the biggest influence on policy and practice developments; however, other theories exist in the literature. Some opposing criminological theories position rape within a psychopathology model, viewing perpetrators as mentally ill and unable to control their sexual urges. Similarly, biological theories of rape consider sexual violence to be motivated by sexual desire and an inability to control that desire. Such theorists are now in a minority; however, there is still work published from this standpoint.

HANNAH BOWS

See also: **Blame and Victims; Gender and Victimisation; Genocide, Harm and Victimisation**

Readings

Chen, L. P., Murad, M. H., Para, M. L. Colbenson, K. M. Sattler, A. L., Goranson, E. N., Elamin, M. B., Seime, R. J., Shinozaki, G. Prokop, L. J. and Zirakzadeh, A. (2010) 'Sexual abuse and lifetime diagnosis of psychiatric disorders: systematic review and meta-analysis', *Mayo Clinic Proceedings*, 85(7): 618–29.

Jütte, S., Bentley, H., Miller, P. and Jetha, N. (2014) *How safe are our children?*, London: NSPCC.

Machado, C.L., De Azevado, R.C.S., Facuri, C.O., Vieira, M.-J.N. and Fernandes, A.-M.S. (2011) 'Posttraumatic stress disorder, depression, and hopelessness in women who are victims of sexual violence', *International Journal of Gynaecology and Obstetrics*, 113: 58–62.

Office for National Statistics (2015) *Violent crime and sexual offences – overview.* London: ONS.

World Health Organisation (2002) *Sexual violence.* Geneva, Switzerland: WHO.

World Health Organisation (2003) *Guidelines for medico-legal care for victims of sexual violence.* Geneva, Switzerland: WHO.

SEX WORKERS AND VICTIMISATION

Sex work is a highly contentious issue that creates massive debate around: choice and lack of agency; abolitionism and rights-based approaches; and arguments for decriminalisation and strengthening existing law. Sex work, in and of itself, is not illegal and is not, in and of itself, inherently dangerous; however, some sectors can be. Street sex workers account for around 25% of all sex workers in the UK, yet around 95% of sex worker homicides occur in this group.

To be a sex worker in the UK today can be 'a risky business' (Sanders, 2004). Sex workers are victims of murder, rape, violence and a range of other crimes but are also subject to cultural issues of stigma, discrimination and the law. They are victims from a range of perpetrators, for example: residents who do not want sex workers in their area; passers-by; and police officers. Kinnell (2009) breaks this down to three types of perpetrators, namely, non-clients, pseudo-clients and bad clients. The non-clients are the general passers-by, the vigilantes, partners, family members, 'muggers', robbers, drug dealers, pimps. Some of these may be violent towards sex workers in non-working situations, but others may simply attack sex workers on the street or throw objects from vehicles or enter indoor premises by force or by posing as some kind of official. This is by far the largest group, but only some of the violence that they commit is likely to be reported to outreach workers, let alone the police. The continuum of abuse by passers-by, residents, young people and so forth is endemic in many street-working areas, and ranges from insults to assaults, robbery and, in some cases, murder.

Pseudo-clients comprise the people posing as clients in order to attack or rob sex workers. These are people who begin by behaving as clients, using the 'client disguise', they pay or offer to pay, but then turn violent and force repayment, force acts that have not been paid for, refuse to use condoms and frequently rob the sex worker of all her money. A client is someone who pays for sex: those who do not pay are therefore not clients but perpetrators. Bad clients are clients who appear to believe that having paid, they are entitled to commit violence. There are a small number of men among the men who have murdered who are known to have paid for sex.

However, even though it is a certainty that sex workers are victims of crime and harm both from a range of perpetrators and through stigma and discrimination, they are not passive victims allowing such victimisation to happen to them. Every day, a proportion of sex workers go to work and do what they have to do to survive. They are resisting victimisation in the form of Ugly Mugs and Dodgy Punter/Bad Date lists throughout the world. Ugly Mugs was set up by the Prostitution Collective in May 1986 in Victoria, Australia. The term 'Ugly Mugs' is used to describe punters, or people posing as punters, who commit violent and other crimes against sex workers or who become problematic. As the majority of Ugly Mugs were not being reported to the police, they realised that sharing descriptions of Ugly Mugs could warn other sex workers about people who posed a danger to them.

The first schemes in the UK started in Birmingham and Edinburgh in 1989 and were run by sex work projects. Since then, similar schemes have been developed by many sex work projects throughout the UK. This is true resistance by sex workers for sex workers and has solved many crimes. There now exists a National Ugly Mugs Scheme in the UK also.

Importantly, what was also known was that crimes against sex workers indicated something deeper than just regular crimes. For sex work projects, these crimes fitted the 'hate crime' mantel because project workers (and the sex workers themselves) felt that the sex workers were being attacked *because* they were sex workers. Merseyside Police (Liverpool, England) agreed with this and in the midst of one of the most famous sex worker murder sprees that the UK has ever seen, the then Chief Constable Bernard Hogan Howe (2006) made the following declaration:

> Merseyside Police are determined to bring all perpetrators of Hate Crime to justice…. We were the first force in the country to recognise and respond to attacks against sex workers as a form of hate crime. The challenge is to build the trust of those vulnerable to attack to report offences and information to us.

In Merseyside, therefore, the police are agents of resistance, fighting for change alongside the sex workers.

In conclusion, sex workers in the UK continue to be discriminated against, culturally stigmatised and subject to an array of crimes, harms and victimisation from a range of perpetrators. Due to resistance on the part of sex workers and sex work projects, some progress is being made in some quarters of the criminal justice process. This can be seen in the recognition of crimes and harms perpetrated against sex workers as a form of hate crime.

MICHELLE STOOPS

See also: **Hate Crime and Victimisation; Resistance to Crime, Harm and Victimisation; Sex Work, Hate Crime and Victimisation**

Readings

Hogan Howe, B. (2006) 'Web address to serving officers', author's private collection.

Kinnell, H. (2009) *Violence and sex work in Britain.* Cullompton: Willan Publishing.

Sanders, T. (2004) *Sex work: A risky business.* Cullompton: Willan Publishing.

SEX WORK, HATE CRIME AND VICTIMISATION

The term 'hate crime' encapsulates a 'type of crime, rather than a specific offence within a penal code'; it 'describes a concept, rather than a legal definition' (OSC and ODIHR, 2009, p 16). Thus, hate crime 'refers to prejudicial or biased criminal acts against a person or property that are motivated by a victim's actual or perceived sexuality, race, ethnicity, disability, religion and gender' (Corteen, 2014, p 175). This definition has also been extended to sex workers (Campbell and Stoops, 2010; Campbell, 2015). The following discussion documents the establishment of the crimes against, and the victimisation of, sex workers as hate crime. It focuses on changes made in the UK by Merseyside Police.

Although the concept of 'hate crime' is contested, it 'has become embedded within law, criminal justice systems, academia, politics and society' (Corteen, 2014, p 175). Hate crime legislation was introduced in the 1980s and 1990s in the UK and the US. Hate crime legislation encourages and enables the infliction of more severe punishments due to crimes being motivated by hate. Problems can occur when seeking justice for victims of hate crimes. However, '[h]ate crime laws are important' in three ways (OSCE and ODIHR, 2009, p 7): first, they explicitly condemn motives of bias and/or hatred on the part of the offender; second, they acknowledge the deep harm caused to an immediate victim, to 'the group with which that victim identifies him or herself' and to communities (OSCE and ODIHR, 2009, p 11); and, third, they convey the message that those affected deserve the protection of the criminal justice system. Such laws are especially important with regard to sex worker hate victimisation as in the UK, the '"othering", marginalisation and criminalisation' of sex workers contribute to a climate in which such victimisation 'can flourish' (Campbell, 2015, p 58).

Sex workers have been 'historically over policed and under protected' (Campbell, 2015, p 57). Amid the various manifestations of sex work, sex workers are at a greater risk of, and have a greater actual experience of, harassment, victimisation and harm than the general public. This is especially so if the sex worker is female and working on the streets (Campbell, 2015). Sex workers are victims of institutional and cultural stigma, discrimination, and the law, and they are subjected to a range of crimes committed by a range of perpetrators (see 'Sex Workers and Victimisation' in this companion). Sex workers (particularly female sex workers) are 'a group whose experiences of victimisation fit within a number of established definitions of hate crime but who have sat outside the established hate crime groups' (Campbell, 2015, p 55). The commission of sex worker hate crime is underpinned by intolerance, bias, discrimination and hatred *because they are sex workers*. Yet, sex workers have been constructed as a deviant, undesirable public nuisance unworthy of criminal justice protection. Sex workers fail to meet the requirements of the 'ideal victim' (Christie, 1986) and their status as victims is denied. The positioning of victimised sex workers as 'deviant victims', 'risky victims' and the 'victimological other' has resulted in their predominant absence from discussions about hate crime within academia and within criminal justice policies and practices.

Research in the city of Liverpool (in Merseyside) documented that 80% of sex workers had experienced violence during the course of their work and that there was vast under-reporting of such crimes to the police (Campbell and Stoops, 2010). In the UK and elsewhere, sex workers are excluded from police policies and practices concerned with such crimes and victimisation (Campbell, 2015). However, in 2006, crimes committed against, and the victimisation of, sex workers was treated as a hate crime for the first time in the UK by Merseyside Police (Campbell and Stoops, 2010; Campbell, 2015). This was in response to concerns about the non-reporting of prevalent violent crimes against sex workers and a number of sex workers being murdered. The linkage between crimes against sex workers and hate crime on the part of police and sex workers underpinned the development of positive partnerships in Liverpool. Police policy specifically comprised of an 'enhanced response with more attention and police resources being allocated to it' (Campbell and Stoops, 2010, p 9).

Writing about homophobic hate crime, Corteen (2014, p 177) concludes that drawing on the violences of the law (harsher punishments) to deal with homophobic hate crime is 'counter-intuitive', possibly 'counter-productive', and that 'institutional and cultural homophobia remains intact'. Yet, with regard to sex workers, according to Campbell (2015, p 55), this predominantly unprotected and criminalised group have derived 'real advantages' from their inclusion in Merseyside hate crime policing policy and practices and their public announcement of this initiative. These included comparable unprecedented increases in the reporting, prosecution and conviction of crimes against sex workers in Merseyside (see Campbell, 2015). The Organisation for Security and Cooperation in Europe and the Office for Democratic Institutions and Human rights (OSCE and ODIHR, 2009, p 7) contend that '[l]aws – especially – criminal laws … are an expression of society's values', and that if enforced, hate crime laws 'express the social value of equality' and promote 'the development of those values'. In this instance, responding to violence against sex workers as hate crime challenges institutional and cultural bias towards, discrimination of and hatred of sex workers on the grounds that they are sex workers. In this instance, the 'real advantages' of a punitive response are not solely short-term 'quick fixes' in the shape of increased convictions and sentences, but potential long-term gains in institutionally and culturally reconstructing sex workers subjected to hate crime as legitimate victims with rights who are deserving of protection and justice. It is therefore important that this progressive response is sustained, developed and extended.

That said, the UK is experiencing a climate of austerity, resulting in cuts in public funding and the marketisation of services. They are hard-hitting and will continue to hit vulnerable and marginalised groups and relevant service providers in a detrimental manner. Thus, sustaining a proactive, collaborative and holistic victim-centred and 'protection-based approach', which embodies an 'inclusive and non-hierarchical hate crime framework' that includes sex workers (and other marginalised victim groups, eg, those with problems with alcohol), will be challenging (Campbell, 2015, p 64). In this economic climate, it is important that the positive partnership working and positive police–sex work community relations continue to be delivered. Further, in order bring justice to sex workers harmed by sex worker hate crime, such policies and practices should be developed nationally. Ultimately, the improvements that have been achieved by treating sex workers as equal or symmetrical victims of hate crime should continue at cultural and institutional levels so as to not necessitate the violences of the law. While the latter is somewhat utopian, the progress that has been made in Liverpool as a result of responding to the victimisation of sex workers as a hate crime teaches important lessons, namely, that investigating and prosecuting crimes against sex workers *and* preventing victimisation and protecting potential and actual victims can be done 'if there is commitment and resources are dedicated to do this' (Campbell and Stoops, 2010, p 10). Also, the longer-term goal of changing cultural and institutional stigma that, at best, enables and, at worst, encourages sex worker hate crime, harm and victimisation in the first instance can be addressed.

KAREN CORTEEN and MICHELLE STOOPS

See also: **Hate Crime and Victimisation; Sex Workers and Victimisation**

Readings

Campbell, R. (2015) 'Not getting away with it: linking sex work and hate crime in Merseyside', in N. Chakraborti and J. Garland (eds) *Responding to hate crime: Bridging the case for connecting policy and research*. Bristol: The Policy Press, pp 55–70.

Campbell, R. and Stoops, M. (2010) 'Taking sex workers seriously: treating violence as hate crime in Liverpool', *Research for Sex Work*, 12 December, pp 9–10.

Christie, N. (1986) 'The ideal victim', in E. Fattah (ed) *From crime policy to victim policy: Reorientating the justice system*. Basingstoke: MacMillan Press, pp 17–30.

Corteen, K. (2014) 'Homophobic hate crime', in R. Atkinson (ed) *Shades of deviance: A primer on crime, deviance and social harm*. London: Routledge.

OSCE (Organisation for Security and Cooperation in Europe) and ODIHR (Office for Democratic Institutions and Human rights) (2009) *Hate crime laws: A practical guide*. Poland: OSCE/ODIHR. Available at: http://www.osce.org/odihr/36426?download=true

SOCIAL ABJECTION AND VICTIMISATION

Social abjection is a process through which groups or individuals come to be considered as objects of disgust. The theory of abjection originated in the work of the Bulgarian–French philosopher Julia Kristeva, who, in her influential text *The powers of horror: An essay on abjection* (Kristeva, 1982), argues that substances such as blood, faeces or vomit elicit disgust reactions that disrupt the boundaries between the perceived limits of the self and things that threaten to overwhelm those limits and engulf us. Abjection is an embodied affect: our physical disgust reactions (we may recoil, shudder or feel nauseous) as we try to distance ourselves from that which compromises our fragile notion of bodily integrity. According to Kristeva (1982), this is a performative process of rejection that allows us to maintain the fantasy of a holistic, proper and clean self. Yet, because disgust arises from objects that are intimate and familiar to us, the rejection is always imperfect: 'a vortex of summons and repulsion' that evidences ambiguity at the heart of the psychic constitution of the self (Kristeva, 1982, p 1).

The theory of abjection has been developed beyond the realm of individual fantasies of discrete subjectivity to explain how states and societies constitute and sustain an imaginary ideal of themselves by designating certain social groups as disgusting outsiders, even as they reside within the community. The sociologist

Imogen Tyler (2013, p 46) argues that the borders of the state – both geopolitical and conceptual – are maintained through processes of *social* abjection through which 'abject subjects' are produced only in order to be excluded. British media and political discourse construct groups such as refugees, migrants, the disabled, the poor, the unemployed and Gypsies and Travellers as disgusting on the grounds that they threaten to overwhelm the limits of British society. Speaking to ITV News on 30 July 2015 (ITV News, 2015), Prime Minister David Cameron's description of Middle Eastern refugees gathering in the northern French port of Calais as a 'swarm' seeking to enter Britain activates abjection's capacity for both producing and unsettling borders via disgust reactions; the swarm's connotations of contamination and engulfment both delineate the fragile border between the revolted British people and disgusting, locust-like intruders and, simultaneously, reveal a fear of dissolution that undermines the border itself. Just as Kristeva (1982) shows how the individual subject asserts her or his own tenuous subjectivity by perpetually embodying the disgusted rejection of the 'other', the British state constructs its borders via the abjection of undesirable populations. The fantasy of the discrete, sanitary self 'is the underpinning of any organization constituted by exclusions and hierarchies' (Kristeva, 1982, p 65).

Social abjection is linked to victimisation because once a group has been established as disgusting, it is easy to treat its members as non-human, to strip them of their human rights and subject them to harm. Writing in *The road to Wigan Pier* (Orwell, 1975 [1937], p 112) George Orwell noted that teaching middle-class children that the working classes were dirty and smelly was far more harmful than other forms of class distinction:

> Very early in life you acquired the idea that there was something subtly repulsive about a working-class body.... You watched a great sweaty navvy walking down the road with his pick over his shoulder; you looked at his discoloured shirt and his corduroy trousers stiff with the dirt of a decade; you thought of those nests and layers of greasy rags below, and, under all, the unwashed body, brown all over (that was how I used to imagine it), with its strong, bacon-like reek. You watched a tramp taking off his boots in a ditch – ugh!... And even 'lower-class' people whom you knew to be quite clean – servants, for instance – were faintly unappetizing. The smell of their sweat, the very texture of their skins, were mysteriously different from yours.

Orwell's 'ugh!' in this evocative passage illustrates abjection – the process through which the embodied disgust of the middle-class subject functions to establish poor people as repulsive objects and therefore deserving of their state of degradation, while concurrently asserting and calling into question the respectable cleanliness (both physical and moral) of the middle-class British populace.

KATHERINE HARRISON

See also: **Human Rights and Victims; Social Harm**

Readings

ITV News (2015) 'PM blames Calais crisis on "swarm" of migrants'. Available at: http://www.itv.com/news/update/2015-07-30/pm-a-swarm-of-migrants-want-to-come-to-britain/

Kristeva, J. (1982) *The powers of horror: An essay on abjection.* New York, NY: Columbia University Press.

Orwell, G. (1975 [1937]) *The road to Wigan Pier.* Harmondsworth: Penguin.

Tyler, I. (2013) *Revolting subjects: Social abjection and resistance in neoliberal Britain.* London: Zed.

SOCIAL EXCLUSION AND VICTIMISATION

Social exclusion involves 'the lack or denial of resources, rights, goods and services, and the inability to participate in the normal relationships and activities, available to the majority of people in a society, whether in economic, social, cultural or political arenas' and affects not only individuals' quality of life but also the 'equity and cohesion of society as a whole' (Levitas et al, 2007, p 25). Social exclusion has consequences in terms of the risks of becoming a victim of crime, the impact and consequences of victimisation, and access to appropriate services and justice. Social and employment status, age, ethnicity, gender, sexuality, and disability each intersect to affect the likelihood and character of victimisation and re-victimisation, as well as influencing societal and official responses to victims and survivors.

The link between social exclusion and crime has been well documented and 'virtually all recent studies find a strong relationship between economic inequality, poverty and violent crime' (Webster and Kingston, 2014, p 6). The limited research available on the social and economic status of victims concurs that people living in more disadvantaged neighbourhoods tend to experience more property and violent crime (Webster and Kingston, 2014). Community-based research pioneered by Left realists in the 1980s challenged official narratives based on large-scale quantitative surveys which indicated that individual risks of victimisation were low by demonstrating the damaging effects of crime and 'anti-social behaviour' on poorer neighbourhoods and highlighting the particular impact of victimisation of young and older people, women, and those from black and minority ethnic (BME) communities (see, eg, Lea and Young, 1984).

Socially excluded individuals also report higher levels of 'fear of crime', for example, older people living in poorer communities are significantly more likely to fear crime than those living in more affluent areas (Croall, 2007). Access to safety and avoidance of risk are also unequal. While wealthier people own possessions that render them vulnerable to property crimes, they also have the means to protect themselves from risk, for example, through buying property in safer areas or purchasing home and vehicle security systems or insurance policies (Hope, 2002).

Homeless people's situation stands in stark contrast; experiencing high levels of victimisation, including violence and sexual assaults, they are routinely excluded from the basic resources that would provide safety and are less likely to report victimisation to criminal justice agencies (Newburn and Rock, 2004). The impact of crime may be greater for socially excluded victims who are less well equipped to regain that which was lost: to replace possessions, pay for medical services or move to a safer area. The situation, however, is not simply reducible to an individual's ability to pay for security: Hummelscheim et al's (2011) review of European-wide data found that lower levels of social and welfare spending correspond with higher levels of public fear about crime. Living in precarious situations of insecurity about employment, health and welfare, and a corresponding loss of social cohesion, may increase people's crime-related anxieties as they doubt their ability to cope with its impact.

Discrimination and marginalisation on grounds of ethnicity, gender, sexuality and disability further exacerbate individual and community experiences of crime victimisation in terms of prevalence, impact and aftermath. People from BME backgrounds are at greater risk of criminal victimisation, particularly those with 'mixed' heritage. This may, in part, be explained by the age demographics of a relatively young population, but also because more people from BME backgrounds live in areas of comparative disadvantage (Francis, 2007). BME communities, as well as lesbian, gay, bisexual and trans (LGBT) and disabled individuals, are also vulnerable to hate crime on a continuum ranging from verbal abuse, threats and harassment, through to violent and sexual assaults. This is a two-way process whereby hate crime is fuelled by discrimination and the structural exclusion of marginalised groups from 'mainstream society', but also whereby the experiences of bullying, intimidation, verbal and physical assaults may lead to further exclusion, for example, through isolation, mental ill-health or homelessness. Social exclusion creates lesser visibility for some victims, for example, isolated older or disabled people, and women and children experiencing domestic and sexual abuse.

Social exclusion not only impacts on primary crime victimisation, but also influences experiences of secondary victimisation, including ineffective or unfair police and criminal justice responses (Croall, 2007). Allegations of police racism, homophobia and sexism may increase victims' reluctance to report victimisation. The Macpherson report (Macpherson, 1999) into the police investigation of the murder of Stephen Lawrence found that institutionalised racism hampered the police response, and allegations of police racism persist. Victims whose legal status is compromised, for example, sex workers, drug users or those whose immigration status is unlawful or uncertain, may be afraid to approach the authorities. Socially disadvantaged individuals also have less recourse to legal representation and may feel intimidated by the formality of court proceedings. Moreover, compensation systems discriminate against those seen as non-deserving victims, for example, ex-offenders and prisoners (Croall, 2007).

The links between social exclusion and victimisation challenge the unreliable dualism of 'victim' and 'offender'. In the case of women who offend in England and Wales, many have led lives of social exclusion and are often themselves the victims of physical, sexual and emotional abuse (Corston, 2007). Perceptions of the 'deserving', 'ideal' victim result in little attention being paid to those most at risk of victimisation, 'the heavily offending, young male, economically disadvantaged' (Green, 2007, p 91). Prisoners and ex-prisoners are a socially excluded group whose experiences of victimisation are often overlooked or seen as justifiable in the light of their offending.

Finally, from a critical perspective, individuals and groups experiencing social exclusion may be victims of a fundamental breach of rights by virtue of their marginalisation from the basic rights to which they are entitled. Social exclusion is, in itself, a form of social harm, with very real physical and emotional consequences for individuals and for society as a whole.

LINDA MOORE

See also: **Blame and Victims; Primary, Secondary and Tertiary Victims and Victimisation; Social Harm**

Readings

Corston, J. (2007) *A report by Baroness Jean Corston of a review of women with particular vulnerabilities in the criminal justice system.* London: Home Office.

Croall, H. (2007) 'Social class, social exclusion, victims and crime', in P. Davies, P. Francis and C. Greer (eds) *Victims, crime and society.* London: Sage, pp 50–77.

Francis, P. (2007) '"Race", ethnicity, victims and crime', in P. Davies, P. Francis and C. Greer (eds) *Victims, crime and society.* London: Sage, pp 109–41.

Green, S. (2007) 'Crime, victimisation and vulnerability', in S. Walklate (ed) *Handbook of victims and victimology*. Cullompton: Willan Publishing, pp 91–117.

Hope, T. (2002) 'Crime victimisation and inequality in risk society', in R. Matthews and J. Pitt (eds) *Crime, disorder and community safety: A new agenda?* London: Routledge, pp 193–218.

Hummelscheim, D., Hirtenlehner, H., Jackson, J. and Oberwittler, D. (2011) 'Social insecurities and fear of crime: a cross-national study on the impact of welfare state policies on crime-related anxieties', *European Sociological Review*, 27(3): 327–45.

Lea, J. and Young, J. (1984) *What is to be done about law and order?*, Harmondsworth: Penguin.

Levitas, R., Pantazis, C., Fahmy, E., Gordon, D., Lloyd, E. and Patsios, D. (2007) *The multi-dimensional analysis of social exclusion*. London: Department for Communities and Local Government.

Macpherson, W. (1999) *Report of the Stephen Lawrence Inquiry*. Available at: https://www.gov.uk/government/publications/the-stephen-lawrence-inquiry

Newburn, T. and Rock, P. (2004) *Living in fear: Violence and victimisation in the lives of single homeless people*. London: London School of Economics.

Webster, C. and Kingston, S. (2014) *Anti-poverty strategies for the UK: Poverty and crime review*. Leeds: Centre for Applied Social Research, Leeds Metropolitan University and Joseph Rowntree Foundation.

SOCIAL HARM

Some scholars – notably, in and around what is known as 'critical criminology' – have argued that a disciplinary approach organised around a concept of 'social harm' may be more theoretically coherent and more progressive politically than a discipline organised around the state-defined notion of crime. An early statement of this approach, drawing on sporadic but longer-term work in and around criminology, can be found in Hillyard et al (2004). Herein, a social harm approach was considered in theoretical and methodological terms, and applied to a broad range of areas of social life, from migration to murder, violence and victimisation.

Several clusters of rationales were set out to establish a social harm approach as distinct from criminology. Crime, it was argued, has no ontological reality, but is a category that has to be constructed through law's complex (and often incoherent) reasonings, and reconstructed through the practices of institutions and agencies of the criminal justice system (Hillyard et al, 2004). Moreover, such constructions of crime simultaneously encompass many petty events and exclude many serious harms. Further, the category of 'crime' gives legitimacy to the expansion of crime control – that is, it supports the extension of processes that, on any stated rationale for them, do not work, but consistently inflict pain, indeed, generate social harm. Overall, 'crime' serves to maintain power relations and criminology, through its perpetuation of the myth of crime, fuels all of these processes.

Importantly, it was further argued that criminology, since its very inception, has enjoyed an intimate relationship with the powerful. This relationship is determined largely by its failure to analyse adequately the notion of crime – and the disciplinary agendas set by this – which has been handed down by the state, and around which the criminal justice system has been organised. For some involved in this project, a social harm approach was designed as a corrective to the limitations of criminology; for others, it was an explicit attempt to develop a new discipline, quite separate from criminology, namely, 'zemiology', with its etymological roots in 'xemia', the Greek word for harm.

Since the publication of Hillyard et al's (2004) edited collection, numerous attempts to engage with the approach set out therein have emerged. One stream of work has sought to develop and operationalise a harm framework in the context of addressing harms caused by criminal justice systems and practices (Greenfield and Paoli, 2013). Others have attempted to develop distinct ontological approaches to defining harm, such as Yar's (2012) framing of social harm within theories of recognition, or to develop a general theory of harm via analyses of narrative accounts of a diverse range of harming and being harmed (Presser, 2013). Other responses have been to dismiss social harm claims as over-introspection, as being clear what is opposed rather than what is proposed, or as redundant since these add nothing to what critical criminologists already do.

Recently, and notably, Pemberton (2015) has sought to refine the definition of social harm. Pemberton (2015, p 9) defines harms 'as specific events or instances where "human flourishing" is demonstrably compromised', a definition very much rooted within Doyal and Gough's (1991) needs framework. This in turn generates a proposal that these harms can be categorised as 'physical/mental health harms; autonomy harms; relational harms' (Pemberton, 2015, p 9). In terms of the 'social', 'socially mediated' harms are viewed as 'preventable harm' insofar as they are either 'foreseeable' events or the result of 'alterable' social conditions (Pemberton, 2015, pp 9–10). This leads Pemberton to argue that harms are not inevitable, but determined by the forms of organisation that our societies take. In this way, Pemberton introduces the notion of 'capitalist harm' – harms that are inherent to the capitalist form of organisation – and develops a useful typology of harm reduction regimes, which draw upon, but supplement, a combination of existing varieties and models of capitalism literatures, and groups nation states according to the harm reduction/production features that they demonstrate.

A social harm approach is very much a work in progress. There remain key issues with the definition of 'social harm', its theoretical justification, its ontological bases and its operationalisation.

STEVE TOMBS

See also: **Zemiology**

Readings
Doyal, L. and Gough, I. (1991) *A theory of human need.* Basingstoke: Palgrave Macmillan.
Greenfield, V. and Paoli, L. (2013) 'A framework to assess the harms of crime', *British Journal of Criminology*, 53(5): 864–85.
Hillyard, P., Pantazis, C., Tombs, S. and Gordon, D. (eds) (2004) *Beyond criminology. Taking harm seriously.* London: Pluto.
Pemberton, S. (2015) *Harmful societies. Understanding social harm.* Bristol: The Policy Press.
Presser, L. (2013) *Why we harm.* New Brunswick, NJ: Rutgers University Press.
Yar, M. (2012) 'Critical criminology, critical theory, and social harm', in S. Hall and S. Winlow (eds) *New directions in criminological theory.* Abingdon: Routldedge, pp 52–65.

SOLDIERS AND VICTIMISATION

The physical and psychological sacrifice made by soldiers is widely acknowledged – such is the nature of soldiering. Throughout history, countries have attempted to count the fallen and quantify the injuries of those who return, which, of course, include psychological injuries. The impact of combat upon combatants' bodies is often framed as a mark of their bravery and courage in popular discourse – a social and cultural expectation. Rock (2007) explains that to frame military personnel who are harmed as victims poses a series of challenges because the image of the soldier does not lend itself easily to the passive, vulnerable and weak connotations of a 'victim'. Further to this, if to be harmed is part of military duty, then a reminder is necessitated in that to cause harm to others is also part of that duty.

Nonetheless, both in the media and academia, the soldier's position is starting to be analysed through victimological frames. As media report the fallen as victims, critical criminologists have proposed that the state is culpable for the harms done to military personnel. These narratives speak to both conflict and post-conflict experiences. During conflict, by placing soldiers in a victimological framework, new light is shed upon the potential consequences that face military personnel during war (McGarry and Walklate, 2011). To begin, those who die or are injured (both psychically and mentally) can be placed into the state crime literature and ask if the state is, indeed, culpable. McGarry et al (2012), however, draw attention to the human rights of soldiers and the practical challenges faced in war that are perhaps not as well known. Experiences such as military equipment and kit that are not satisfactory and the reality of fatigue, hunger and sustained anxieties upon the body are analysed. As such, while performing their military duty on behalf of the state, soldiers can be victimised by the state (Ruggerio, 2005).

Walklate and McGarry (2015) argue that lasting experiences of war can be found post-deployment; they refer to these as 'traces' of the violence of war. The repatriation of military personnel and the counting of those fallen is the first trace. For those soldiers who return home, the violence of war is often still visible. The physiological trace can be found in rising levels of post-traumatic stress disorder (PTSD) and other mental disorders such Brain Blast Injury, while the physical trace can be found in the large numbers of soldiers wounded. Their analysis questions whether or not some of those injuries are attributable to military equipment, encouraging questions as to whether or not, even during combat, there is to some extent an expectation of safety through equipment. When that equipment is not up to the necessary standard, the state should be liable for those breaches.

The complexity of this framing continues to be realised as the significant number of ex-armed forces embroiled in the criminal justice system is acknowledged. Many of those who commit an offence post-war, commit a violent offence and are diagnosed with PTSD. A victimological frame encourages a consideration of both the perpetrators of crime and their victims as casualties of war (Treadwell, 2010). Is this violence also a trace of war that manifests as soldiers return? McGarry and Walklate (2011, p 14) contend that victimology is able to look 'beyond the domain assumptions of crime per se and explore the experiences of those who may be on the fringes of the discipline but are nonetheless very much within its capacity to understand'. While framing the soldier as a victim is not without its challenges, it directs a critical criminological and victimological understanding of the effects of war and an all too often obscured culpability.

EMMA MURRAY

See also: **Criminology and War; Victimology**

Readings
McGarry, R. and Walklate, S. (2011) 'The soldier as victim: peering through the looking glass', *British Journal of Criminology*, 51(6): 900–17.

McGarry, R., Mythen, G. and Walklate, S. (2012) 'The soldier, human rights and the military covenant: a permissible state of exception?', *International Journal of Human Rights*, 16(8): 1182–95.

Rock, P. (2007) 'Theoretical perspectives on victimisation', in S. Walklate (ed) *Handbook of victims and victimisation*. Cullompton: Willan Publishing, pp 37–61.

Ruggiero, V. (2005) 'Criminalising war: Criminology as ceasefire', *Social and Legal Studies*, 14: 239-257.

Treadwell, J. (2010) 'COUNTERBLAST: more than casualties of war? Ex-military personnel in the criminal justice system', *Howard Journal*, 49: 73–7.

Walklate, S. and McGarry, R. (2015) 'Competing for the trace: the legacies of war's violence', in S. Walklate and R. McGarry (eds) *Criminology and war: Transgressing the borders*. London: Routledge, pp 180–97.

SPORT, CRIME AND HARM

An accidental kick in the head hurts as much as a deliberate one; some martial arts may involve an individual consenting to a kick in the head, and other sports at least the possibility. Sport is a human activity; therefore, in common with all other human activities, deviance, crime or harm will be associated with it. In his discussion on the relative nature of deviance, Durkheim did not talk of footballers, but of saints. Though of human society, sport is often given some separate jurisdictional sovereignty its top stars are expected to be role models or even to be saint-like.

While sports law is a growing field and the sociology of sport is long established, criminology and victimology has tended to ignore sport. Thus, few textbooks mention sport unless talking about football hooliganism or crowd violence, or the potential of sport in crime prevention or desistance (Meek, 2014). There is now some recognition of various forms of cheating/corruption that are harmful to sport (or at least its reputation with the public and sponsors) and a growing recognition of the harms of sport – for example, the recognition of the dangers of concussion in the US by the National Football League and in the UK on the part of the Rugby Football Union.

Many of the precursors of modern sports were fairly bloody affairs before they were codified on the playing fields of British public schools and universities. The blood of animals is still shed in what opponents call 'blood sports' and supporters call 'field sports'. Much of the crime now associated with sport is not on the field, but in violence on the streets and terraces, although some attention is now paid to the boardroom (Hopkins and Treadwell, 2014).

The folk history of sport is replete with connections to gambling (a moral or actual harm in its own right for some), and much horse and dog racing only exists to be legally bet on, and dog and cock fighting to be illegally bet on. Haberfeld and Sheehan (2013) survey the scene of match- and spot-fixing as 'sports-related crime'. Online, in-match betting on cricket run rates, the score spread of a basketball match or the timing of a yellow card make for apparently harmless actions by greedy or fearful sports players that can see them benefit even while the team still wins.

Such corruption often involves cheating to lose. Doping involves cheating to win. Dimeo (2007) shows the long history of such practices and Yar (2014) uses the growing numbers of star autobiographies to reflect on how they manage the crime-like stigma that they live under. The key and ongoing exemplar in all this is US cyclist, and one-time record-breaking Tour de France-winner, Lance Armstrong, but he also examines the case of British sprinter Dwain Chambers.

Meek (2014) carefully assesses the possibility that sport in prison may lead to desistance (at times and with the right sport and circumstances), and many sportspeople claim that it prevented them going into crime. However, a growing area of interest is in the criminogenic link or, at least, correlation between violence on and off the field. Some have tried to directly link action on the field to that off the field by spectators in imitation of their 'heroes'. Much recent feminist-influenced work picks up on the homosocial masculinity of male sports teams. Thus, Waterhouse-Watson (2013) found that Australian Rules and Rugby League Football stars enjoyed a protective culture of immunity among their 'mates', management and media. There was a culture of celebratory group sex and alcohol that rendered the issue of consent even more difficult for juries to decide while the media carried out their own 'trial' of the women.

Sport is harmful/harmless depending on time and circumstance, and who has the power to define. Sport also usefully illustrates the limits of criminal–civil distinctions in legislating against harm.

NIC GROOMBRIDGE

See also: **Victimology**

Readings

Dimeo, P. (2007) *A history of drug use in sport: 1876–1976: Beyond good and evil.* Abingdon: Routledge.
Haberfeld, M. and Sheehan, D. (eds) (2013) *Match-fixing in international sports: Existing processes, law enforcement, and prevention strategies.* Switzerland: Springer.

Hopkins, M. and Treadwell, J. (eds) (2014) *Football hooliganism, fan behaviour and crime: Contemporary issues*. Basingstoke: Palgrave Macmillan.

Majid, Y. (2014) *Crime, deviance and doping: Fallen sports stars autobiography and the management of stigma*. Basingstoke: Palgrave Macmillan.

Meek, R. (2014) *Sport in prison: Exploring the role of physical activity in correctional settings*. London: Routledge.

Waterhouse-Watson, D. (2013) *Athletes, sexual assault, and 'trials by media': Narrative immunity*. Abingdon: Routledge.

STATE-CORPORATE CRIME AND HARM

The term 'state-corporate crime' first appeared in 1990, when Kramer and Michalowski (2006, p 15) defined this phenomenon as signifying 'illegal or socially injurious actions that occur when one or more institutions of political governance pursue a goal in direct co-operation with one or more institutions of economic production and distribution'. For Michalowski, Kramer and other scholars, state-corporate crime and harm can be initiated and facilitated by states. Thus, corporations engage in illegality at the prompt, or with the approval, of state institutions, while state actors fail to prevent or respond to, or, indeed, collude with, such illegality. More recently, Lasslett (2010, para 4) has usefully expanded upon this concept thus: 'Corporate-initiated state crime occurs when corporations directly employ their economic power to coerce states into taking deviant actions'. 'Corporate-facilitated state crime' occurs 'when corporations either provide the means for state's criminality (e.g. weapons sales), or when they fail to alert the domestic/international community to the state's criminality, because these deviant practices directly/indirectly benefit the corporation concerned' (Lasslett, 2010, para 4). These are important conceptual developments in the study of the crimes of the powerful.

The conceptual lens of state-corporate crime and harm has been applied to a range of events and contexts. From the explosion of the space shuttle Challenger and the crash of Valujet Flight 592, to the technological underpinnings of the Holocaust, the contemporary seizure of natural resources in occupied Iraq and beyond, and the oil spill in the Gulf of Mexico, to a variety of harms and crimes committed in conflict zones, occupation and the 'war on terror', as well as to diverse sectors such as the Latin American shrimp industry, the Nigerian oil sector and the arms trade (see Green and Ward, 2004; Michalowski and Kramer, 2006), these various indicative areas make it immediately clear how state-corporate activities can produce harms that affect vast numbers of people and other organisations, emanating from a range of activities and sectors, across local, national and even global contexts.

Noting the extent to which the concept of state-corporate crime and harm has proven productive and significant, Tombs (2012) recently sought to extend and develop it. In so doing, he stressed the interdependencies – the symbiotic relationships – between states and corporations. First, he emphasised the fact that the corporation is a creation of the nation-state, and is maintained through a great deal of state activity. Corporations are wholly artificial entities whose very existence is provided for, and maintained, through the state via legal institutions and instruments, which, in turn, are based upon material and ideological supports. Certainly, it is the case that maintaining the conditions of existence of contemporary corporations, even, or perhaps especially, in 'free' markets, requires an enormous amount of state activity. The logical corollary of this claim is that just as states create and sustain markets, so, too, can and do they create and sustain criminogenic markets, that is, markets that are conducive to, or facilitate, the production of harms and crimes. The corporate form and the state are thus inextricably linked to the extent that, in contemporary capitalism, each is a condition of existence of the other.

At the most basic and manifest level, states appear complicit in corporate crime and harm production through omissions, specifically in terms of their failures to: put into place more effective legal regimes; enforce adequately existing laws; and respond effectively to violations of such laws. A second way in which states may be and appear complicit in corporate crime and harm production is through their formal, often intimate, relationships with the corporate sector. These relationships take various forms, such as states' (local, regional, national) effective role as joint partners with the private sector in various forms of economic activity, as outsourcers and contractors of economic activity, and as key purchasers of corporate goods and services. These generally proceed through contracts, new regulatory regimes, regulatory reform or a combination of each. The significance of such relationships increases as states formally withdraw from directly providing goods and services, both under longer-term conditions of neoliberalism and, more specifically, within the claims for fiscal crisis upon which the economics and politics of austerity are based.

If, then, states and corporations produce crime and harms via their symbiotic relationships to the extent that these symbioses become deeper and more prevalent, then it is expected that such crimes and harms will proliferate.

STEVE TOMBS

See also: **Legal Crimes – Lawful But Awful; White-Collar Crime, Harm and Victimisation**

Readings

Green, P. and Ward, T. (2004) *State crime: Governments, violence and corruption.* London: Pluto.

Kramer, R.C. and Michalowski, R.J. (2006) 'The original formulation', in R.J. Michalowski and R.C. Kramer (eds) *State-corporate crime.* New Jersey, NJ: Rutgers University Press, pp 18–26.

Lasslett, K. (2010) 'A critical introduction to state-corporate crime', International State Crime Initiative. Available at: http://statecrime.org/state-crime-research/state-corporate-crime-crit-intro/

Michalowski, R.J. and Kramer, R.C. (eds) (2006) *State-corporate crime.* New Jersey, NJ: Rutgers University Press.

Tombs, S. (2012) 'State–corporate symbiosis in the production of crime and harm', *State Crime,* 1(2): 170–95.

SURVIVOR STIGMATISATION

Survivor stigmatisation centres on the societal response to victimisation and problematises the notions of blame and responsibility. As Rock (2002, p 13) notes: 'a victim is one who is defined voluntarily or involuntarily, directly or indirectly, abruptly or gradually, consequentially or inconsequentially, by the proven or alleged criminal or crime-like actions of another'. The social construction of victim identity can affect who is considered to be deserving of being recognised as such, potentially also influencing the self-perception of those victims. The victim label is both practical and symbolic, but it is not afforded to all who experience victimisation. The attribution or lack of victim status can have substantial repercussions. The former can allow an individual to benefit from concern and understanding, enable them to feel validated, place them in a position of power, or allow them recourse to financial compensation. However, the latter has the potential to exclude, blame, weaken, deny agency and stigmatise. For some, the term 'survivor' has become preferable because it can avoid devaluing connotations of being weak and passive that have been linked with the term 'victim'. However, using the term 'survivor' does not exempt the individual from stigmatisation.

Survivor stigmatisation can be particularly problematic for women who experience sexual assault and domestic violence. For example, in cases of domestic abuse, there is rarely a discreet one-off incident. Decisions to remain in or return to abusive relationships can be perceived as something that goes against expectations of how a 'good' victim should behave, neglecting concerns or complexities that influence these decisions. Blame is a complex notion that encourages 'all-or-nothingness' and attributing it in this way is 'unhelpful, lacks nuance and focuses on extremes, placing people at polar opposites' (Lamb, 1999, p 12).

The consideration of victim behaviour as being inextricably linked to the criminal act is not a new phenomenon. Forms of stigmatisation have roots in the work of early victimologists, including Von Hentig's (1940, p 303) discussion of the 'reciprocal action between perpetrator and victims'. This was also evidenced in Amir's (1971, p 259) later work on the theory of 'victim-precipitated rape', in particular, the manner in which it outlined a set of typologies of victims, involving the 'accidental victim' and the 'unconsciously seductive victim' (Amir, 1971, p 260). These approaches have been heavily criticised, not least for perpetuating the idea of 'good' and 'bad' victims, and working with extreme and unsubstantiated stereotypes. The work of Christie (1986) on the 'ideal victim' has exemplified the rigidity of the victim label. For the victim to be considered 'ideal', Christie suggested that they needed to fit within a set of attributes, including being relatively weak, blameless for their victimisation, unrelated to the offender and representing no threat to existing vested interests, so that they are afforded full, unambiguous victim status.

While it is suggested that the victim identity is more fluid than Christie (1986) suggested, it is clear that many of those who do not fit within the normative expectations of what a victim/survivor should be can find themselves excluded from receiving this label and consequently stigmatised and blamed for their behaviour. Taking a more nuanced approach to understanding the role of gender and victimisation is not a straightforward task, with some 'tricky questions' to consider, and the potential risk of being accused of resorting back to victim-blaming approaches, similar to those associated with the early victimologists, or of weakening the substantial gains made by the feminist movement (Davies, 2007, p 184).

However, it is evident that alternative perspectives that can tread the thin line of comprehending victimisation and its impact while avoiding apportioning blame between victim and offender would avoid a reductionist approach and aid a better understanding of victimisation and responses to it. Stigmatisation may not take into account the victim's resourcefulness, visible and invisible forms of resistance, or the complex motivations that may influence behaviours. In turn, this may result in the individual not meeting the cultural ideals around victim behaviour.

CLAIRE FOX

See also: **Blame and Victims; Deviant Victims; Survivorology**

Readings
Amir, M. (1971) *Patterns in forcible rape.* Chicago, IL: University of Chicago Press.
Christie, N. (1986) 'Ideal victim', in E.A. Fattah (ed) *From crime policy to victim policy: Reorientating the justice system.* Basingstoke: MacMillan Press, pp 17–30.

Davies, P. (2007) 'Lessons from the gender agenda', in S. Walklate (ed) *Handbook of victims and victimology*. Oxon: Routledge.

Lamb, S. (1999) *The trouble with blame: Victims, perpetrators, and responsibility*. Cambridge: Harvard University Press.

Rock, P. (2002) 'On becoming a victim', in C. Hoyle and R. Young (eds) *New versions of victims*. Oxford: Hart Publishing, pp 1–22.

Von Hentig, H. (1940) 'Remarks of the interaction of perpetrator and victim', *Journal of Criminal Law and Criminology*, 31(3): 303–9.

SURVIVOROLOGY

The term 'survivor' used to be applied mostly to persons who lived through traumatic ordeals and near-death experiences, especially duels, shipwrecks, plane crashes and the concentration camps run by the Nazis during the Holocaust. However, ever since the start of the 1980s, some people harmed by criminals (especially those who have endured child abuse, incest, sexual assaults and repeated beatings by intimate partners) have preferred to be called 'survivors' rather than 'victims'. This is because the term 'survivor' contains positive connotations – that harmed or wronged individuals are overcoming obstacles, exercising 'agency' to regain control of their lives, thus successfully coping with adversity and making a comeback. Many see the label 'victim' as a negative, demoralising and stigmatising term carrying negative connotations, such as being 'helpless' and 'defeated'.

Victimology is unavoidably preoccupied with death, injury, pain, loss, grief, hostility and recriminations. 'Survivorology' – a term coined by Karmen (2013) – can embody a new, alternative, positive, upbeat line of inquiry within victimology. Survivorology can be defined as the scientific study of resiliency and recovery from the physical and emotional wounds and economic costs inflicted by criminals on their targets (Karmen, 2016). Victimologists seeking to launch research projects in survivorology could begin by focusing on success stories about individuals whose lives looked so bleak during the downward spiral in the immediate aftermath of a terrible crime, and how they transformed a crisis into an opportunity to make impressive strides to reconstruct their shattered lives. The overarching themes of survivorology could be to discover the common threads that underlie the sources of their upward trajectories, and to uncover the social, economic, political, cultural and personal factors that either facilitate or impede resiliency and recovery.

To initiate studies in survivorology, researchers must first define, recognise and then operationalise the two key dependent variables – 'resilience' and 'recovery' – as potential responses to interpersonal violence. Resilience (the ability to rebound from serious setbacks) and recovery (the process of recuperating, regaining lost ground and returning to the conditions that the person experienced before the crime took place) are contextual, and the rate and degree of recovery varies from victim to victim. An additional challenge is to define, identify and then operationalise the loosely applied designation of 'survivor' so that it is not so inclusive as to automatically include virtually all individuals who have suffered from a particular type of serious crime, regardless of their degree of resilience and the extent of their recovery, and not so restrictive as to exclude nearly all victims as subjects worthy of study. Once the degree of resilience and the degree and rate of recovery of specific survivors becomes identifiable and measurable, then empirically oriented investigations can start out by asking: 'How did they do it? What enabled them to make the transition from victim to survivor?'

Researchers might pose questions about individuals and their resilience and recovery, such as: 'What aspects of a person's character and which personality traits foster resiliency and recovery?'; 'What coping skills, inner resources, sources of solace and encouragement, stress reduction techniques, comforting rituals, and belief systems enabled these victims who endured shattering experiences to emerge from a period of turmoil, bereavement, depression, and anger as exemplary role models whose achievements are widely recognised as admirable and impressive, even inspiring?'; and 'Was their ability to rebound facilitated by faith and spirituality, inner strengths and outstanding character traits, an immersion into activism, or some other basis for courage and perseverance?' A richer and more detailed and critical qualitative analysis of narratives could yield insights about the structural contexts that both positively and negatively influence an individual's struggle to regain lost ground.

Research questions that enable comparisons to be made could include: 'Which types of victims (in terms of social variables such as age, sex, race and ethnicity, education, income, occupation, and religiosity) show the greatest resilience?'; 'Which kinds of victims (eg of molestations, incest, rapes and shootings) face the best prospects for recovery?'; 'What forms of social support (such as strong family ties, close bonds with friends, comradeship provided by fellow sufferers in a self-help group, financial reimbursement, community assistance and governmental aid and benefits) and therapeutic interventions maximise the chances of making a successful "re-entry" back into society?'; 'What impact does the criminal justice system's handling of the case (arrest, conviction, appropriate sentencing) have on the rate and degree of the victims' emotional healing?'; and 'What role did their pursuit of "justice" play – whether to seek retribution through the courts and imprisonment or alternatively to pursue reconciliation and forgiveness through offender rehabilitation, restitution and apology by participating in a restorative justice programme?'

As survivorology develops due to the insights and findings derived from both quantitative and qualitative studies, it could transcend the limitations of being an offshoot or area of concentration within victimology and might broaden its focus to investigate what all sorts of resilient people who made great strides towards recovery have in common, whatever the origins of their suffering: from vicious interpersonal crimes, political violence and torture, natural disasters, disabling diseases, even tragic accidents. The pragmatic aim would be to identify the best practices that provide immediate and short-term relief, as well as to devise long-term strategies that could empower more victims to achieve their goals of becoming survivors.

ANDREW KARMEN

See also: **Victim Hierarchy; Victim Recovery; Victimology**

Readings

Karmen, A. (2013) *Crime victims: An introduction to victimology* (8th edn). Boston, MA: Cengage Learning.
Karmen, A. (2016) *Crime victims: An introduction to victimology* (9th edn). Boston, MA: Cengage Learning.

T

TERRORISM AND VICTIMISATION

Terrorism is often a sudden, extreme event. Victims of terrorism are likely to experience trauma as a result of being completely overwhelmed by their experiences. Traumatic symptoms include intrusive memories, flashbacks of the event, avoidance of reminders of what happened, heightened arousal and trouble in concentrating, and persistent distorted thoughts (Spalek, 2016).

Terrorism can lead to wide-scale and widespread victimisation. Individuals directly harmed by the terrorist incident comprise primary victims, while their direct family members are secondary victims. A wider group of victims includes the emergency service personnel who respond to the terrorist attack and who themselves may be exposed to danger and extreme images. People watching images through traditional and newer forms of media can also be tertiary victims of terrorism in that they may also be exposed to shocking images that can trigger traumatic symptoms. Governments have introduced victim compensation schemes specifically for victims of terrorism. These schemes can lead to controversy in relation to how payments are calculated. Also, victims of terrorism can be dissatisfied with the amount of compensation that they have received because terrorism can often leave lifelong impacts upon their lives (Spalek, 2016).

Terrorists may justify their attacks by identifying themselves with a particular social, religious, political or ethnic group. Terrorists may claim that their actions are vengeance for the historical and/or contemporary victimisation of the group that they identify with. This can victimise a large group of people because it may be that the social, religious, political or ethnic group that terrorists highlight is attacked by groups and individuals in society that directly blame the group for the terrorist incident. In a post-9/11 world, where Al Qaeda-linked terrorists and Islamic State/ISIS-based terrorists try to justify their actions with reference to the suffering of Muslims across the world, the risk of Muslim minorities becoming the victims of hate crimes is heightened. Negative stereotypes of Muslim and Arab communities continue to pervade Western perceptions of Islam, where Islam is interpreted as 'the other' and 'inhumane' – the antithesis of Western society (Spalek, 2013).

Reactions to terrorism can also victimise large groups of people. The notion of a 'suspect community' (Hillyard, 1993) has been introduced, whereby security responses in the prevention of terrorism may focus predominantly on one particular social, political, ethnic or religious group. This means that particular people are singled out for heightened security measures such as police stop and search tactics, surveillance technologies, and airport security measures. Here, victimisation might be thought of in relation to differentiated citizenship, in that security measures may mean that 'suspect communities' experience different, reduced, citizenship according to legal, political and social status. Securitisation involves increased security measures, and governments often justify these by arguing that there is a heightened risk from terrorism. Securitisation can impact differentially upon different groups. For example, in relation to Republican-linked terrorism in Northern Ireland and Britain, Irish Catholic communities were often targeted for security measures and interventions. Post-9/11, it has been argued that Muslim communities have become the new 'suspect communities', experiencing hard-edged counter-terrorism policies and practices. This illustrates that state responses to terrorism can involve the victimisation of groups and individuals (Choudhury and Fenwick, 2011).

Victimisation can help to radicalise people as a result of them being traumatised, repressed and victimised by state responses to terrorism. Indeed, colonisation and harsh contemporary economic and political realities, including the violent state repression of certain political parties, can help to radicalise people (see, eg, Githens-Mazer, 2010). While not everyone who is radicalised will engage in violence, a small minority may become terrorists. This illustrates how terrorism and victimisation are linked, and that oppressive state responses to terrorism can play a significant role in producing and sustaining terrorism. Oppressive state practices might be thought of as having a traumatising effect on an individual's collective identity, which may be different from trauma that is experienced from violence relating to a person's individual identity (Spalek, 2013, 2016). Victimisation at the level of collective identity may comprise of everyday humiliations and insults, alongside severe victimisation in the form of targeted killing, group punishment or torture. The cumulative aspects of these must be considered when exploring links between the co-production of terrorism and victimisation.

BASIA SPALEK

See also: **Culture and Victimisation; Ethnic Minorities and Victimisation; Primary, Secondary and Tertiary Victims and Victimisation**

Readings

Choudhury, T. and Fenwick, H. (2011) *The impact of counter-terrorism measures on Muslim communities*. London: Equality & Human Rights Commission.
Githens-Mazer, J. (2010) 'Islamic radicalisation amongst North Africans in Britain', *British Journal of Politics and International Relations*, 10(4): 550–70.
Hillyard, P. (1993) *Suspect community: People's experience of the prevention of terrorism acts in Britain*. London: Pluto Press.
Spalek, B. (2013) *Governing terror: Trust, community and counter-terrorism*. London: Bloomsbury Academic Press.
Spalek, B. (2016) *Crime victims and trauma: Theory, policy and practice*. Hampshire: Palgrave Macmillan.

TRANSNATIONAL ORGANISED CRIME, HARM AND VICTIMISATION

Transnational organised crime is a threat to both national and international security. Such organised criminal syndicates operate using complex and sophisticated methods to carry out crimes on a transnational scale; therefore, preserving national and international security requires the cooperation and effective intelligence sharing of various nations. These criminal organisations vary in size and objectives and tend to operate using corrupt and violent methods in more than one nation-state, favouring those with profitable market environments, economic inequalities and low risk of detection. Globalisation and regional integration has facilitated the rise in transnational organised crimes due to criminal organisations being able to take advantage of the ease of international travel, growth of international trade, technological advances and sophisticated international financial networks (Bagley, 2004). Transnational organised crime takes on many forms and includes criminal acts such as human smuggling and the trafficking of humans, drugs and arms. Such crimes result in an array of harms and various levels of victimisation.

It can be said that such organised groups contribute to national wealth by creating jobs and generating profits that go back into local and national economies

(Williams, 1994). Nonetheless, the existence of criminals undoubtedly results in the creation of victims and harms; therefore, transnational organised crime oppresses and harms both individuals and nation-states. Although the prime aim of transnational criminal organisations is not to seize control of the state, they disrupt and pose a challenge to national authority and control. They aim not to aid in the development of society, but purely to benefit themselves to the detriment of a nation and its people. Furthermore, such criminal networks are often able to manipulate corrupt law enforcement and state officials, which aids in the facilitation of their criminal objectives (UNODC, 2010) and their subsequent victimisation.

It is the responsibility of nation-states to ensure the protection of its citizens from fear, violence and harm. Many transnational and organised criminal groups carry out their objectives through the threat and use of violence, which can therefore result in a catastrophic effect on a nation's citizens. Crimes committed by these groups, such as the trafficking and smuggling of people, also result in significant numbers of victims on a national and international scale. Such groups thrive on weak state structures and on the resulting opportunities to manipulate vulnerable individuals. At the time of writing, this is evident in the ongoing humanitarian crisis in Syria, where criminal offences such as trafficking and smuggling are on the rise due to criminal syndicates taking advantage of the number of vulnerable individuals seeking refuge. The depth of harm and victimisation has been witnessed through news media around the globe. Furthermore, certain illegal activities such as drugs and arms trafficking can appear to be victimless crimes but profits made from such activities can be used to fund further criminal activities.

By its nature, transnational organised crime impacts upon multiple nation-states. Therefore, to combat such criminal organisations, effective cooperation among states on an international level is crucial. One suggested approach to ensure such cooperation is the harmonisation of legislation in areas affected by transnational organised crime (Shelley, 1995). Such a move would ensure that the criminal investigations of nation-states affected by transnational organised crime are dealt with in a similar manner, thereby preventing offenders from circumventing the law in one nation and not another. Cooperation among law enforcement agencies is a crucial element in this fight. For example, there is a need to tighten intelligence sharing and data collection among nations in order to ensure an efficient flow of information on criminal organisations among nation-states (Le et al, 2014).

AKILAH JARDINE

See also: **Human Trafficking and Victimisation**

Readings

Bagley, B. (2004) 'Globalization and transnational organized crime: the Russian mafia in Latin America and the Caribbean', in M. Vellinga (ed) *The political economy of the drug industry: Latin America and the international system.* Gainesville, FL: University of Florida Press, pp 261–96.

Le, V., Bell, P. and Lauchs, M. (2014) 'Elements of best practice in policing transnational organised crime: critical success factors for international cooperation', *International Journal of Management and Administrative Sciences*, 2(3): 24–34.

Shelley, L. (1995) 'Transnational organized crime: an imminent threat to the nation-state?', *Journal of International Affairs*, 48(2): 463–89.

UNODC (United Nations Office on Drugs and Crime) (2010) 'The globalization of crime: a transnational organized crime threat assessment', 17 June.

Williams, P. (1994) 'Transnational criminal organisations and international security', *Survival*, 36(1): 96–113.

U

UNITED NATIONS DECLARATION OF THE BASIC PRINCIPLES OF JUSTICE FOR VICTIMS OF CRIME AND ABUSE OF POWER

The Declaration of the Basic Principles of Justice for Victims of Crime and Abuse of Power (hereinafter, the Victims' Declaration) was adopted by the United Nations General Assembly on 29 November 1985. It recognised that such victimisation affects millions of people globally, impacting not only on victims themselves, but also on families, friends, communities and witnesses to the offence. The impetus for the Victims' Declaration came from the energy and persuasive power of the flourishing 'victims' movement' in the 1970s. Its origins lie in discussions at the Fifth United Nations Congress on the Prevention of Crime and the Treatment of Offenders in 1975 regarding crimes committed by the rich and powerful. Following from this, at the Sixth Congress in 1980, a paper produced by the Secretariat attempted to broaden the conception of crime to cover the activities of transnational corporations. This also introduced the new category of offences of 'abuse of power': activities that although not necessarily breaches of the criminal law, are nonetheless harmful to society, ranging from financial practices, dangerous consumer goods and economic pollution, through to torture and the maltreatment of political opponents by the state (Clark, 1994). Given the politically contentious nature of 'victimhood', the document went through a process of drafting and redrafting by various authors, the final product being a 'somewhat unhappy accommodation' between the 'interests of victims of crime and those of victims of abuse of power' (Clark, 1994, pp 180–1).

The Victims' Declaration requires that victims be treated with compassion and dignity, emphasising the prevention of offending and the importance for victims of effective detection, prosecution and sentencing processes. Part A deals with victims of crime, defined as those who have individually or collectively experienced physical, mental or emotional harm, and economic loss or breach of rights, through violations of the criminal law, whether as a result of acts or omissions. People may be considered victims whether or not the perpetrator has been identified or brought to justice. Victims of crime are entitled to 'access to the mechanisms of justice' and to 'prompt redress' (Article 4), through procedures that are 'expeditious, fair, inexpensive and accessible' (Article 5), and delay should be avoided (Article 6(e)). To facilitate access to justice, victims must be made aware of their legal rights and their views should be heard in proceedings (Articles 6(a) and 6(b)). Informal methods of resolving disputes, including mediation, should be used where appropriate (Article 7). Victims are entitled to appropriate restitution from the perpetrator (Article 8) and states should provide financial compensation when this is not available from the offender (Article 12). Finally, effective 'medical, psychological and social assistance' (Article 14) should be provided and police, criminal justice, health and welfare professionals should be adequately trained in dealing sensitively with victims (Article 16).

Part B focuses on victims of 'abuse of power' who have individually or collectively suffered harms that 'do not yet constitute violations of national criminal laws', but do breach international human rights norms (Article 18). States must incorporate remedies for abuse of power into their national laws, for example, through compensation or medical or social support (Article 19). While stressing the immediate and long-term significance of 'meeting fundamental victim needs, speeding recovery, restoring community vitality and securing justice', the *Handbook on justice for victims* of the United Nations Office (1999, p v) also acknowledges that, in some environments, the guidance 'may appear unrealistic' given the resource implications.

Regarding impact, some, but by no means all, jurisdictions reacted promptly to implement the principles contained within the Victims' Declaration through the introduction of victim-focused legislation and policy, notably, in New Zealand, Canada and South Africa. In general, where states have chosen to implement the Victims' Declaration, this has been through the adoption of statutory and non-statutory victims' charters. For example, in England and Wales in 1990, a charter set out the standards of treatment that victims should expect from the criminal justice system, but with 'no enforcement structures to guarantee such treatment' (Hall, 2010, p 23). In reviewing the impact of the Victims' Declaration, Hall (2010, p 63) concludes that although not legally binding on states, it remains the 'most wide-ranging and influential document on the issue of crime victims' at an international level, and acts as a baseline 'against which national policies across jurisdictions can be measured and compared' (Hall, 2010, p 65).

LINDA MOORE

See also: **Victims' Charters**

Readings

Clark, R.S. (1994) *The United Nations crime prevention and criminal justice program: Formulation of standards and efforts at their implementation.* Philadelphia, PA: University of Pennsylvania Press.

Hall, M. (2010) *Victims and policy making: A comparative perspective.* Cullompton: Willan Publishing.

United Nations General Assembly (1985) 'Declaration of Basic Principles of Justice for Victims of Crime and Abuse of Power', adopted 29 November, UN Doc A/Res/40/ 34, annex Arts 1, 2.

United Nations Office (1999) *Handbook on justice for victims.* New York, NY: United Nations Office for Drug Control and Crime Prevention.

UNIVERSAL DECLARATION OF HUMAN RIGHTS

The Universal Declaration of Human Rights (UDHR) was ratified by the General Assembly of the United Nations on 10 December 1948 in the aftermath of the Second World War. The UDHR was drafted within a context of global concerns about the 'widespread and horrendous violations of the most basic rights which had characterised the Second World War', coupled with hopes surrounding the new authority vested within the United Nations (Johnson and Symonides, 1998, p 26). There was also pressure from many countries to ensure that the UDHR would result in 'not just talk', but also 'the necessary machinery of implementation and realisation' (Morsink, 1999, p 12). Being the first international document to set out universal civil, political, economic, social and cultural rights, the UDHR provides the foundation for subsequent international human rights law. Its provisions, together with the International Covenant on Civil and Political Rights (1976) and its optional Protocols and the International Covenant on Economic, Social and Cultural Rights (1976), form what is known as the 'International Bill of Rights'. Although the UDHR is not legally binding, it has been highly influential, being 'frequently referred to in international, regional, and national human rights instruments and jurisprudence' (Smith, 2007, p 36).

The preamble to the UDHR celebrates the 'inherent dignity' and 'equal and inalienable rights' of all people as the 'foundation of freedom, justice and peace in the world'. There are several rights with particular relevance to the criminal justice process. Article 1 proclaims that 'all human beings are born free and equal in dignity and rights'. Article 2 expresses the entitlement to these rights without discrimination. Article 3 protects 'life, liberty and security of the person', while slavery (Article 4), and 'cruel, inhuman or degrading treatment or punishment' (Article 5) are expressly prohibited. Article 8 contains the right to 'an effective remedy' at the national level whenever fundamental rights have been violated. The UDHR forbids 'arbitrary arrest, detention or exile' (Article 9). Any person who is charged with a criminal offence has the right to a 'fair and public hearing by an independent and impartial tribunal' (Article 10). Innocence must be presumed until guilt is proven in court and individuals may not be punished for anything that was not an offence at the time, nor may a heavier penalty be imposed than was applicable when the offence was committed (Article 11). To some extent, many of these rights contain protections against suspects or offenders being harmed or victimised during the criminal justice process. Other articles include the right to private and family life (Article 12), freedom of movement, the right to a nationality and the right to claim asylum (Articles 13–15), the right to 'social security' and an adequate standard of living (Articles 22 and 25), employment and trade union rights (Article 23), the right to rest and leisure (Article 24), and the right to education (Article 26).

The right to restitution contained within Article 8 is especially relevant to victims of crime and abuse. The origins of this Article lie in the post-war recognition of the importance of protection for individuals against abuse by the authorities (Morsink, 1999). Starr (2010, p 479) observes that following the introduction of the UDHR 'came a series of binding human rights treaties, each containing provisions establishing an individual right to an effective remedy' so that, in recent decades, the right to reparation 'has assumed a significant place in international human rights law'. Despite this, however, on the 50th anniversary of the UDHR, then United Nations High Commissioner for Human Rights Mary Robinson commented that 'the gap between human rights rhetoric and reality must be closed' and 'despite all the legislation, procedures and mechanisms that were in place, millions were still routinely deprived of their basic rights' (General Assembly of the United Nations, 1998).

LINDA MOORE

See also: **Human Rights and Victims; Victims' Rights**

Readings

General Assembly of the United Nations (1998) 'Marking fiftieth anniversary of Universal Declaration of Human Rights, Assembly notes need to overcome obstacles to their full enjoyment', Press Release, 10 December. Available at: http://www.un.org/press/en/1998/19981210.ga9533.html

Johnson, G. and Symonides, J. (1998) *The Universal Declaration of Human Rights: A history of its creation and implementation 1948–1998*. Paris: UNESCO.

Morsink, J. (1999) *The Universal Declaration of Human Rights: Origins, drafting and intent*. Philadelphia, PA: University of Pennsylvania Press.

Smith, R. (2007) *International human rights* (3rd edn). Oxford: Oxford University Press.

Starr, S. (2010) 'The right to an effective remedy: balancing realism and aspiration', in M. Ssenyonjo and M. Baderin (eds) *International human rights law: Six decades after the UDHR and beyond*. Farnham: Ashgate Publishing.

V

VICTIM HIERARCHY

Victims' experiences of the criminal justice system (CJS) may differ according to a number of subjective and objective factors, within or beyond their control. Subjective factors include: the nature/severity/frequency of harm that they have incurred; the identity characteristics embodied by the victim (which, in turn, may impact on their experiences or subsequent needs); their knowledge of, and ability to access, available criminal justice processes; and their willingness to engage with the CJS to seek redress for the harm that they have incurred. Objective factors include: whether the harm that they have experienced is deemed criminal; the perceived severity of the offence; the criminal justice processes available to offer reparation for that particular harm; the perceived level of blamelessness attributed to the victim in relation to the harm; and their level of cooperation with the criminal justice process.

This discrepancy in treatment was first critiqued by Christie (1986), who recognised that some victims were deemed more 'deserving' than others in statutory and social imagery. Christie identified six key characteristics that informed the socially constructed 'ideal victim', which involved being: weak in relation to the offender (ideally female, sick, very old or very young); virtuous or engaged in legitimate, everyday activities; blameless for what had happened to them; unrelated to the offender (this 'stranger' element also implies that it is a person, not an organisation, who has committed the offence and that it is likely to be a single incident); opposite to the offender (who is 'big and bad'); and able to elicit unqualified sympathy through their attained victim status.

In Christie's (1986) typology, the weak, vulnerable and disempowered victim is contrasted to the strange, scary and motivated perpetrator in a way that provides clear divisions, which may then be used to rationalise increased criminal justice responses. These victims – such as children, the elderly and those who have been subject to excessive violence – are often the most visible in media imagery and political rhetoric. In comparison to this, victims who belong to socially marginalised groups – such as street-sleeping homeless people, drug addicts or alcoholics, and street sex workers – occupy the lower end of this hierarchy. When they are the victim of a crime, not only may they find their victim status invalidated, but they may also even be implicated or deemed culpable for the harm that they have incurred as a result of victim-blaming prejudice.

The processes underpinning this illustrate the existence of social and statutory 'victim hierarchies' based on identity, experience and the level of 'deservedness' inferred. However, seemingly 'ideal victims' with similar backgrounds or who experience similar crimes/harms may also experience different treatment as a result of other forms of prejudice. A stark example of this was when in the fortnight following the disappearance of four-year-old Madeleine McCann in Portugal in 2007, a high-profile media campaign raised over £2.6 million in public donations. By contrast, when nine-year-old Shannon Matthews disappeared in Dewsbury, England, a similar two-week media campaign raised £25,500, £20,000 of which was donated by the campaigning newspaper *The Sun*. Despite both being children (at the time of their disappearance) typified as 'ideal victims', the marked differences in responses indicated a hierarchy based on 'virtuousness' (in this case, social class). Although not initially included in Christie's (1986) typology, class identity may have a significant impact on how victims of crime are considered and responded to in society and the CJS.

With the establishment of 'hate crime' legislation (which refers to crimes fuelled by racial, religious, sexual orientation, disability or transgender prejudice), claims of victim hierarchies have emerged as a result of the differing sentencing tariffs available. Enhanced criminal justice services exist for victims of crime based on one (or more) of these demarcated 'minority' characteristics, but the punishments available differ significantly. Assault, for example, may incur a higher penalty if seen to be based on racial, rather than transgender, prejudice.

The development in victim hierarchies illustrates the contemporary reimagining of victims and victimisation along the lines of demarcated identities. These victims may experience enhanced treatment when encountering the CJS; others, it appears, remain overlooked entirely if they do not fit the re-imagined, politically prioritised, 'ideal victim' typology.

MARIAN DUGGAN and VICKY HEAP

See also: **Blame and Victims; Deviant Victims; Victimological Other**

Readings

Christie, N. (1986) 'The ideal victim', in E. Fattah (ed) *From crime policy to victim policy: Reorientating the justice system.* Basingstoke: Macmillan Press, pp 17–30.

Duggan, M. and Heap, V. (2014) *Administrating victimisation: The politics of anti-social behaviour and hate crime policy.* Basingstoke: Palgrave Macmillan.

VICTIM IMPACT STATEMENTS

The first victim impact statement was presented in 1976 in California, US. Since then, such statements have been implemented across the US, Australia, Britain, Canada and New Zealand, among other countries. Some victims describe their victim impact statements (or personal statements in England and Wales) as a powerful participatory tool in criminal court sentencing, whereas critics assert that incorporating such subjective (even emotional) statements is contrary to the objectivity that underpins the law and the aims of sentencing. Research on such statements provides support for both those against and those in favour of victim impact statements.

Initial research focused on whether allowing victims to participate in sentencing would: distract from the objectivity of the sentencing process and instead introduce the subjective personal perspectives of victims; further delay court proceedings, thus having practical and financial implications; lead to longer terms of imprisonment or harsher sentences, and cause greater disparity on sentences; and unnecessarily raise victims' expectations, only to see them dashed. Researchers also sought to identify victims' reasons for making, or not making, impact statements and whether those who made such statements were more satisfied than those who did not with their criminal justice experience and/or sentences.

Victims' most common reasons for making a statement vary across jurisdictions (Erez and Roberts, 2007). In one Australian state, over two thirds of victims made statements in order to ensure that justice was done, and 5% sought to influence the sentence given to the offender. In Canada, victims were twice more likely to state that they wanted the court to understand the effect of the offence than thought that their statement would affect the sentence. Likewise, in England and Wales, most victims wanted to communicate a message to the court and the offender; however, some victims wished to influence the severity of the sentence imposed (Roberts and Manakis, 2011). In Scotland, just over one third made a statement to express feelings about the offence and just under one third wanted to influence the court outcome (Leverick et al, 2007).

The greater weight of research findings in common law jurisdictions (eg Australia, Canada, England and Wales, Scotland, and the US) indicates that victim involvement and the opportunity to voice their views and concerns likely improves victim satisfaction with justice; however, satisfaction is, of itself, an incomplete measure and a notion that should be unpacked. It seems that victims' satisfaction is associated with more than simply the process of making their statement. Rather, victims' satisfaction increases when the presiding magistrate or judge who receives or listens to the statement then acknowledges the harm done by referring to the victim's statement and its content. Furthermore, it is evident in Australia and Canada that some magistrates and judges are aware of that effect and therefore seek to validate the harm done by acknowledgement in remarks on sentence (Victim Support Agency, 2009).

Giving victims a voice via impact statements potentially reduces victims' feelings of helplessness and sense of loss of control (Erez and Roberts, 2007). It also appears to help with victims' psychological well-being, as well as sensitising offenders to the pain and suffering inflicted on victims (Fattah, 2015), without unduly affecting sentencing patterns. Thus, such statements might aid victim and offender rehabilitation. Further, victims' input can advance other sentencing aims (Pearl, 2013). Victim input, for example, might increase the certainty of sanctions (deterrence), enhance the proportionality of sanctions (retribution), afford an insight into offenders' potential to reoffend (incapacitation) and quantify victims' losses (restitution).

In addition to individual victim impact statements, several countries with adversarial criminal justice systems have introduced community or neighbourhood impact statements during the sentencing process. Proponents of these statements assert that they draw attention to the consequences of offending for particular groups or communities, thereby improving judicial awareness of the broad social ramifications of offenders' offences (Webster, 2011). Arguably, these statements might help courts to construe harms and impose a proportionate sentence. Canada, England and Wales, some states of the US, and South Australia provide for such statements, which inform the court of the impact of an offence on a particular group of people, neighbourhood or society. For example, in Canada and the US, information has been tendered on the effects of dealing or trafficking in drugs in certain neighbourhoods during the sentencing of drug offenders; in Canada and South Australia, information on the ramifications of interpersonal violence has been tendered. South Australia differentiates neighbourhood and social impact statements. A neighbourhood impact statement has been tendered on the effects on students, teachers and others of child sex offences that happened at their school, and a social impact statement was tendered in a homicide matter to highlight the prevalence of domestic violence and the emotional, physical, personal and economic costs. Like victim impact statements, community impact statements may complement the various aims of sentencing.

MICHAEL O'CONNELL

See also: **Justice and Victims; Victims of Crime**

Readings

Erez, E. and Roberts, J. (2007) 'Victim participation in the criminal justice system', in R. Davis, A. Lurigio and S. Herman (eds) *Victims of crime* (3rd edn). New York, NY: Sage, pp 277–97.

Fattah, E. (2015) 'On some important yet neglected issues in victim research: a modest attempt to revive interest in theoretical victimology', in T. Tollefson (ed) *Victimological advances in theory, policy and services: A festshrift in honor of John Peter Joseph Dussich, PhD, Professor Emeritus.* California, CA: California State University, Dumont Printing, pp 67–77.

Leverick, F., Chalmers, J. and Duff, P. (2007) 'An evaluation of the pilot victim statement schemes in Scotland', Research Findings No 92, Social Research, Crime and Justice, Scottish Executive Social Research, Edinburgh.

Pearl, T.H. (2013) 'Restoration, retribution, or revenge? Time shifting victim impact statements in American judicial process', Florida International University Legal Studies Research Paper Series, August, Research Paper No 13-15, pp 1–25.

Roberts, J. and Manakis, M. (2011) *Victim personal statements: A review of empirical research,* report for the Commissioner for Victims and Witnesses in England and Wales. Oxford: Oxford University.

Victim Support Agency (2009) *A victim's voice: Victim impact statements in Victoria – findings of an evaluation into the effectiveness of victim impact statements,* Melbourne: Department of Justice. Available at: http://assets.justice.vic.gov.au/voc/resources/14331837-4a33-45b0-b1b8-fb02205335a4/a_victims_voice-victim_impact_statements_in_victoria.pdf

Webster, A. (2011) 'Expanding the role of victims and the community in sentencing', *Criminal Law Journal,* 21, University of Adelaide Law Research Paper No 2014-09. Available at: http://ssrn.com/abstract=2404745

VICTIM RECOVERY

In daily life, people are confronted with routine stressors, conditions that cause varying levels of anxiety that are usually resolved with coping skills acquired over the course of their life that serve to maintain psychosocial equilibrium.

Some are caused by the physical environment; some by psychosocial interactions. Victimisation is a stressor that occurs out of the norm and can range from low to high magnitudes. Victimisations require coping skills that are unique and not part of one's normal coping repertoire. Some persons are not able to cope adaptively and cannot protect themselves effectively. The usual result is anxiety and a range of suffering that can last a long time, produce psychosocial trauma and require professional treatment (Takahashi and Dussich, 2010).

Recovery is a primary goal of most responses to victims. Recovery is often used to describe the process of psychosocial healing that starts with cognitive and emotional dysfunction, including the application of a range of interventions designed at reducing confusion, suffering and dysfunction, with the objectives of arriving at a point of normalcy in daily life activities, an improved sense of well-being and without significant symptoms. Recovery in clinical practice is a concept that is usually subjective; however, it can be made objective with the use of empirical indicators. Not only is recovery the process of healing, but it is also the end state at which a victim reaches a measured level of normalcy, well-being and significantly fewer symptoms (Maekoya and Dussich, 2010).

The first phase of recovery requires a comprehensive objective psychosocial evaluation of the victim prior to providing treatment. Ideally, this evaluation should involve multiple aspects of the victim's psychological condition, including measures of: personality, intelligence, coping skills, victimisation impact, previous victimisation experience, physical and cognitive handicaps, and degree and character of trauma and post-traumatic stress disorder (PTSD). It should also include primary social aspects of the person's life, including: cultural and ethnic affiliations, neighbourhood influences, family status, and the extent of friendships and other relationships, which include those with work colleagues, school mates and professional contacts. To complete the assessment, it is important to take note of those unique victim coping resources linked to their own special life-space, being mindful of how these influenced their victimisation. The ultimate objectives of the assessment are to identify the extent and character of injury, discover which resources need to be changed and/or strengthened to facilitate achieving the end state of recovery, and to create a treatment plan to maximise the quality of the intervention (Andrews, 1990).

The second phase of recovery involves treating the victim with an array of evidence-based protocols that will reduce suffering, confusion, fear, anger, dysfunction, trauma, PTSD and other related symptoms. As some of these symptoms continue to worsen the victim's condition, it becomes imperative to act as soon as possible to prevent further victimisation by reducing risk and hastening progression towards the end state of recovery. The key to effective intervention is to provide protocols that are tailored to the specific needs of each victim based on an accurate assessment. For the initial contact with most victims, information, support and crisis intervention are recommended, even though many victims will not experience crisis. Follow-up victim protocols can include: stress reduction; psychosocial education for the victim, family and peer groups; and psychotherapy and cognitive-behavioural treatment (Andrews, 1990; Cook et al, 2013). In the final phase of recovery, a determination should be made as to whether the victim has achieved end-state recovery. This means that a measured criterion is used to ascertain whether the victim has returned to normalcy in their everyday life, has reclaimed their self-esteem and does not have significant symptoms. When the agency-agreed-upon set of measured recovery standards are reached, it is time to cease treatment. In some cases, due to a variety of barriers, there can be premature dropout of those in treatment (Rogers et al, 2015). Periodic follow-up checks using evidence-based measures, within a few weeks, after a month and after a year following the cessation of treatment, are recommended.

JOHN P.J. DUSSICH

See also: **Survivorology**

Readings

Andrews, A.B. (1990) 'Crisis and recovery services for family violence survivors', in A.R. Roberts (ed) *Helping crime victims: Research, policy, and practice.* Newbury Park, CA: Sage, pp 206–32.

Cook, J.M., Thompson, R., Harb, G.C. and Ross, R.J. (2013) 'Cognitive-behavior treatment for posttraumatic nightmares: an investigation of predictors of dropout and outcome', *Psychological Trauma: Theory, Research, Practice, and Policy,* 5(6): 545–53.

Maekoya, C. and Dussich, J.P.D. (2010) 'Exploring possible indicators of recovery', *International Perspectives in Victimology,* 5(1): 37–45.

Rogers, M.S., Zeigler, S., Tuerk, P.W., Cunningham, P.B. and Acierno, R. (2015) 'Barriers to completing treatment for veterans with PTSD', in T. Tollefson (ed) *Victimological advances in theory, policy and services.* Fresno, CA: Dumont Printing, pp 249–60.

Takahashi, Y. and Dussich, J.P.J. (2010) 'Assessing the impact of coping resources on the degree of recovery from negative critical life events: a study of Japanese college students', *International Perspectives in Victimology,* 5(1): 29–35.

VICTIM SERVICES

Simply stated, globally, victim services are those helping activities provided directly to victims. Victim services are a relatively new profession also referred to as victim advocacy, victim support and victim assistance. The primary function of victim services is to serve as first responders, mostly to crime victims. However, while most victim service generalist programmes provide services to the full spectrum of victims of crimes, many programmes provide services to other victim types: human trafficking, terrorism, traffic accidents, human rights violations, armed conflicts and wars, disasters and others. The persons who perform victim services are usually university graduates who have studied in the social sciences, with some having also received specialised training in victimology, victim rights and victim services. Most of these victim service providers are full-time or part-time paid employees, although some are full-time or part-time volunteers. Volunteers are a major part of victim services. Many of these care providers are themselves victim survivors who have experienced similar suffering to those they now care for.

The main activities of victim services include: assuming immediate responsibility as a first responder; performing psychological first-aid; referring and facilitating emergency medical and psychosocial services; serving as a victim advocate during the aftermath of victimisation; helping to protect victims from media exploitation; ensuring the adequate delivery of other forms of public assistance to victims; supporting crime victims with their role as witnesses; providing reality-oriented counselling; assisting victims to avoid re-victimisation; rendering hotline services; offering crisis intervention; and ensuring victim safety during the aftermath, especially during a criminal trial. With regard to crime victims specifically, services promote victim compensation and restitution and, when appropriate, restorative options, aiding victims as the primary conduit for their case-related information. While these activities are high-priority services provided directly to victims, other activities are provided that serve the needs of the host agencies (mentioned earlier) and the community, such as: developing victim awareness programmes; conducting community research with victimisation surveys; engaging in pre-victim-oriented prevention programmes focused on vulnerable groups using survey results; and lobbying on behalf of victim rights and systemic policy reforms in all areas of government (Dussich, 1976).

Most victim service organisations started out as grassroots entities. However, today, victim services are carried out at the community and state levels by a wide range of organisations: some are not-for-profit and some are government entities serving the needs of the criminal justice system. These generalist crime victim service organisations may be hosted by different components of the criminal justice system: the police, the prosecution and the courts (other organisations such as religious groups may also play a part in different jurisdictions). Most specialty crime victim service programmes focus exclusively on unique types of victims: sexual assault, intimate partner violence, child abuse and elder mistreatment. The funding of these organisations is mostly the responsibility of local government and private donors; however, some national governments provide special funding for a wide range of victim services. Resulting from closer collaborations between the private and public sectors, in many jurisdictions, the trend over the past three decades has been away from grassroots non-profit organisations towards government organisations. This has led to more established organisations or what can be called the 'institutionalization of victim support' (Van Dijk, 1988, p 120). In recent years, local criminal justice systems in the US have become more victims-friendly. This has evolved to the point where there are victim advocates in each of the three components: police, courts and corrections (Karmen, 2015). Although these results have greatly improved the protection of victims' needs and rights, the legal standing of victims in most countries does not yet fulfil the promises of existing victim rights legislation. Of special concern is that victim services and victim protections are still not being fully honoured by the courts. The irony of this condition is that the violators of some of these rights are agents of the criminal justice system, which continue to be burdened by the weight of conservative attitudes resisting the changes intended by recent victim rights legislation (Beloof et al, 2006).

JOHN P.J. DUSSICH

See also: **Victims of Crime; Victims' Rights**

Readings

Beloof, D.E., Cassell, P.G. and Twist, S.J. (2006) *Victims in criminal procedure* (2nd edn). Durham, NC: Carolina Academic Press.

Dussich, J.P.J. (1976) 'Victim service models and their efficacy', in E.C. Viano (ed) *Victims and society.* Washington, DC: Visage Press, pp 471–83.

Karmen, A. (2015) 'Assessing the victim-friendliness of a local criminal justice system: an inventory for use by advocates and activists', in T. Tollefson (ed) *Victimological advances in theory, policy and services.* Fresno, CA: Dumont Printing.

Van Dijk, J.J.M. (1988) 'Ideological trends within the victim movement: an international perspective', in M. Maguire and J. Pointing (eds) *Victims of crime: A new deal?* Milton Keynes: Open University Press.

VICTIMOLOGICAL OTHER

This is a shorthand way of delineating the ways in which different versions of victimology give visibility to some kinds of victims and render others invisible. This concept captures who is included, counted and acquires the label of 'victim' and who is not. Who is included and excluded from understandings of victimhood is important for understanding the nature and extent of criminal victimisation and what might be done about it. Who constitutes the 'victimological other' varies according to what kind of victimisation is the focus of concern (see Walklate, 2007). For example, it is easy to assume from some feminist work on sexual violence that victim equals female, and perpetrator equals male. This assumption renders the sexual victimisation of men hidden from view. In relation to this particular issue, men constitute the 'victimological other'. Perversely, this is a view endorsed by much mainstream victimological work. Historically, the white, heterosexual, reasonable male has been the measuring stick against which to compare those most likely to be victims and those most likely not to be. However, this is not the only dimension along which a victimological other might be constructed.

The notion of the 'innocent' victim of crime has also informed much policy and practice in response to victimisation. The notion of innocence, while informed by earlier distinctions made between 'deserving' and 'undeserving' victims, removes what Miers (2007) has referred to as 'delinquent victims' from the purview of policy. An innocent victim cannot be blamed for what happened to them and is deserving of help and support, but a delinquent victim certainly can be.

Lying behind the construction of the victimological other are conceptions of an 'ideal victim', first articulated by Christie in 1986 (Christie, 1986). This concept centres on notions of innocence, legitimacy and deserving and led Carrabine et al (2004) to identify what they termed a 'hierarchy of victimisation'. At the bottom of this hierarchy would be the homeless, the street prostitute and the drug addict, indeed, all those categories of people for whom it is presumed that they expose themselves to victimisation. These people are not innocent, legitimate or deserving and certainly comply with a conservative understanding of who might comprise the 'victimological other'. At the top of this hierarchy would be the elderly person robbed in their own home, the child abused by their parents and perhaps increasingly an elderly person abused by their children. These people are innocent, legitimate and deserving and their claim to victim status would be considered non-problematic.

This hierarchy of victimisation can be applied in different contexts and can be used to facilitate an understanding of the ways in which victimhood changes shape and form over time. Some groups and/or individuals acquire victim status and others lose it. McGarry and Walklate (2011), for example, make the case for soldiers being recognised as victims in the UK as a result of the illegal engagement in conflict in Iraq and Afghanistan from 2003 to 2014: a group for whom the victim label was previously considered anathema. In a similar vein, Aradau (2004) deploys the idea of a 'politics of pity' to make sense of the ways in which trafficked women came to be constructed as victims, rather than women seeking work, in order for their abuse to be recognised. They were constructed as innocent, legitimate and deserving rather than delinquent and 'other'. Similarly, there is evidence to suggest that the political complexities lying behind the mass victimisations in Darfur inhibited international recognition of those experiences as genocide

(Hagan and Rymond-Richmond, 2009). Those victims remained 'othered' until those complexities changed. In all of these examples, being acknowledged as a victim is a complex process, with the constitution of the victimological other being context-dependent and variable over time.

SANDRA WALKLATE

See also: **Blame and Victims; Deviant Victims; Victim Hierarchy**

Readings

Aradau, C. (2004) 'The perverse politics of four-letter words: risk and pity in the securitisation of human trafficking', *Millennium: Journal of International Studies*, 33(2): 251–77.

Carrabine, E., Iganski, P., Lee, M., Plummer, K. and South, N. (2004) *Criminology: A sociological introduction*. London: Routledge.

Christie, N. (1986) 'The ideal victim', in E.A. Fattah (eds) *From crime policy to victim policy: Reorientating the justice system*. Basingstoke: MacMillan Press, pp 17–30.

Hagan, J. and Rymond-Richmond, W. (2009) *Darfur and the crime of genocide*. Cambridge: Cambridge University Press.

McGarry, R. and Walklate, S. (2011) 'The soldier as victim: peering through the looking glass', *British Journal of Criminology*, 46(6): 900–17.

Miers, D. (2007) 'Looking beyond Great Britain: the development of criminal injuries', in S. Walklate (eds) *The handbook of victims and victimology*. Cullompton: Willan Publishing, pp 337–62.

Walklate, S. (2007) *Imagining the victim of crime*. Maidenhead: Open University Press.

VICTIMOLOGY

Criminology is the study of offenders, the people they victimise, the operations of the criminal justice system and the social reaction to crime. Therefore, victimology can be considered a sub-discipline or area of specialisation within criminology, and victimologists are criminologists who pay close attention to the physical wounds, emotional turmoil and financial hardships inflicted by lawbreakers. Victimisation is an asymmetrical interpersonal relationship that is unfair, parasitical, oppressive, exploitative, abusive, painful, destructive and forbidden by law.

Victimologists have generally focused their attention on individuals and groups who have endured acts of violence and theft, especially murders (including at workplaces, on campuses and of officers in the line of duty), aggravated assaults like shootings and stabbings, hate crimes, terrorist attacks, intimate partner violence, forcible rapes (and other sexual assaults and molestations), child abuse, elder abuse, kidnappings, robberies, burglaries, motor vehicle thefts, identity thefts, and other larcenies.

Some criminologists focus on the 'kinds of people' most at risk of committing acts of violence or theft; victimologists carry out research, often by using self-report surveys, to discover 'differential risks' – estimates of the degree of danger faced by specific groups based on their common geographic and demographic factors. Just as other criminologists scrutinise how the legal system handles suspects, defendants and convicts, victim-oriented researchers study how injured parties are handled by officials and agencies. The primary practical goal of victim-centred studies is to devise ways to help them recover: to find out how effectively they are being assisted, supported, served, compensated, rehabilitated and educated to avoid further trouble.

Reacting emotionally to the suffering of victims might be categorised as a subjective approach; issues are approached from the standpoint of morality, ethics, philosophy and personal experiences. Victimologists examine these same incidents through a social science lens as objectively as possible by striving to be fair, open-minded, even-handed, impartial, dispassionate, neutral and unbiased. The value of reserving judgements and resisting the urge to readily identify with those who were harmed might not be self-evident and could even appear to be insensitive, if not callous. However, victimologists cannot be automatically, unabashedly and consistently pro-victim because real-life confrontations often do not generate simple clear-cut cases that neatly fall into the dichotomies of complete innocence and overwhelming guilt. Not all individuals who end up wounded or even killed were weak, defenceless, unsuspecting prey targeted by vicious predators. Some clashes can be characterised as 'criminal versus criminal', in which it is far from clear to detectives, prosecutors, reporters or jurors which of the two combatants is worthy of support and protection and which should be stigmatised as the villainous aggressor deserving of condemnation, arrest and punishment. The designations 'victim' and 'offender' are not always at opposite poles, but can sometimes be pictured as overlapping categories near the middle of a continuum bounded by total blamelessness (such as being in the wrong place at the wrong time) and full legal responsibility. The status of being a legitimate, bona fide or 'ideal type' of victim is surely socially constructed and conferred.

Striving for objectivity is also important because crime victims can and do become embroiled in conflicts with other persons and groups besides offenders: journalists reporting about their cases; police officers and detectives investigating their complaints; prosecutors ostensibly representing their interests in court; defence lawyers working on behalf of the accused; juries and judges deciding how to resolve their cases; probation, parole and corrections departments supervising convicts who harmed them; lawyers handling their lawsuits in civil court; state-run compensation programmes set up to reimburse them; governmental agencies and legislative bodies shaping their legal rights; social movements either speaking on their behalf or opposing their wishes; and businesses viewing them as customers for security products and services. Impartiality helps social scientists to understand why friction can develop in these situations and how to find solutions if these relationships become antagonistic.

Controversial issues for research include: accusations of shared responsibility (victim facilitation, precipitation, provocation); contentions that not all victims receive equal protection under the law (perhaps because of their age, race, class and sex); exhortations that victims should arm themselves for self-protection; contentions that victims should vigorously pursue their recently gained legal rights to play a more influential role (especially concerning conditions of bail, plea negotiations, sentences, restitution obligations and parole decisions); and recommendations that they resolve their cases in victim–offender reconciliation programmes that pursue restorative justice rather than retributive justice.

ANDREW KARMEN

See also: **Blame and Victims; Victims of Crime**

Readings

Karmen, A. (2016) *Crime victims: An introduction to victimology* (9th edn). Boston, MA: Cengage Learning.
Schafer, S. (1977) *Victimology: The victim and his criminal.* Reston, VA: Reston Publishers.

VICTIMS' CHARTERS

In England and Wales, the first Victims' Charter in 1990 was one of a series of charters produced by John Major's Conservative government, heralding the age of consumerism, with victims repositioned as consumers of criminal justice services as they shed their Cinderella status. Published to a fanfare of publicity, the charter was described as setting out for the first time the rights and entitlements of victims of crime. This was misleading. Rather, with few exceptions, it set out a code of good practice, listing the ways in which victims should be treated by both state bodies and non-governmental organisations (NGOs). However, it was innovative in that, for the first time, it applied standards to agencies with respect to their treatment of victims. The Victims' Charter was updated and extended in 1996, covering the services that victims should expect, what should happen at different stages of the process and how to complain if services were found wanting. The charter was then supplemented by specialist leaflets.

The interest in victims and victims' services gained increased momentum under the New Labour years, where victim-oriented justice became the pivotal feature of Home Office thinking on crime and disorder. Subsequently, a raft of discussion papers and policy documents focusing on victims emerged. Many of these initiatives were drawn together in the third version of the charter, *The code of practice for victims of crime* (Home Office, 2005), first published in 2005, which described the minimum level of services that victims should expect. In a move to a more rights-based agenda, the code promised a complaints system, culminating in the Parliamentary Ombudsman, should agencies fail to deliver an appropriate standard of service. In a significant change of emphasis, the code focused almost exclusively on public sector bodies, largely ignoring the voluntary sector except where they were engaged in multi-agency partnerships, or where public sector bodies were required to liaise with, or refer victims to, NGOs like Victim Support. In 2008, services for witnesses were detailed separately in a Witness Charter, based on 34 standards that set out the level of service that witnesses could expect. The charter applied to all agencies providing services to witnesses in criminal proceedings, including the police, Witness Care Units, the Crown Prosecution Service, Her Majesty's Courts Service and the Witness Service.

The recent Coalition government's views on victim policies were set out in Paper CP3/2012 (Ministry of Justice (2012) and reiterated after a period of consultation. The need to update both charters was accepted, although the government favoured the 'outcome-based approach' of the Witness Charter to the 'process-oriented' approach of the victims' code, which it perceived as being too rights-based. This is reflected in the updated versions of each charter, published in 2013. The new code sets out the minimum standards that victims should expect, distinguishing between different subgroups of victim, with an emphasis upon support for the most vulnerable victims, following the spirit of CP3/2012. Again, the code refers to public sector agencies and excludes NGOs, but includes an additional focus on restorative justice services and specifies that the code applies to business victims as well as individuals. Alongside it, the revised Witness Charter sets out the standards of service/care that witnesses should expect at six stages: during police investigation; for pre-trial information; when going to court; on arrival at court; in the courtroom; and post-trial. It also contains details of additional support for vulnerable and intimidated witnesses.

As a means of summarising the range of services that victims and witnesses should expect from the different public sector agencies, and as a means of directing victims to further information, charters in England and Wales were an excellent innovation, and similar charters and codes have been introduced in Northern

Ireland and, recently, Scotland, and in a range of other countries. However, contrary to the message implied in their title, they rarely deliver victims' rights: rights to help, to information, to compensation and to be heard. Indeed, the 2013 code in England and Wales illustrates this, with the availability of financial compensation and personal help for victims restricted to the allegedly most vulnerable and 'blame-free' victims. The virtual exclusion of NGOs from the code is also a weakness. Nevertheless, as a statement of the way in which the criminal justice system has moved towards the recognition of victims' importance to that system, charters and codes signify progress.

ROB I. MAWBY

See also: **Code of Practice for Victims in England and Wales; Victims of Crime**

Readings

Home Office (2005) *The code of practice for victims of crime*, London: Home Office.
Ministry of Justice (2012) 'Getting it right for victims and witnesses: the government response'. Available at: www.gov.uk/government/publications/getting-it-right-for-victims-and-witnesses-the-government-response
Ministry of Justice (2013a) 'Code of practice for victims of crime, October'. Available at: www.gov.uk/government/uploads/system/uploads/attachment_data/file/254459/code-of-practice-victims-of-crime.pdf
Ministry of Justice (2013b) 'The Witness Charter: standards of care for witnesses in the criminal justice system'. Available at: https://www.gov.uk/government/publications/the-witness-charter-standards-of-care-for-witnesses-in-the-criminal-justice-system
Walklate, S. (ed) (2007) *The handbook of victims and victimology*. Cullompton: Willan Publishing.
Williams, B. (1999) 'The Victim's Charter: citizens as consumers of criminal justice services', *Howard Journal*, 38(4): 384–96.

VICTIMS' MOVEMENTS

The beginnings of the victims' movement can be linked to the increase in academic work on victimisation, which would place the origins with early victimologists (Hall, 2010). However, victims' movements are generally associated with a more politicised approach, involving campaigning for a prominent role for victims within the criminal justice process and for greater support (Goodey, 2005). So, while pinpointing the exact origins of victims' movements is not a straightforward task, it is generally thought to be during the 1960s and 1970s when a noticeable focus on victims' issues began to emerge and gain traction (Shapland et al, 1985; Mawby and Walklate, 1994).

It would be a mistake to see the development of the victims' movement internationally as 'an uncomplicated series of simple, chronological breakthroughs' (Hall, 2010, p 22). In reality, a complex picture of competing interests and multiple drivers underpinned the resurgence of interest in the victim. Goodey (2005) cites three key developments that coincided to foster this increased interest and helped to establish a victims' movement: first, the growing crime rates and the disillusionment with rehabilitation as a response to offending; second, the move to centre-right governments on both sides of the Atlantic, accompanied by a more punitive approach to law and order; and, third, the second wave of feminism, which had a specific interest in placing the victimisation of women and children on the public and policy agenda. Other notable factors included the growth in academic research and knowledge about the victim experience, the recognition of victims as important to policymaking initiatives within criminal justice, and the influence of developments occurring internationally upon the UK context (Hall, 2010).

Shapland et al (1985) have suggested that within the victims' movement, a number of different components can be identified that help to conceptualise and understand the significant developments that have occurred, including: some states establishing a compensation scheme and offender contributions to aid reparation; recognising victim experiences of criminal justice processes and seeking to improve these; and the provision of support and aid through the creation of victim support initiatives.

The character of victims' movements differs quite substantially at the international level (Hall, 2010). While there are variations in how the provision of aid and assistance for victims has manifested itself in European countries and in the US, there has been a general theme of providing emotional as well as more practical support, which has been the case for the services offered by Victim Support in the UK (Goodey, 2005).

The victims' movement does not represent a unified political group. There are differences in the ideologies and the motivations of those who campaign for victim concerns. Goodey (2005) notes how diverse groups such as feminist activists and right-wing lobbyists may come together to promote victims' rights in the criminal justice system, but will do so from different perspectives and for different reasons. For example, feminist campaigners may lobby for additional protections for rape victims in court, whereas those from a right-wing perspective might argue for the use of victim personal statements prior to sentencing (Goodey, 2005). The two approaches do not sit comfortably together under the banner of victims' rights.

The needs of victims are varied and subjective, which is not always recognised. With elements of the victims' movement not necessarily based upon the experiences and views of victims themselves (Shapland et al, 1985), there is a risk of movements inadvertently perpetuating the notion of an 'ideal victim' (Christie, 1986), marginalising those who do not fall within this category who may therefore be unable to benefit from the support, compensation and other rights and services that the movements may have campaigned to secure.

There have been concerns raised over the political and ideological manipulation of the victims' movement in the UK and in the US by those wishing to promote an agenda that does not necessarily have the victims' interests at its centre (Mawby and Walklate, 1994; Hall, 2010). The politicisation of victims can be perceived as a way of engendering support from the electorate, and championing victims' rights can also be used as a means to support more punitive law-and-order measures, which has the potential to do more harm than good (Goodey, 2005).

With more campaign groups emerging, the continuing provision of support for victims, more research focusing on victims, and further legislation and policy initiatives, the development of this diverse movement shows no sign of abating.

CLAIRE FOX

See also: **Criminal Justice and Victims; Victim Services; Victims' Rights**

Readings

Christie, N. (1986) 'Ideal victim', in E.A. Fattah (ed) *From crime policy to victim policy: Reorientating the justice system*. Basingstoke: MacMillan Press, pp 17–30.

Goodey, J. (2005) *Victims and victimisation: Research, policy and practice*. Harlow: Pearson Longman.

Hall, M. (2010) *Victims and policy making: A comparative perspective*. Oxon: Willan.

Mawby, R.I. and Walklate, S. (1994) *Critical victimology*. London: Sage.

Shapland, J., Willmore, J. and Duff, P. (1985) *Victims of crime in the criminal justice system*. Aldershot: Gower.

VICTIMS OF CRIME

While the term 'victim' is commonly applied to someone who has suffered from some kind of misfortune, over the last 50 years, that common usage has been increasingly co-joined with crime. 'Crime', as a concept, is itself problematic;

nonetheless, for the purposes of this discussion, its use with the term 'victim' is more often than not connected with those kinds of behaviours rendered illegal by law. Thus, the victim of crime is an individual who has suffered as a result of the illegal behaviour of another individual. It should, of course, be noted that once a crime has been recognised and acted upon by the criminal justice process, the term 'victim' becomes problematic since in the legal process, there are complainants, witnesses and defendants, not victims and offenders. In addition to the different ways in which a victim of crime might be referred to in law, there are other problematic issues associated with the notion of a 'victim' of crime.

Historically, feminists have challenged the use of the term 'victim', especially in relation to women's experiences of sexual violence, since this term implicitly attributes passivity and powerlessness to the individual concerned. These attributes are also, by definition, associated with being female. Thus, feminists express a preference for the term 'survivor' as a better way to capture women's resistance to male power. In putting to the fore the concept of survivor, feminism also draws our attention to appreciating that being a victim of crime, and acquiring this label, is a process and not necessarily a label achieved simply because an individual has been subjected to an act that has caused them suffering. In this respect, Christie (1986) reflects on how this process of acquiring the victim label is informed by our understandings of the 'ideal victim'.

The concept of the ideal victim points to the important connections to be made between acquiring victim status and whether or not an individual is understood as a 'deserving' or an 'undeserving' victim. These social processes are a reminder that there can be 'good' and 'bad' victims, as well as 'good' and 'bad' offenders. These additional distinctions between victims prompted Carrabine et al (2004, p 117) to talk of a 'hierarchy of victimisation'. In this hierarchy, some victims of crime are more visible and easily recognised as victims, and find themselves at the top of the hierarchy in terms of responses to their suffering, with others being more invisible finding themselves at the bottom. Clearly, victim status is not easily achieved, especially for those who fall short of the ideal victim stereotype. This is equally the case for those victims whose experiences of victimisation are the result of the victimisation of a collective or group.

Genocide and atrocity crimes have increasingly drawn attention to the fact that victims of crime are not always or necessarily individuals. In an interesting application of the notion of the 'ideal victim' to such international crimes, Van Wijk (2013) posits that in order for a victim status to be assigned successfully to such crimes, certain conditions need to be met: the conflict must not be complex, it must be unique, it must be short and it must be well-timed. In particular, the role and use of the media is pertinent to understanding the conditions for the successful acquisition of victim status for these kinds of crime, with 'good' and 'bad' victims featuring prominently in that process. Hence, the concepts of ideal victim, deserving and undeserving victims, and the hierarchy of victimisation underpin and inform who is considered and/or not considered to be legitimate in their claim for victim status.

SANDRA WALKLATE

See also: **Deviant Victims; Primary, Secondary and Tertiary Victims and Victimisation; Victim Hierarchy; Victimological Other**

Readings

Carrabine, E., Iganski, P., Lee, M., Plummer, K. and South, N. (2004) *Criminology: A sociological introduction*. London: Routledge.

Christie, N. (1986) 'The ideal victim', in E.A. Fattah (ed) *From crime policy to victim policy: Reorientating the justice system*. Basingstoke: Macmillan Press, pp 17–30.

Van Wijk, J. (2013) 'Who is the "little old lady" of international crimes? Nils Christie's concept of the ideal victim re-interpreted', *International Review of Victimology*, 19(2): 159–79.

VICTIMS' RIGHTS

The modern debate on victims' rights emerged from a 'rights revolution' fuelled by a 'rights consciousness' (Friedman, 1985) that began after the Second World War with the international community endorsing a Universal Declaration on Human Rights. It is the root for other rights proclamations for women, prisoners, children, minority groups, people with mental illnesses, people with disabilities, older persons, indigenous peoples and victims of gross violations of human rights and humanitarian law, as well as for victims of terrorism. Each proclamation recognises entitlements, provides standards to govern the treatment of individuals and collectives of people, and imposes obligations on those in authority. Some proclamations also provide for an enforcement mechanism, which might be a body charged with monitoring the operation of the proclamation or a grievance procedure.

Crime victims' rights evolved out of the 1960s' civil rights movement in the US but the push for these rights soon became a prominent feature of public policy in other developed nations. Rising crime rates, coupled with a heightened fear of crime, the outcries of disenfranchised victims who felt shut out of the criminal justice system, a perception that too much attention was being paid to defendants' rights, and a diminished confidence in criminal justice systems, contributed to assertions that victims were the 'forgotten people' in such systems. Moreover, especially in those nations that inherited the British adversarial approach to criminal justice, it was argued that victims they had been relegated to mere witnesses for the state–as-prosecutor.

Victims' rights are intended to empower victims and to obligate police, prosecutors, magistrates and judges, correctional officers and others. The United Nations Declaration of the Basic Principles of Justice for Victims of Crime and Abuse of Power (1985) (the declaration) enshrines 10 rights for crime victims, which are a mix of negative rights and positive rights. The former prohibit certain actions, for instance, public officials should not unnecessarily intrude on victims' privacy, whereas the latter require the provision of certain actions, for instance, governments should provide material and therapeutic assistance to victims. Furthermore, when enacted in domestic law, these rights are frequently constructed as passive rights, so victims are required to, for example, ask for information about the investigation before a police officer is obligated to provide it or ask to be notified on prosecutorial decisions before a prosecutor is obligated to consult.

Service and information rights have been widely welcomed, whereas participatory rights are said to be fraught with difficulties, especially in adversarial criminal justice systems. An evaluation on the implementation of the declaration and studies on the effectiveness of domestic victims' rights instruments in several countries reveal that, in spite of better recognition of victims' standing in criminal proceedings and improvements in their treatment, too many victims continue to be denied their entitlements. In addition, their interests remain peripheral to those of the state and those of defendants.

As a consequence, demand for stronger and enforceable victims' rights has gained traction. Such rights have been enacted in the US and promised in other places. Victims have standing as participants in proceedings in the International Criminal Court and some international tribunals. In Austria, victims' right to legal counsel has been reintroduced; in Japan, crime victims (like those in Germany) have become co-accusers. Independent statutory officers in Britain, Canada and Australia, among other functions, inquire into victims' grievances and recommend remedies.

A US study, however, suggests that stronger rights laws do not necessarily produce better outcomes (US Department of Justice, 1998; see also Davis and Mulford, 2008). Perhaps instead of stronger rights, there should be greater investment in the current regime of crime victims' rights. Groenhuijsen (2014) says that if public officials are already not meeting their obligations, it is ludicrous to assume that simply increasing their obligations will improve the operation of victims' rights laws. It is also unclear whether victims genuinely benefit from the 'rights industry' and the culture it fosters. Some commentators, for example, allege that the victims' right agenda has been co-opted by the law-and-order lobby. Others point to crime victims' unrealistic expectations, which might be driven by vested interests such as lawyers who profit from victims attaining legal status in criminal proceedings. Zur (2015) warns that victims' rights should neither be the sole preoccupation nor a distraction if the dynamic between victims and victimisers and the social, economic, political and cultural context in which the crime happens, or happened, is to be genuinely tackled, and victimisation is thus to be prevented.

The concept of victims' rights remains contentious, and the growth of enforceable victims' rights is not yet well informed. That said, the genie of victims' rights is 'out of the bottle' and unlikely to be returned. Giving victims rights, especially participatory rights, can alleviate their sense of disenfranchisement and prevent secondary victimisation. Thus, ensuring that all crime victims throughout the world are treated fairly and equitably, as well as having access to justice, is paramount.

MICHAEL O'CONNELL

See also: **Victims of Crime**

Readings

Davis, R.C. and Mulford, C. (2008) 'Victim rights and new remedies – finally getting victims their due', *Journal of Contemporary Criminal Justice*, 24(2): 198–208.

Friedman, L.M. (1985) *Total justice*. New York, NY: Russell Sage Foundation.

Groenhuijsen, M. (2014) 'The development of international policy in relation to victims of crime', *International Review of Victimology*, 20: 31–48. Available at: https://pure.uvt.nl/portal/files/1577224/The_development_of_international_policy_in_relation_to_victims_of_crime.pdf

Matrix Insight and Andersson Elfers Felix (2010) *The study for an impact assessment on ways of improving the support, protection and rights of victims across Europe*. Brussels: Council of Europe, Directorate-General Justice, Freedom and Security. Available at: http://ec.europa.eu/justice/criminal/files/matrix_2010_ia_final_report_en.pdf

United Nations (1985) 'Declaration of the Basic Principles of Justice for Victims of Crime and Abuse of Power', General Assembly Resolution 40/34, annex. Available at: http://www.un.org/documents/ga/res/40/a40r034.htm

US Department of Justice (1998) *Victims' right compliance efforts: Experiences in three states, report*. Washington, DC: US Department of Justice. Available at: http://ojp.gov/ovc/publications/infores/vrce.pdf

Zur, O. (2015) *Rethinking 'don't blame the victim': The psychology of victimhood*. Sonoma, CA: Zur Institute. Available at: www.zurinstitute.com/victimhood.html

VICTIMS, SURVIVORS OR COMPLAINANTS?

The word 'victim' has itself become the centre of arguments about terminology. Victims of sexual offending, in particular, have said that they prefer to be called 'survivors'. The word 'victim' is said to imply a certain passivity and acceptance of one's position. The word 'survivor', on the other hand, implies an element of agency and inner strength on the part of the person concerned to take at least some control over their circumstances and to take action to survive the trauma that has come their way.

In a 2015 parliamentary debate, all the MPs referred to 'survivors' rather than 'victims'. Caroline Lucas MP noted this change of terminology:

> The Home Secretary and all hon. Members have used repeatedly the word 'survivor', which is wonderful. May I make a quick plea to the press and the media who are following this debate and this issue to use the word 'survivor' and not the word 'victim', because every time they use that word, it adds to the hurt and the disrespect? (Hansard House of Commons Debates, 4 February 2015, col 285)

Home Secretary Theresa May responded that:

> ... the hon. Lady is absolutely right about language. It is important that we use the language of survivors or, in some cases, of victims and survivors ... I say to the House and to all outside who comment on this matter that we should be very careful about the language we use. We should not use inappropriate terms that are hurtful and that could cause harm to individuals. (Hansard House of Commons Debates, 4 February 2015, col 285)

If 'victims' was the wrong word, to be replaced by 'survivors', 'survivors' was considered by some to be the wrong word when used in the early stages of the criminal justice process. Critics argued that the word was being used prematurely and before any due process of law and court proceedings had been started to determine whether someone was actually 'a victim' or not. The correct word, it was suggested, was 'complainant' until such time as proof had been established.

In light of the sexual offences committed against children by celebrity Jimmy Savile, a joint report was written by the National Society for the Prevention of Cruelty to Children (NSPCC) and the Metropolitan Police in 2013. It reported on investigations into Jimmy Savile's activities and it explained why they used the word 'victim' rather than 'complainant':

On the whole victims are not known to each other and taken together their accounts paint a compelling picture of widespread sexual abuse by a predatory sex offender. We are therefore referring to them as 'victims' rather than 'complainants' *and are not presenting the evidence they have provided as unproven allegations.* (Gray and Watt, 2013, para 2.4, emphasis added)

Barbara Hewson, a barrister, accused both the police and NSPCC of playing the roles of judge and jury:

What neither acknowledges is that this national trawl for historical victims was an open invitation to all manner of folk to reinterpret their experience of the past as one of victimisation. It's time to end this prurient charade, which has nothing to do with justice or the public interest. Adults and law-enforcement agencies must stop fetishising victimhood. (Hewson, 2013, para 19)

The arguments have continued. In December 2014, the Metropolitan Police sought possible victims of sexual abuse from the 1970s, and a Detective Superintendent went on television to reassure any victims who might come forward that '*you will be believed*, you will be supported' (BBC News, 2014, emphasis added). What appeared to be missing was any recognition that people could lie and make false statements that needed to be examined in court; at worst, this could result in miscarriages of justice. The better terminology, it was suggested, might have been 'you will be taken seriously, you will be supported' and the increasing ease with which testimony might be uncritically 'believed' spread concern among critics who thought that such testimony should always be questioned to arrive at the truth. Not everyone is happy about this move to 'believe' complainants before their evidence and statements have been exposed to rigorous cross-examination in the interests of justice (see, eg, Gittos, 2014).

TERRY THOMAS

See also: **Survivorology**

Readings

BBC News (2014) 'Child abuse inquiry: police investigate three alleged murders', 18 December. Available at: http://www.bbc.co.uk/news/uk-30534235

Gittos, L. (2014) 'The "I believers": a law unto themselves', *Spiked*, 23 December. Available at: http://www.spiked-online.com/newsite/article/the-i-believers-a-law-unto-themselves/16403#.VODhCpWzV9C

Gray, D. and Watt, P. (2013) *Giving victims a voice: Joint report into sexual allegations made against Jimmy Savile.* London: Metropolitan Police and NSPCC.

Hewson, B. (2013) 'Yewtree is destroying the rule of law', *Spiked*, 8 May. Available at: http://www.spiked-online.com/newsite/article/13604#.VMlYa5WzV9A

VISUAL VICTIMOLOGY

The media plays a fundamental role in ideological struggles and agenda setting. It entertains, seeks to make profits and is an important communicative tool. For Cavender (2004, p 336), this 'is what the media do in contemporary society; they help define what we think about, what we see as problems and the solutions we consider'. Many individuals do not have direct experience of crime, the criminal justice system and agents of social control; therefore, the media play a fundamental role in the public's understanding or misunderstanding of crime, victims and victimisation.

Rawlings (1998) and Rafter (2007) recognised the popularity and impact of factual and fictional accounts of crime and thus their worthiness of academic study. Similarly, Stevens (2011, p 7) states that what most people 'know about crime and its history can often be traced to motion pictures, popular television dramas, and news reports'. Whether representations of crime are mediated in the format of entertainment or news, 'crime sells', even though, in the main, it has 'virtually no relationship to the reality of crime itself or the functioning of the criminal justice system' (Potter and Kappeler, 2012, p 4).

Yet, narratives about and representations of crime have always been, and continue to be, a prime feature of the media (Cavender, 2004; Reiner, 2007; Marsh and Melville, 2009; Jewkes, 2015). New and old media are littered with images of 'crime, harm and punishment', and subsequently, over the past 10 years or so, 'there is growing recognition that criminology needs to rethink its relations with ascendant power of the spectacle' (Carrabine, 2012, p 463). Hayward (2009) called for a *visual criminology* in order to understand the power and influence of visual culture in the context of an increasing mediascape. Carrabine (2012, p 464) refers to this development as the 'visual turn in criminology'. However, is there a *visual turn* regarding *victimology* and, if so, is a *visual victimology* necessitated and desirable? This is a question to which this discussion will return. First, victim representations need exploring.

Bissler and Conners (2012, p 1) contend that one 'unreality' of 'television crime drama' comprises the following: 'a crime is committed, and a suspect is identified, apprehended and brought to justice in just one hour'. While this is true with regard to such representations, what about the victim of crime and the type of victimisation being portrayed? Where there is a crime – real or imagined – there is a victim – real or imagined or a combination of both. For example, the crime drama *Amber* is a four-part series set in the suburbs of Dublin, Ireland, depicting a parent's worst nightmare – the disappearance of their 14-year-old daughter (and school girl). It highlights the devastating impact on her family and the impact on many others who knew her. It also shows the impact of the intense media spotlight that the family is confronted with. This 'fictitious' representation of real-life events prompted mixed audience responses as it raised more questions than answers. Moreover, it did not give the audience the desired closure as Amber Bailey remains missing and the audience do not even know if she is dead or alive.

One factor that theorists agree on with regard to victim representations is that the media make a distinction between, and produce and reproduce the idea of, 'deserving' and 'undeserving' victims (Marsh and Melville, 2009; Jewkes, 2015). Victims of child abuse and murder are presented as the most deserving of criminal justice, public and political support, and this is especially so when the perpetrator is a stranger. However, children can be represented as 'innocent victims', on the one hand, and as 'evil monsters', on the other, especially when they have offended (Jewkes, 2015). Thus, whether the victim is a child, a female or of another social category, the more a primary victim is seen to have played a role in their victimisation, the less deserving they become.

The media also features secondary victims as well as primary victims – and this is increasingly so regarding 'fictitious' victims such as *Amber* and real victims, especially when they are children. In Britain, the media response to the abduction and killing of Sarah Payne was to get behind Sarah's parents campaign for Sarah's Law. Likewise, the parents of Madeleine McCann used the media in a similar manner after their daughter was allegedly abducted while on a family holiday in Portugal (for more detail, see Marsh and Melville, 2009).

Various theorists have come to highlight how news media, in particular, have come to focus less on criminal justice responses to victimisation and harm, and more on victims' families and the grief and emotion that emanates from the wider community and the rest of society. Wardle (2007 in Marsh and Melville, 2009) researched press coverage of high-profile child murders over a 70-year period. Marsh and Melville (2009, p 106) describe how Wardle noted a change 'from photographs of the offender being the most regularly used images to photographs of the victim and victims' families being the most common'.

Höijer (2004) points out how the victims of human suffering feature in highly popular charity programmes such as Children in Need, Comic Relief and Live Aid. Höijer (2004, p 513) draws attention to how the media is increasingly exposing audiences to 'pictures of distant victims of civil wars, genocide, massacres and other violence against civil populations' and, in so doing, plays 'a basic role in giving publicity to human suffering'. She goes on to comment how 'extensive media coverage' of 'distant human suffering' has meant that images of such suffering 'have become part of ordinary citizens' perceptions of conflicts and crises in the world' (Höijer, 2004, p 514). Again, a change in focus is documented from one that concentrated on representing 'military aspects, such as strategies and weapon systems', to a greater focus on 'the people who provoke them, the people who fight them and the people who suffer from them' (BBC war reporter Martin Bell, 1998, cited in Höijer, 2004, pp 515–16). This is especially the case regarding innocent victims of war, political conflicts and other violence.

The importance of national and international representations of victims, both primary and secondary, and depictions of human suffering, especially when they involve innocent children, can be seen in the recent still and moving visual representations of the drowned Syrian boy Aylan Kurdi, aged three, in September 2015. Smith (2015, para 2) commented that the 'images of the lifeless body of a young boy' who was one of 12 Syrians who had drowned attempting to reach the Greek island of Kos 'brought home' the 'full horror of the human tragedy unfolding on the shores of Europe'. The image sparked an array of shared and mixed public and political reactions too complex to be explored here.

The preceding illustrates that as visual representations of crime have been increasing, so too have images of victims, both fictitious and real. Representations of primary and secondary, national and international, real and imagined victims have become a media staple – whatever its format. Further, the victims and victimisation that are being represented entail more than those resultant from crime as encompassed within the criminal law. Crime victims through to zemiological victims are articulated, rearticulated and dearticulated; thus, a *visual victimology* is necessary and desirable in order to understand the intention, reception, ethics and impacts of such still and moving visual images. It is important to critically evaluate the impact on the public and the political, policy and practical responses within and beyond criminal justice through a victimological as well as criminological lens. Finally, given how *the visual* has become an integral and embedded part of criminal justice practitioners' work (Haywood, 2009), the manner in which *the visual* is used to represent and support victims by criminal justice agencies (eg closed-circuit television and the use of video-camera evidence in courts) also warrants investigation.

KAREN CORTEEN

See also: **Primary, Secondary and Tertiary Victims and Victimisation**

Readings

Bissler, D.L. and Conners, J.L. (2012) 'Preface', in D.L. Bissler and J.L Conners (eds) *The harms of crime media: Essays on the perpetuation of racism, sexism and class stereotypes*. London: McFarland and Company, pp 1–2.

Carrabine, E. (2012) 'Just images: aesthetics, ethics and visual criminology', *British Journal of Criminology*, 52: 463–89.

Cavender, R. (2004) 'Media and crime policy: a reconsideration of David Garland's "The culture of control"', *Punishment and Society*, 6(3): 335–48.

Hayward, K. (2009) 'Visual criminology: cultural criminology style', *Criminal Justice Matters*, 78(1): 12–14.

Höijer, B. (2004) The discuss of global compassion: the audience and media reporting of human suffering, *Media, Culture and Society*, 26(4): 513–531.

Jewkes, Y. (2015) *Media and crime* (3rd edn). London: Sage.

Marsh, I. and Melville, G. (2009) *Crime, justice and the media*, London: Routledge.

Potter, G.W. and Kappeler, V.E. (2012) 'Introduction: media, crime and hegemony', in D.L. Bissler and J.L. Conners (eds) *The harms of crime media: Essays on the perpetuation of racism, sexism and class stereotypes*. London: McFarland and Company, pp 3–17.

Rafter, N. (2007) 'Crime, film and criminology: recent sex-crime movies', *Theoretical Criminology*, 11(3): 403–420.

Rawlings, P. (1998) 'True crime', British Society of Criminology Conferences 1. Available at: http://www.britsoccrim.org/volume1/010.pdf

Reiner, R. (2007) 'Media-made criminality: the representation of crime in the mass media', in M. Maquire, R. Morgan and R. Reiner (eds) *The Oxford handbook of criminology*. Oxford: Oxford University Press, pp 189–231.

Smith, H. (2015) 'Shocking images of drowned Syrian boy show the tragic plight of refugees', *The Guardian*, 2 September. Available at: http://www.theguardian.com/world/2015/sep/02/shocking-image-of-drowned-syrian-boy-shows-tragic-plight-of-refugees

Stevens, D.J. (2011) *Media and criminal justice: The CSI effect*. London: Jones and Bartlett.

WHITE-COLLAR CRIME, HARM AND VICTIMISATION

White-collar crime is complex and subject to a range of interpretations. For some theorists, it comprises crimes committed by trusted individuals against an organisation. For other scholars, and as shown here, the concept encapsulates a far more extensive list of offending, for example, corporate, professional and occupational crime.

Victimisation by white-collar offenders is a global problem that impacts people of all ages, race/ethnicity and gender. Despite the large population harmed by white-collar offenders, scholarly research directed at actual victims and explorations of the aftermath of people's experiences is limited. Countless victims of financial frauds, insider trading, corporate wrongdoing and medical malfeasance are often ignored. This lack of acknowledgement occurs for a variety of reasons, including a scarcity of data and misconceived notions that white-collar crime is non-violent and less harmful compared to street crime. Crimes involving unsafe working conditions, dangerous products or toxic dumping endanger and physically injure larger groups of vulnerable populations than burglary, robbery or homicide.

Victimisation with regard to white-collar crimes is a largely underexplored area in criminology and jurisprudence. The lack of knowledge and data may be attributed to disagreements about what constitutes white-collar crime and who is the real victim. Using a broad definition means that corporations, banks, politicians, financiers, medical practitioners, governments and individuals may all be victimised by crimes such as embezzlement, Ponzi Schemes, economic 'meltdowns', poor manufacturing, toxic dumping, insider trading or unsafe drugs. The diffuse nature of white-collar crimes often results in unknown victims, and many people may be unaware of the wrongdoing or reluctant to report to criminal justice officials or regulatory agencies. Other victims, such as corporations or banks, are collective entities with no 'real person' to identify as the victim (or the perpetrator).

Unfortunately, white-collar crimes often result in victim blaming. In financial fraud, for example, the victims are viewed as greedy because they invested in high-risk ventures. Consequently, the loss of retirement accounts or savings is misconceived as just deserts for their own seemingly misguided participation in the fraud. Medical fraud also results in victim blaming, particularly in cases of cosmetic surgery, prescription drug use or reproductive medicine. Similar to early attitudes towards rape and domestic violence incidents, victims are blamed for placing themselves in dangerous situations with questionable outcomes. A so-called 'real victim', as viewed by the media or the public, is an innocent person harmed by a dangerous or unknown offender (Friedrichs, 2010). While victims of white-collar crime may be denied victim status, they experience physical injury, emotional trauma, distress and self-blame.

The number of women and children victimised by white-collar crime is staggering and many scholars believe that women are disproportionately harmed in the medical field because of their reproductive abilities (Dodge, 2009). Numerous case studies and research in Norway, German, Australia and the US suggest that corporate and medical crime against women is promulgated by social expectations and patriarchal control of the female body. Wrongdoing against women in developing world countries remains largely unexplored (Hartmann, 1995). In one case, infant formulas, marketed as safer than breastfeeding, were distributed to developing countries and resulted in hundreds of babies dying from starvation and infections. Wyeth-Ayerst/Pfizer, a pharmaceutical company in the US, intentionally downplayed the risks of the implanted contraceptive Norplant and distributed it to more than 5 million women worldwide. Women using the device suffered from headaches, depressions, weight gain, hair loss and prolonged menstrual bleeding. Similarly, the Dalkon Shield intrauterine device (IUD) scandal in the US caused serious health problems and death, endangering over 1 million women in 80 countries. Also, the pharmaceutical company shipped the devices from the US to developing world countries in non-sterile packs with one applicator per thousands of devices despite known dangers.

White-collar crime victimisation often involves hundreds of investors who suffer financially from illegal or unethical schemes by corporations, financiers or investment advisors. Financial schemes in the US are estimated to cost US$1 million to US$3.5 million in losses annually (Barak, 2012). Restitution for the victims is difficult to obtain. A class action lawsuit more often benefits attorneys and the legal system than the victim. Pursuing a lawsuit against large corporations in civil courts may result in monetary settlements or verdicts, but the expenses are prohibitive for individual victims.

Globally, progress is being made to identify and compensate victims of white-collar crime. Officials in England and Wales have developed the 'fraud justice network', designed to implement remedies for victims of fraud (Buttons et al, 2012). Also, large monetary settlements with the US Justice Department are contributing to victim restitution, although direct compensation remains relatively minimal and may fail to deter large companies, which view fines as just a cost of doing business. International efforts to identify and compensate victims of white-collar crime, including corporate crime, are increasing, but recognition of the serious nature of these crimes requires continued research, better narratives of those who have suffered serious losses and greater legal intervention and state regulation.

MARY DODGE

See also: **Blame and Victims; Social Harm; State-Corporate Crime and Harm**

Readings

Barak, G. (2012) *Theft of a nation: Wall Street looting and federal regulatory colluding.* Lanham, MD: Rowman & Littlefield.

Buttons, M., Tapley, J. and Lewis, C. (2012) 'The "fraud justice network" and the infra-structure of support for individual fraud victims in England and Wales', *Criminology and Criminal Justice*, 13: 37–61.

Dodge, M. (2009) *Women and white-collar crime.* Upper Saddle, NJ: Prentice Hall.

Friedrichs, D.O. (2010) *Trusted criminals: White-collar crime in contemporary society.* Belmont, CA: Wadsworth Cengage Learning.

Hartmann, B. (1995) *Reproductive rights and wrongs.* New York, NY: Harper & Row.

WITNESSES AND WITNESS PROTECTION

Witnesses are an essential part of the court process. However, there are competing rights between protecting witnesses and ensuring justice for the accused. Newburn (2007) identified three issues that affect witness testimony: *acquisition*, which refers to the time between the event and making the testimony in court, whereby the shorter the time period, the more accurate the recollection; *retention*, which is about how witnesses remember information and supports a shorter time span between processes; and *retrieval*, which makes connections between types of offences witnessed and the accuracy of recall. Within all of these stages, core questions arise about the reliability and validity of witnesses.

There are also differences between types of witnesses, and the complexity of the roles they play within the criminal justice process. Witnesses are not necessarily just bystanders to crime, but may be victims or perpetrators. For most people, the courtroom is an 'alien situation' due to the formal procedures and unfamiliar environment, but this may be more challenging for some witnesses, such as children, the disabled, sufferers from mental illness or those who are 'vulnerable' in some way. There are also particular issues for victims of serious sexual assaults (McEwan, 2002).

It is, however, essential that witnesses feel able to participate in court proceedings, this being a fundamental part of the due process of law. Witnesses may therefore require protection from those involved in the alleged crime, and also from the rigours of the court system. Sanders and Jones (2007, p 282) identify problems in offering witnesses the opportunity to 'tell their story' while also reflecting that their appearance in court can be a form of 'secondary victimisation'. This is partly because court procedures in England and Wales employ an 'adversarial system' of justice. This means that witnesses should be physically available and identifiable in court in order to be cross-examined, face to face, by the defence and/or the prosecution (Goodey, 2005). Challenging and sometimes aggressive cross-examination is seen as normal in the adversarial system, where the defence tries to undermine the credibility of prosecution witnesses. Witnesses are also usually only permitted to speak when questioned (Goodey, 2005), which often makes it difficult for them to 'tell their story' in the way they want.

Recent initiatives have attempted to improve the witness experience. The Witness Support Service run by Victim Support, the Domestic Violence Crime and Victims Act 2004 and the 'No Witness, No Justice' initiative, which developed new 'witness units', with multi-agency support, have potentially improved provision for witnesses (Davis et al, 2010). These provide information about court processes and may allow visits to the courts before a trial in order to decrease the level of anxiety that witnesses might experience. Article 6 of the European Convention on Human Rights also denotes the need to protect the private life of witnesses by restricting publication of personal details, particularly where publicity would undermine the quality of evidence (Goodey, 2005). A key policy for improving witness protection, especially for children and those perceived as vulnerable witnesses, was the Youth Justice and Criminal Evidence Act 1999. This Act created a number of special measures for witnesses in court and expanded the definition of what constitutes a 'vulnerable witness' (McEwan, 2002). However, measures such as giving evidence through a video-recording or live video-link can be problematic as the fact that the witness is separated from the courtroom may both imply their need for protection and imply that the defendant is guilty (Goodey, 2005). McEwan (2002), however, argues that there is no evidence to suggest that using video-links increases or decreases the prospects of conviction. Affording anonymity to witnesses is also allowed in limited cases involving crimes such as murder and manslaughter. However, risks include the defence not being able to identify whether the witness has a history of unreliability, or whether they have an undisclosed relationship with the defendant that might be the source of a prejudiced attitude (Goodey, 2005), both of which, while protecting the witness, may undermine the rights of the defendant to a fair trial.

JILL JAMESON and KATE STRUDWICK

See also: **Primary, Secondary and Tertiary Victims and Victimisation; Victims' Rights**

Readings
Davies, M., Croall, H. and Tyrer, J. (2010) *Criminal justice* (4th edn). London: Longman.
Goodey, J. (2005) *Victims and victimology: Research, policy and practice.* London: Longman.
McEwan, J. (2002) 'Special measures for witnesses and victims', in M. McConville and G. Wilson (eds) *The handbook of the criminal justice process.* Oxford: Oxford University Press, pp 231–51.
Newburn, T. (2007) *Criminology.* Cullompton: Willan Publishing.
Sanders, A. and Jones, I. (2007) 'The victim in court', in S. Walklate (ed) *Handbook of victims and victimology.* Cullompton: Willan Publishing, pp 282–308.

X

XENOPHOBIA

The word 'xenophobia' means a fear of strangers – of those who are regarded as different, as 'other', as not one of 'us'. The basic meaning of 'phobia' is fear, but it has also come to refer to hostility, as in the term 'homophobia'. Indeed, fear and hostility are closely related emotions: hostility often evokes fear (on both sides) and fear may well lead to hostility. To identify people as 'other' often has harsh and oppressive consequences for them: they may be treated quite differently from 'us', have social opportunities denied to them and may even find it hard to sustain their own sense of self-worth and to avoid internalising the hostility and discrimination that they encounter. Like other forms of oppression, experiencing xenophobia can be profoundly damaging for emotional and psychological well-being.

The social and psychological origins of xenophobia are complex and contested. It may be that it is an extreme expression of a tendency to favour one's own kin, tribe and community and to be suspicious of others (Greene, 2013). Porter (2002, p 62) refers to 'deep-seated and perhaps unconscious needs to order the world by demarcating self from other.... The construction of such "them-and-us" oppositions reinforces our sense of self-identity and self-worth through the pathologisation of pariahs'. In this process of demarcation, individuals mark out people as different, as deviant and perhaps as threatening.

Xenophobia is commonly experienced by people who are believed to be of different nationality or ethnicity. The American Psychological Association (2012) uses the term to draw attention to the psychological vulnerability of immigrants. The experience of immigration – the unfamiliarity of a new land, uncertainties about status in the host community, acclimatising, as it were, to a different culture, and economic challenges – is, typically, intrinsically stressful. When this is aggravated by hostility and rejection from the 'hosts', overt or latent, the effects on mental well-being can be seriously detrimental. Meeting the psychiatric needs of people from different countries and cultures in any case calls for considerable sensitivity and wisdom (Fernando, 2010). Yet, xenophobia can persist in subsequent generations, where the children and grandchildren of immigrants may continue to be met with suspicion and racism.

People believed to be mentally ill or disabled have often been regarded as 'other', so those who are already marked out as different are doubly vulnerable. At first sight, it may seem surprising that xenophobic hostility towards people with mental disorders should persist when mental distress is being increasingly recognised as common and something that many people will experience in their lifetime. However, arguably, this very closeness fuels our fear and makes demarcation all the more 'necessary': the closer we feel ourselves to be, the more we may feel a need to create a distance and to set (exaggerated and artificial) boundaries. Psychiatrists – the accredited guardians of the borders between mental health and madness – have been criticised for their historical contribution to these processes. 'Homosexuality', for example, was a listed disorder in the psychiatric diagnostic manuals until the 1970s, referred to by the Diagnostic and Statistical Manual or Mental Disorders as a 'sexual deviation'. Generally, it is wise to be cautious of a tendency to 'pathologise' difference and reduce it to a medical category (Kutchins and Kirk, 1999).

The concept of xenophobia, then, may help an understanding of the basis of discrimination against people with mental distress. For example, while anxieties about the risk posed by people with mental illness are familiar – and largely misplaced – the oppression and victimisation that they experience attracts much less public concern. Yet, people with schizophrenia are stigmatised and experience discrimination in many countries (Thornicroft et al, 2009), and the same seems true for people with major depressive disorders (Lasalvia et al, 2013). Mentally ill people are vulnerable to hate crime on the basis of their mental ill health or disability (Clement et al, 2011), are three times more likely than average to be victims of crime (BBC, 2013), and are five times more likely to be murdered (*The Independent*, 2013). Xenophobia is part of the explanation as to why many people withhold their empathy and acquiesce in this state of affairs, which is seldom raised as an issue of political concern. Xenophobia may also be part of an explanation of hate crime, constituting either a motive to attack others or as a way of insulating perpetrators from the constraints that would normally check them from malice and cruelty. Empathy is more readily applied to 'us' and easier to withhold from 'them' (Greene, 2013).

As well as undermining the well-being of its victims, xenophobia has a corrosive and corrupting influence on everyone, undermining the trust, reciprocity and mutual respect on which society and community ultimately depend.

ROB CANTON

See also: **Hate Crime and Victimisation**

Readings

American Psychological Association (2012) 'Crossroads: The psychology of immigration in the new century', report of the APA Presidential Task Force on Immigration. Available at: http://www.apa.org/topics/immigration/immigration-report.pdf

BBC (2013) 'Crime victims with mental illness ignored, research suggests', 7 October. Available at: http://www.bbc.co.uk/news/uk-24420430

Clement, S., Brohan, E., Sayce, L., Pool, J. and Thornicroft, G. (2011) 'Disability hate crime and targeted violence and hostility: a mental health and discrimination perspective', *Journal of Mental Health*, 20(3): 219–25.

Fernando, S. (2010) *Mental health, race and culture* (3rd edn). Basingstoke: Palgrave Macmillan.

Greene, J. (2013) *Moral tribes: Emotion, reason, and the gap between us and them.* New York, NY: Penguin.

Kutchins, H. and Kirk, S. (1999) *Making us crazy: DSM – the psychiatric bible and the creation of mental disorders.* London: Constable.

Lasalvia, A., Silvia Zoppei, S., Van Bortel, T., Bonetto, C., Cristofalo, D., Wahlbeck, K., Bacle, S. V., Van Audenhove, C., Van Weeghel, J., Blanca Reneses, B., Germanavicius, A., Economou, M., Lanfredi, M., Ando, S., Sartorius, N., Lopez-Ibor, J. J., Thornicroft, G., the ASPEN/INDIGO Study Group.(2013) 'Global pattern of experienced and anticipated discrimination reported by people with major depressive disorder: a cross-sectional survey', *The Lancet*, 381(9860): 55–62.

Porter, R. (2002) *Madness: A brief history.* Oxford: Oxford University Press.

The Independent (2013) 'Mentally ill people nearly five times more likely to be victims of murder than general population', 6 March. Available at: http://www.independent.co.uk/life-style/health-and-families/health-news/mentally-ill-people-nearly-five-times-more-likely-to-be-victims-of-murder-than-general-population-8521493.html

Thornicroft, G., Brohan, E., Rose, D., Sartorius, N., Leese, M. and INDIGO Study Group (2009) 'Global pattern of experienced and anticipated discrimination against people with schizophrenia: a cross-sectional survey', *The Lancet*, 373(9661): 408–15.

YOUNG PEOPLE, CRIME, HARM AND VICTIMISATION

The forms of victimisation that young people may face can be complex and specific in their form and impact upon this population. Children and young people are relatively powerless within society, and they can therefore be vulnerable to abuse. They may also be susceptible to being exploited, sexually, through forced migration, through child labour or by being manipulated into committing criminal acts. It can also be argued that young people experience a range of social harms, due to changes in policy and practice, at the hands of the state and those associated with it (Muncie, 2003).

In many ways, the impact of victimisation for young people is no different than it is for those who are older. However, the labelling and treatment of young people who experience victimisation may vary dramatically. The social construction of childhood and young people is subject to change across time, place and space. It is particularly reactive to key events, which can have a substantial impact on the perception of young people, harm and victimisation, for example, the death of two-year-old James Bulger in 1993 in the UK, which was perpetrated by two 10-year-old boys. Subsequently, the political discourse around young people has tended to construct them as a 'threat' or a 'risk' to society, rather than as group who are at risk of being victimised, often within the hidden 'private' sphere of the home or within institutional settings. The labelling of this population as posing a risk to society has been applied to ever-younger age groups (Brown, 1998), to the extent that young people can find themselves represented in the polarising forms of either 'evil' or 'innocent', with the conflation of youth and offending behaviour being commonplace. There is a paradoxical positioning of young people as an over-controlled, yet under-protected, population, subject to regulation and monitoring but often not readily recognised as victims or as a group to be consulted with over their experiences (Muncie, 2003).

The labelling of young people's victimisation has an impact upon how those offences become categorised and the ensuing responses to them. As Brown (1998, p 116) has suggested: 'the pre-dominant categorizations of youth do not sit easily within a "victim" discourse ... in popular and policy discourse such issues are often treated with cynicism, disdain or vehement denial'. For example, Morris (1987) cited a fourfold typology of the different ways in which child sexual abuse has been explained. This included viewing the abuse as a figment of the child's imagination, or the abuse being considered as relatively harmless because the child was too young to comprehend what was happening. Blaming the parents of the child, usually the mother, for colluding in the abuse or casting the child into the role of the 'seducer' were other methods of downplaying or denying the victimisation. The emphasis was on labelling the child as dysfunctional or dishonest, opting to see the abuse through a social work, health care or psychological lens, while obscuring their criminal victimisation. While the victims may be seen as blameless and innocent, they are also seen as victims of *harm* rather than crime (Brown, 1998).

Despite the issue of young people and crime featuring heavily in the media, relatively scant attention has been paid to their victimisation. Most academic studies focus on young people as offenders rather than as victims. There have, however, been a growing number of quantitative and qualitative studies looking at children's and young people's victimisation. Mawby's (1979) quantitative study on youth victimisation was one of the first to investigate this topic. In Britain, the 1990s saw a more concentrated approach to understanding young people and victimisation, with the British Crime Survey including questions on young people's victimisation in 1992, and a number of key academic studies beginning to focus on the issue (eg Carlen, 1996).

While there have been studies into this area of victimisation, young people are often not seen as occupying the role of both offender *and* victim. This state of affairs highlights the complexities involved in understanding the victimisation of this relatively powerless population.

CLAIRE FOX

See also: **Age and Victimisation; Child Protection and Children's Rights**

Readings

Brown, S. (1998) *Understanding youth and crime: Listening to youth?* Milton Keynes: Open University Press.

Carlen, P. (1996) *Jigsaw: A political criminology of youth homelessness*. Buckingham: Open University Press.

Mawby, R. (1979) 'The victimization of juveniles: a comparative study of three areas of publicly owned housing in Sheffield', *Journal of Research in Crime and Delinquency*, 16(1): 98–113.

Morris, A. (1987) *Women, crime and criminal justice*. Oxford: Blackwell.

Muncie, J. (2003) 'Youth, risk and victimisation', in P. Davies, P. Francis and V. Jupp (eds) *Victimisation theory, research and policy*. Basingstoke: Palgrave, pp 46–60.

Z

ZEMIOLOGY

While the notion of social harms have long concerned critical and Marxist criminologists, this concept (harm rather than crime) now constitutes a distinct alternative field of study, one that compliments and underpins traditional criminology and social science analysis. Academic concern with social harm has been gaining momentum in recent years. From early origins in the late 1990s, Zemiology (from the Greek *zemia* for harm) has emerged as a separate and distinct academic subject that provides a more accurate analysis of the vicissitudes of life generally (see Pemberton, 2015).

As a critical scholarly movement, 'zemiology' (re-)emerged during the 2000s as part of contemporary global criminology (Hillyard et al, 2004). Its early adherents, drawn from a range of social science-linked subjects, were largely united by the concern that the undue attention given to those acts commonly defined as 'crimes' distracts attention from much more pressing serious social harms and injurious behaviour. While this point was one made by a few traditionally in criminology (eg Schwendinger and Schwendinger, 1970), the 2000s saw a renewed rift with criminology as zemiologists argued for a separation and sought to make a distinct break with criminology and the notion of crime (irrespective of legal categorisations). Zemiologists instead seek to fashion responses through progressive and democratic social policies comprising truly inclusive and progressive alternatives (Hillyard et al, 2004). Academics such as Hillyard (Hillyard et al, 2004) championed the focusing of academic study of the range of the social harms that people experience from the cradle to the grave, only a small proportion of which, they argued, were regulated or captured by the criminal law. Hence, zemiological approaches attempt to broaden public and sociological focus to the plethora of harms encountered in daily life in capitalist societies, where much less obvious problems are frequently much more serious and damaging than those caused by crime and criminal activity.

For example, often, legally available drugs like alcohol and tobacco products kill more than prohibited drugs; yet, in contrast with prohibited narcotics, the producers of such harmful legally endorsed products are rarely considered criminal. Hence, zemiology examines the contemporary world in which neoliberal business practices associated with free trade are linked to avoidable environmental problems and intergenerational injustices that separate the socially privileged from the majority of the global populace, underpinning a range of subjects, from green and environmental criminology, to political and terrorist violence, poverty, and inequality.

Zemiological critique of traditional criminology also involves the latter discipline's ability to endorse punishment and perpetuate social harms and injustice. For example, some zemiologists argue that the criminal justice system and government systems have many stages that can inflict pain in a discrete manner: defining, classifying, broadcasting, disposing and punishing, and stigmatising individuals (see Pemberton, 2015). Furthermore, these social control processes can create wider societal problems and harms that bear little relationship to the initial crime or problem and cause or exacerbate excessive suffering that is disproportionate to the original problem. For example, jailing an individual for personal drug possession may lead to a loss of job, family problems and a lack of employment opportunities in the future, in effect, doing more harm than good.

As an emergent discipline, important aspects of this notion remain under active construction, in particular, the classification of social harm, questions of accountability and the empirical and methodological apparatuses for its investigation remain emergent (Pemberton, 2015). Yet, with growing global inequity and increased recognition of the harms that neoliberal global capitalism can cause, zemiological calls for consideration of harm generally have not only crafted a distinct new perspective in its own right, but reinvigorated the subject more broadly as new critical and ultra-realist criminologists are inspired to think more generally about harms rather than crimes per se and credit zemiological thinking as a potential inspiration in the reinvigoration of the criminological project (see, eg, Hall and Winlow, 2015).

JAMES TREADWELL

See also: Social Harm

Readings

Hall, S. and Winlow, S. (2015) *Revitalizing criminological theory: Towards a new ultra-realism*. London: Routledge.

Hillyard, P., Pantazis, C., Tombs, S. and Gordon, D. (2004) *Beyond criminology: Taking harm seriously*. London: Pluto Press.

Pemberton, S. (2015) *Harmful societies: Understanding social harm*. Bristol: The Policy Press.

Schwendinger, H. and Schwendinger, J. (1970) 'Defenders of order or guardians of human rights', *Issues in Criminology*, 5: 123–57.

Appendix

International campaign groups and sources of interest

Acid Survivors Trust International: http://www.acidviolence.org/

Alliance of NGOs on Crime and Criminal Justice: http://cpcjalliance.org/

American Society of Criminology (ASC): http://www.asc41.com/

American Society of Victimology: http://www.american-society-victimology.us/

Amnesty International: https://www.amnesty.org/en

Anti-Slavery: http://www.antislavery.org/

Asian Criminological Society: http://www.acs001.com

Asociación Latinoamericana de Derecho Penal y Criminología (ALPEC): http://www.alpecweb.org

Australasian Society of Victimology: http://www.victim.org.au/

Australian and New Zealand Society of Criminology (ANZSOC): http://www.anzsoc.org/

Australian Institute of Criminology: http://www.aic.gov.au/

Australian Women Against Violence Alliance: http://awava.org.au/

British Nuclear Test Veterans Association: https://bntva.com

British Society of Criminology (see Victims Network): http://www.britsoccrim.org/

Campaign Against Prison Slavery: http://www.againstprisonslavery.org/

Canadian Centre for the Victims of Torture: http://www.ccvt.org/

Canadian Criminal Justice Association: http://www.ccja-acjp.ca/

Canadian Resource Centre for Victims of Crime: http://crcvc.ca/en

Centre for Crime and Justice Studies: http://www.crimeandjustice.org.uk/

Centre for Research into Violence and Abuse (CRiVA) at Durham University, UK: https://www.dur.ac.uk/criva/

Children of Prisoners Europe: http://childrenofprisoners.eu/

Chinese Society of Criminology: http://www.ccunix.ccu.edu.tw/~clubcrime/

Climate Change Database Clearinghouse: http://ccrm.vims.edu/climate_change/ index.html

Coalition Against Wildlife Trafficking: http://www.cawtglobal.org/

Commissioner for Victims' Rights, South Australia: http://www.voc.sa.gov.au/

Commission for Victims and Survivors (Northern Ireland): http://www.cvsni. org/

Criminal Justice Alliance: http://www.criminaljusticealliance.org/

Criminological and Victimological Society of Southern Africa (CRIMSA): http://www.crimsa.ac.za/

Criminology Association of Ireland: http://criminologyireland.webs.com

Crisis (UK): http://www.crisis.org.uk/

Critical Criminology: http://critcrim.org/

Critical Resistance: http://criticalresistance.org/

Croatian Victimology Society: http://inavukic.com/tag/croatian-victimology-society/

Czech Society of Criminology (CKS): http://www.ok.cz/iksp/cks_o.html

Dutch Society of Criminology: http://www.criminologie.nl

Embrace – Child Victims of Crime (UK): http://www.embracecvoc.org.uk/

End Violence Against Women: http://www.endviolenceagainstwomen.org.uk/

Equality and Human Rights Commission (UK): http://www.equalityhumanrights. com/

European Group for the Study of Deviance and Social Control: http://www. europeangroup.org/

European Society of Criminology (ESC): http://www.esc-eurocrim.org

European Union Agency for Fundamental Rights (FRA): http://fra.europa.eu/

Freedom from Torture: http://www.freedomfromtorture.org/

French Society of Criminology (Association française de criminologie [AFC]): http://www.afc-asso.fr

Friends of the Earth: http://www.foe.co.uk/

General Assembly of the United Nations (Declaration of Basic Principles of Justice for Victims of Crime and Abuse of Power): http://www.un.org/documents/ ga/res/40/a40r034.htm

German, Austrian and Swiss Society of Criminology: http://www.krimg.de

German Society for Interdisciplinary Scientific criminology: http://www.giwk. de/

Gift from Within: http://www.giftfromwithin.org/

Green Criminology: http://greencriminology.org/

Hillsborough Family Support Group: http://www.liverpoolfc.com/hillsborough/ contact

Hillsborough Independent Panel: http://hillsborough.independent.gov.uk/

Hillsborough Justice Campaign: http://www.contrast.org/

Hong Kong Society of Criminology: http://www.crime.hku.hk/HKUcrime%204/ HKUcrime/index.html

Howard League for Penal Reform: https://www.howardleague.org/

Humane Society of the United States: http://www.humanesociety.org/

Human Rights and Justice Group: http://www.justicegroup.us/

Human Rights Watch: https://www.hrw.org/

Hungarian Society of Criminology: http://www.kriminologia.hu

Indian Society of Victimology: http://www.indiansocietyofvictimology.com/

Innocence Network: http://www.innocencenetwork.org.uk/

Inquest: http://inquest.org.uk/

Interdisciplinary Centre for Research on Victimology and Security: http://www.cirvis.eu/

International Association of French Speaking Criminologists (Association internationale des criminologues de langue française [AICLF]): http://www.aiclf.umontreal.ca/

International Bureau for Children's Rights: http://www.ibcr.org/

International Campaign for Justice in Bhopal: http://www.bhopal.net/

International Committee of the Red Cross: https://www.icrc.org/

International Critical Incident Stress Foundation: http://www.icisf.org/

International Prison Watch Network: http://www.prisonwatchnetwork.org/

International Society for Criminology (ISC): http://www.isc-sic.org/web/

International Society for Traumatic Stress Studies: http://www.istss.org/

International Victimology Institute Tilburg (INTERVICT): https://www.tilburguniversity.edu/research/institutes-and-research-groups/intervict/

Interpol Environmental Crime: http://www.interpol.int/Crime-areas/Environmental-crime/Environmental-crime

Italian Society of Criminology (Società Italiana di Criminologia): http://www.criminologiaitaliana.it

Make Justice Work: http://www.makejusticework.org.uk/

Mexican Society of Criminology of the State of Nuevo Leon (Sociedad Mexicana de Criminología Capítulo Nuevo León): http://www.somecrimnl.es.tl

NACRO (Crime Reduction Charity): https://www.nacro.org.uk/

National Association of Atomic Veterans Inc: http://www.naav.com/

Orchid Project (Female Genital Cutting): http://orchidproject.org/

Pakistan Society of Criminology: http://www.pakistansocietyofcriminology.com/

Pakistan Society of Victimology: http://pakistansocietyofvictimology.org/

Penal Reform International: http://www.penalreform.org/

Policy Exchange (UK): http://www.policyexchange.org.uk/

Portuguese Society of Criminology (Sociedade Portuguesa de Criminologia): http://granosalis.blogspot.com/2008/05/infromao-da-sociedade-portuguesa-de.html

Prison Reform Trust: http://www.prisonreformtrust.org.uk/

Prison Watch UK: http://prisonwatchuk.com/

Quebec's Society of Criminology: http://www.societecrimino.qc.ca/

Redress: http://www.redress.org/

Reprieve: http://www.reprieve.org.uk/

Romanian Society of Criminology (SRCC): http://www.criminologie.ro

Societat Catalana de Victimologia (SCV): http://www.victimologia.cat/

South Asian Society of Criminology and Victimology (SASCV): http://www.sascv.org/

Spanish Society of Criminological Research (Sociedad Española de Investigación Criminológica [SEIC]): http://www.criminologia.net/

Sports Criminology: http://sportscriminology.blogspot.co.uk/

Statewatch: http://www.statewatch.org/

Stonewall: http://www.stonewall.org.uk

Stop Violence Against Women (The Advocates for Human Rights): http://www.stopvaw.org/Stop_Violence_Against_Women

Swiss Group of Criminology: http://www.kriminologie.ch/siteWeb/anglais/anglais.htm

The John Howard Society of Canada: http://www.johnhoward.ca

Tokiwa International Victimology Institute (TIVI): http://www.tokiwa.ac.jp/~tivi/english/about/index.html

Traffic (Wild Plant and Animal Movement Monitoring): http://www.traffic.org/

UK Network of Sex Work Projects: http://www.uknswp.org/

Unicef: http://www.unicef.org.uk/

United (European Network Against Nationalism, Racism, Fascism and in Support of Migrants and Refugees): http://www.unitedagainstracism.org/

United Nations Greenhouse Gas Inventory Data: http://unfccc.int/ghg_data/items/3800.php

United Nations International Hazardous Waste Generation Report: http://unstats.un.org/unsd/environment/hazardous.htm

United Nations Office for the Coordination of Humanitarian Affairs: http://www.unocha.org/

United Nations Office on Drugs and Crime: https://www.unodc.org/

United Nations Wildlife Enforcement Monitoring System Initiative: http://wems-initiative.org/

United States Global Change Research Program: http://www.globalchange.gov/

Victim Justice Network (Canada): http://www.victimjusticenetwork.ca/

Victimology Society of Serbia: http://www.vds.org.rs/indexEng.html

Victims' Rights Alliance: http://victimsrightsalliance.com/

Victim Support (UK): https://www.victimsupport.org.uk/

Violence and Exploitation Research Program at the Australian Institute of Criminology (AIC): http://www.aic.gov.au/

Vital Voices: http://www.vitalvoices.org/

Walk Free (Modern Slavery): http://www.walkfree.org/

Water Aid: http://www.wateraid.org/

World Health Organization: http://www.who.int/

World Society of Victimology: http://www.worldsocietyofvictimology.org/

Legislation and policy index

Subject index

C

Cameron, David 83, 189, 214
Campbell, R. 210, 211–12
Canada
  common law legal system 195
  compensation 66
  victim impact statements 245, 246
  victims' rights 238, 262
capitalist harm 219
Carrabine, E. 252, 260, 266
Casey, Louise 160
Cavender, R. 266
Centre for Corporate Accountability 29
Chambers, Dwain 219
Chelmsford Crown Court 204
Chicago School 39
child protection 21–4
children 281–3
  abduction 146
  female genital mutilation 79
  giving evidence 203–5
  media representations of 267
  rights 21–4
  sexual abuse 2, 33–4, 206, 282
  trafficking 104
  see also young people
China 47
Christie, N. 18, 110, 227, 243–4, 252, 260
Citizens Advice Bureau 31, 81
Clark, P. 116
Clark, R.S. 237
Clarke, J. 141–2
clinical iatrogenesis 107, 134
Codd, H. 110
Cohen, E. 171–3
Cohen, L.E. 2, 193
Cohen, S. 108, 110
Colover, S. 29
Commercial Victimisation Survey 156
Commissioner for Victims and Witnesses 24,
  58, 115, 116, 160
common law jurisdictions 195–8
community impact statements 246–7
Community Rehabilitation Companies 154,
  170
compensation 25–8, 34–6, 44, 66, 231
complainants 264–5
Concerned Health Professionals of NY
  (CHPNY) 83
conflict see war
Conners, J.L. 266
Connolly, P. 73
Conrad, P. 135
consensus theory 40–1
corporate crime
  environmental victimology 68
  legal crimes 125–7
  state-corporate crime 224–6
corporate manslaughter 28–30

Corteen, A. 171–3
Corteen, K. 166, 167, 171–3, 210, 211
Council of Europe 103
court-ordered compensation 26–7
courts
  sexual offence cases 203–5
  and victims 30–2, 65
  witnesses 274–5
crime
  international law 199–200
  legal crimes 125–7
  prevention 163–5
  property crime 174–7
  and social harm 218–19
  and sport 222–4
  victimisation and vulnerability 32–4
  young people 281–3
  see also harm; offending; victimisation;
    victims
crime statistics 155–7
Crime Survey for England and Wales 156
  anti-social behaviour 8–9
  hate crime 92
  and homelessness 97
  young people 282
Criminal Cases Review Commission
  (CCRC) 10, 11
Criminal Injuries Compensation Authority
  (CICA) 34–6, 116, 141
Criminal Injuries Compensation Scheme
  (CICS) 34, 35, 36
Criminal Justice Joint Inspection Board 51
criminal justice system (CJS)
  and disability hate crime 51, 52
  Justice for All 115–17
  offenders as victims 151–3
  and social exclusion 217
  survivorology 229
  and victims **36–8**, 93–5, 159–61, 195–8,
    243–4, 251
  wrongful conviction 10–11, 137
  see also courts; Crown Prosecution Service;
    police; sentencing
criminology
  and critical victimology 40–2
  cultural 42–3
  green 6, 69–70
  and social harm 218–19
  social harm approach 12
  visual 266
  and war 38–40
  and zemiology 285, 286
  see also victimology
critical criminology 218
critical victimology 40–2
Croall, H. 193
Crown Court Witness Service 159
Crown Prosecution Service 94
  riots 152

T

U

V